"The book provides a reflection quality, writ large, where the authors and teachers they interviewed offer a tantalising narrative for teacher education, interweaving scholarship and teachers' voices while describing insights that extend complexities and clarify contradictions (e.g., actions), challenges (e.g., policy), and comforts (e.g., institutions). The book is an asset to the international NARRES project providing Australia as context, highlighting resilience (variously), and offering a strong example of narrative as reflection both theoretically and practically."

Associate Professor Robert C. Kleinsasser, *Mary Lou Fulton College for Teaching and Learning Innovation, Arizona State University, United States; Co-Editor-in-Chief of Teaching and Teacher Education (2019–2024)*

"This book is both a celebration of teachers and teaching and a sophisticated analysis and evaluation of the current zeitgeist of the profession. A 'must-read' for aspiring teachers and those who work beside them."

Associate Professor Glenda McGregor, *Deputy Head of School (Learning & Teaching), School of Education & Professional Studies, Griffith University, Australia*

Understanding Australian Teachers' Success Strategies

This book presents new insights into the success strategies of Australian teachers. It analyses interviews with 42 experienced teachers across a range of school contexts to examine "what works" in those contexts. The authors organise teachers' work and identities around ten distinct roles: designers for learning, emotional labourers, narrative constructors and deconstructors, pandemic navigators, policy refractors, relationship brokers, self-regulated learners, situated ethicists, teaching idealists and technology reframers.

The chapters explore two separate but interrelated arcs of analysis simultaneously. Teachers' work is examined around four nodes: complexities, challenges, contradictions and comforts. Five dimensions of that work are considered as well: psychosocial; profession and professionalism; changes and continuities; naming, framing and shaming; and teaching by design. The Australian study is part of a five-nation international research project focused on teacher motivation and resilience, with the other countries including Brazil, Chile, Ecuador and Spain. The authors are affiliated with the University of Southern Queensland, Central Queensland University and the Queensland University of Technology.

What emerges is the understanding that Australian teachers acknowledge the challenging complexity of their work, while they mobilise their constrained agency in innovative ways in diverse contexts. Their success strategies cluster around four distinct types—value-driven, agentic, adaptable and relational—with important implications for current and future teachers alike. It is an essential read for both in-service and pre-service teachers, as well as a viable resource for education researchers and research students, and general lay readers with an interest in the future of education.

Karen L. Peel is a Senior Lecturer in the School of Education at the University of Southern Queensland, Australia. She is an experienced teacher, having taught in Australian schools across decades of educational transformations. Her research interests include implementing practices for effective teaching and self-regulated learning.

Deborah L. Mulligan is an Honorary Postdoctoral Researcher at the University of Southern Queensland, Australia. Her research interests include gerontology, where she has published on older men and suicide ideation. Deborah has a strong interest in community capacity-building through examining marginalised societal cohorts.

R. E. (Bobby) Harreveld is Professor Emerita at Central Queensland University, Australia. Her interests include socio-cultural understandings of education in diverse contexts; research education and ethics (politics, theory, practice); professional and vocational education and employment transition pathways; and distance, open and online teaching and learning.

Nick Kelly is Associate Professor in Design Science in the School of Design at Queensland University of Technology, Australia. He conducts interdisciplinary research across the fields of design and education, with a focus upon design cognition and design science in teacher education and schooling.

Patrick Alan Danaher is Professor in Education in the School of Education at Excelsia University College, and Professor Emeritus at the University of Southern Queensland, Australia. His research interests include academics', educators' and researchers' work and identities, and education research ethics, methods, politics and theories.

Critical Perspectives on Teaching and Teachers' Work

Series Editors: Nina Bascia, Denisha Jones, Arlo Kempf, and Rhiannon Maton

Teachers' Work During the Pandemic
Nina Bascia

Critical Perspectives on White Supremacy and Racism in Canadian Education
Dispatches from the Field
Edited by Arlo Kempf and Heather Watts

Disrupting Secondary STEM Education
Educator Experiences of Teaching for Globally Just Futures
Edited by Margery Gardner

Handbook on Teachers' Work
International Perspectives on Research and Practice
Edited by Nina Bascia and Rhiannon M. Maton

Understanding Australian Teachers' Success Strategies
Narratives of Motivation and Resilience
Karen L. Peel, Deborah L. Mulligan, R. E. (Bobby) Harreveld, Nick Kelly, and Patrick Alan Danaher

For more information about this series, please visit: https://www.routledge.com/Critical-Perspectives-on-Teaching-and-Teachers-Work/book-series/CPTTW

Understanding Australian Teachers' Success Strategies
Narratives of Motivation and Resilience

Karen L. Peel, Deborah L. Mulligan,
R. E. (Bobby) Harreveld, Nick Kelly,
and Patrick Alan Danaher

LONDON AND NEW YORK

Designed cover image: Conor Moore

First published 2026
by Routledge
4 Park Square, Milton Park, Abingdon, Oxon OX14 4RN

and by Routledge
605 Third Avenue, New York, NY 10158

Routledge is an imprint of the Taylor & Francis Group, an informa business

© 2026 Karen L. Peel, Deborah L. Mulligan, R. E. (Bobby) Harreveld, Nick Kelly, and Patrick Alan Danaher

The right of Karen L. Peel, Deborah L. Mulligan, R. E. (Bobby) Harreveld, Nick Kelly, and Patrick Alan Danaher to be identified as authors of this work has been asserted in accordance with sections 77 and 78 of the Copyright, Designs and Patents Act 1988.

All rights reserved. No part of this book may be reprinted or reproduced or utilised in any form or by any electronic, mechanical, or other means, now known or hereafter invented, including photocopying and recording, or in any information storage or retrieval system, without permission in writing from the publishers.

For Product Safety Concerns and Information please contact our EU representative GPSR@taylorandfrancis.com. Taylor & Francis Verlag GmbH, Kaufingerstraße 24, 80331 München, Germany.

Trademark notice: Product or corporate names may be trademarks or registered trademarks, and are used only for identification and explanation without intent to infringe.

British Library Cataloguing-in-Publication Data
A catalogue record for this book is available from the British Library

ISBN: 9781032931975 (hbk)
ISBN: 9781032895123 (pbk)
ISBN: 9781003564850 (ebk)

DOI: 10.4324/9781003564850

Typeset in Galliard
by KnowledgeWorks Global Ltd.

Dedication

For those who teach, for those whom they teach and for those who research their teaching, and for their common commitment to rendering the world a more empowering, inclusive and transforming place.

Contents

List of Figures	xvi
List of Tables	xvii
List of Contributors	xviii
Foreword: How Teachers Cope with Complexity by Marc Clarà	xx
Acknowledgements	xxiv
List of Acronyms and Abbreviations	xxv
Data Availability Statement	xxvi

1 Conceptualising and Contextualising Australian Teachers' Success Strategies   1

Introduction 1
The International NARRES Study 4
The Australian Research Project 5
The Research Design 6
   Data Collection 6
   Data Analysis 8
   Research Ethics 12
The Book 12
Conclusion 13
References 14
Recommended Further Reading 16

2 Teachers as Designers for Learning   17

Introduction 17
Selected Literature 18
   Design and Teaching 18
   Design Cycles, Frames and Activities 19
   Design Expertise and the Basic Psychological
     Needs of Teachers 22

xii *Contents*

    Data Analysis 24
       Teachers Framing Their Design for Learning 25
       Cycles of Design for Learning 28
    Implications 30
    Conclusion 31
    References 31
    Recommended Further Reading 33

3 Teachers as Emotional Labourers   34

    Introduction 34
    Selected Literature 35
    Data Analysis 37
       Complexities 39
       Challenges 41
       Contradictions 43
       Comforts 45
    Implications 46
    Conclusion 47
    References 48
    Recommended Further Reading 48

4 Teachers as Narrative Constructors and Deconstructors   50

    Introduction 50
    Selected Literature 51
    Data Analysis 53
       Complexities 54
       Challenges 56
       Contradictions 59
       Comforts 60
    Implications 63
    Conclusion 64
    References 64
    Recommended Further Reading 66

5 Teachers as Pandemic Navigators   67

    Introduction 67
    Selected Literature 68
    Data Analysis 70
       Complexities 71
       Challenges 73
       Contradictions 76
       Comforts 77

Implications 79
Conclusion 80
References 80
Recommended Further Reading 82

6 Teachers as Policy Refractors   83

Introduction 83
Selected Literature 84
Data Analysis 86
  Audrey: A Case of Complexities, Challenges,
    Contradictions and Comforts 86
  Complexities 88
  Challenges 89
  Contradictions 91
  Comforts 92
Implications 93
Conclusion 94
References 95
Recommended Further Reading 96

7 Teachers as Relationship Brokers   97

Introduction 97
Selected Literature 98
Data Analysis 100
  Complexities 101
  Challenges 102
  Contradictions 104
  Comforts 106
Implications 107
Conclusion 108
References 109
Recommended Further Reading 110

8 Teachers as Self-Regulated Learners   111

Introduction 111
Selected Literature 112
Data Analysis 114
  Complexities and Comforts 115
  Challenges and Comforts 118
  Contradictions and Comforts 121
Implications 124
Conclusion 126

xiv Contents

    References 127
    Recommended Further Reading 130

9 Teachers as Situated Ethicists   131

    Introduction 131
    Selected Literature 132
    Data Analysis 134
      Complexities 135
      Challenges 137
      Contradictions 139
      Comforts 141
    Implications 142
    Conclusion 143
    References 144
    Recommended Further Reading 145

10 Teachers as Teaching Idealists   147

    Introduction 147
    Selected Literature 148
    Data Analysis 150
      Complexities 151
      Challenges 153
      Contradictions 155
      Comforts 157
    Implications 159
      Adhering to Social Conscience 159
      Believing in the Ideal of Education and the Societal
        Value of Effective Teaching Methodology 159
      Building and Working on Relationships (Connections) 160
      Finding and Maintaining Professional Satisfaction
        and Purpose 160
      Sustaining Passion 160
    Conclusion 160
    References 161
    Recommended Further Reading 161

11 Teachers as Technology Reframers   162

    Introduction 162
    Selected Literature 163
    Data Analysis 165
      Complexities 166
      Challenges 168

Contradictions 169
Comforts 170
Implications 171
Conclusion 173
References 173
Recommended Further Reading 175

12 Celebrating Teachers: Lessons for Teachers and Teaching Nationally and Globally   176

Introduction 176
Value-Driven Success Strategies 178
Agentic Success Strategies 180
Adaptable Success Strategies 182
Relational Success Strategies 183
Discussion 185
Conclusion 186
References 186
Recommended Further Reading 188

Appendix: Interview Protocol: Emotional Experiences of Australian Teachers   189
Index   192

List of Figures

2.1	Design as cycles of learning and creating (adapted from Berkun, 2020)	20
2.2	Teachers design by framing a problem, conducting activities and drawing on resources (adapted from Kelly & Grace, 2025)	21
2.3	How design capabilities lead to satisfaction of basic psychological needs	23
8.1	The triadic reciprocation view of self-regulatory functioning	113
12.1	A representation of four categories for teachers' success strategies: value-driven, agentic, adaptable and relational	178

List of Tables

1.1	Interview Participants	9
1.2	Data Analysis Matrix	11
1.3	Chapter Titles, Authors and Coverage of Data Dimensions	13
2.1	Data Analysis Matrix for Teachers as Designers for Learning	24
3.1	Data Analysis Matrix for Teachers as Emotional Labourers	38
4.1	Data Analysis Matrix for Teachers as Narrative Constructors and Deconstructors	54
5.1	Data Analysis Matrix for Teachers as Pandemic Navigators	71
6.1	Data Analysis Matrix for Teachers as Policy Refractors	86
7.1	Data Analysis Matrix for Teachers as Relationship Brokers	100
8.1	Data Analysis Matrix for Teachers as Self-regulated Learners	115
9.1	Data Analysis Matrix for Teachers as Situated Ethicists	135
10.1	Data Analysis Matrix for Teachers as Teaching Idealists	151
11.1	Data Analysis Matrix for Teachers as Technology Reframers	165

List of Contributors

Marc Clarà is Associate Professor and Serra Húnter Fellow in the Facultat d'Educadió, Psicologia i Treball Social at the Universitat de Lleida, Catalonia. His research addresses some key problems faced by teachers, putting special emphasis on representation, interaction and the mediating role of digital technologies.

Patrick Alan Danaher is Professor in Education in the School of Education at Excelsia University College and Professor Emeritus at the University of Southern Queensland, Australia. His current and recent adjunct and honorary positions include at Central Queensland University, James Cook University and the University of the Sunshine Coast, Australia and the University of Helsinki, Finland.

R. E. (Bobby) Harreveld is Professor Emerita at Central Queensland University, Australia. As a researcher and teacher, her interests include sociocultural understandings of education in diverse contexts; research education and ethics (politics, theory, practice); professional and vocational education and employment transition pathways; and distance, open, and online teaching and learning.

Nick Kelly is Associate Professor in Design Science in the School of Design at Queensland University of Technology, Australia. He conducts interdisciplinary research across the fields of design and education, with a focus upon design cognition (how designers think) and design science in teacher education and schooling (design pedagogy, design for learning, learning by design).

Deborah L. Mulligan is an Honorary Postdoctoral Researcher at the University of Southern Queensland, Australia. Her research interests include the field of gerontology, where she has published and presented widely on older men and suicide ideation. Deborah has a strong interest in community capacity-building through examining psychosocial groups targeted at marginalised societal cohorts.

Karen L. Peel is a Senior Lecturer in the School of Education at the University of Southern Queensland, Australia. She is an experienced classroom teacher, having taught in Australian schools across decades of educational transformations. Her research interests include the implementation of practices for effective teaching and self-regulated learning.

Foreword: How Teachers Cope with Complexity

Marc Clarà

Teacher burnout is an important problem for educational systems worldwide. It has been estimated that, internationally, about 30% of teachers experience high levels of stress or burnout (Agyapong et al., 2022). In Australia, the Teachers and School Leaders as Lifelong Learners (TALIS) 2018 survey showed that 57.6% of lower secondary education teachers experienced "quite a bit" or "a lot" of stress and that 21.7% of these teachers wanted to leave the profession in the following five years. Similar numbers were found among primary education teachers: 55.5% experienced "quite a bit" or "a lot" of stress and 22.8% wanted to leave the profession in the coming five years (OECD, 2018).

This emotional reality of teachers has important impacts on educational systems and societies. For example, high levels of teacher burnout have been found to be related to students' higher stress and negative emotions, lower motivation and achievement, and higher levels of disruptive behaviour, as well as to poorer relationships between teachers and students, poorer teaching strategies, high rates of teacher attrition and absenteeism, and serious teacher health problems (Frenzel et al., 2021; Klusmann et al., 2016; Madigan & Kim, 2021; Oberle & Schonert-Reichl, 2016; Redín & Erro-Garcés, 2020; Salvagioni et al., 2022; Shen et al., 2015).

Research has consistently found that teacher burnout is related to certain conditions of teachers' work, such as students' disruptions and other emotional demands, workload, role ambiguity, lack of autonomy and lack of social and institutional support (Clarà et al., 2022). In short, teacher burnout is partly due to the fact that teaching is complex and challenging. Some of this complexity can and should be structurally reduced by improving societies, policies, educational contexts and the conditions of teachers' work; however, complexity is also, in part, intrinsic to teaching, and understanding how teachers cope with it is fundamental to addressing the teacher burnout problem.

Between 2018 and 2022, a group of researchers from different countries conducted a research project called NARRES (La relación entre las narrativas y el desarrollo de la resiliencia en los profesores—http://www.erims.udl.cat/index.php/2021/11/03/narres-2/), aimed at investigating this issue. A point of departure for our approach in that project was the fact that many teachers, when facing the same kinds of complexities and adversities related to teacher burnout, instead experience feelings of professional growth and commitment. We wondered, therefore, how these teachers distinctively cope with adversity to generate such a different experience.

To explore this question, we used the concept of teacher resilience, which was also further conceptually developed in the project. Teacher resilience was defined, in our approach, as a type of relationship between a teacher and an adverse situation that generates simultaneous improvements both in the situation and in the teacher's emotional experience (Clarà, 2018; Vallés & Clarà, 2023). We assumed, based on previous theoretical developments and empirical evidence (Clarà, 2015, 2020), that the nature of this relationship between the teacher and the adverse situation is mediated by narrative meaning. In other words, our hypothesis was that the narratives that teachers use to relate to their professional situations are the key to understanding both how teachers will feel and how they will be able to act within these situations. Our research, therefore, focused on studying these narratives, to understand how teachers make sense of their situations and how that enables them to thrive.

The study of the narratives was conducted by different teams, who used complementary approaches. For example, a team in Chile studied these narratives from the point of view of professional identity, looking at how teachers narratively positioned themselves and others when making sense of their situations (Chávez et al., 2024). A team working in Catalonia (Spain) studied the semantic structure of the narratives and looked for the relationships between certain structures and several indicators of teacher resilience (Clarà et al., 2023, 2024), as well as for the semio-narrative mechanisms through which some teachers structurally transformed their narratives—and their emotional experiences—regarding their professional situations (Clarà et al., 2025). In Australia, a five-person team—the authors of this book—analysed the narratives looking at how teachers explained their coping strategies within different dimensions of teachers' work. This book presents the results of this analysis.

The analysis conducted by the Australian team constitutes an important contribution to the NARRES general endeavour since it presents several distinctive characteristics. First, it studies the work of teachers from a multifaceted and novel perspective, which considers the psychosocial aspects of teaching, aspects related to professionalism, aspects related to the dynamism of work, the political and institutional nature of work, and aspects related to designing and enacting teaching and learning. Second, in each facet of work, the analysis disentangles teachers' experience by distinguishing among complexities, challenges, contradictions and comforts. This offers a useful classification that helps to clarify experience. Third, the analysis identifies specific coping strategies that can be linked to each facet of work and type of experience. This offers a very useful set of coping resources for teachers experiencing difficulty, which the authors cluster around four key impulses: agentic, relational, adaptable and value-driven strategies. The coping strategies identified and explained in this book complement, at a more macro level, the resources offered at a more micro level within the NARRES project, such as the identification of semio-narrative mechanisms and key structural and positioning characteristics of the narratives.

In short, this book constitutes an important contribution to understanding how teachers may cope with the complexities and adversities of teaching to generate positive outcomes, both in terms of the teacher's emotional experience and in terms of the improvement of the situation. The results can become an important resource to assist teachers dealing with complexity and adversity, contributing to the development of teachers' resilience and, as a consequence, to the improvement of educational systems.

References

Agyapong, B., Obuobi-Donkor, G., Burback, L., & Wei, Y. (2022). Stress, burnout, anxiety and depression among teachers: A scoping review. *International Journal of Environmental Research and Public Health*, 19(17), Article 10706. https://doi.org/10.3390/ijerph191710706

Chávez, J., Barril, J. P., López, T., Clarà, M., Ramos, F. S., Peel, K., & Justiniano, B. (2024). Navigating burnout: A study of teacher identity in Chile, Ecuador, Brazil, Spain and Australia. *Pedagogy, Culture & Society*, 33(2), 729–745. https://doi.org/10.1080/14681366.2024.2302314

Clarà, M. (2015). Representation and emotion causation: A cultural psychology approach. *Culture & Psychology*, 21, 37–58. https://doi.org/10.1177/1354067X14568687

Clarà, M. (2018). *La resiliencia de los profesores: Una conceptualización [Teacher resilience: A conceptualization]* [Invited conference presentation]. Universidad de la Frontera, Temuco, Chile. Available at: https://youtu.be/9EkEE9aRtl0

Clarà, M. (2020). Meaning and the mediation of emotional experience: Placing mediational meaning at the center of psychological processes. *New Ideas in Psychology*, 58. https://doi.org/10.1016/j.newideapsych.2019.100776

Clarà, M., Vallés, A., Cavalcante, S., Franch, A., Coiduras, J., Silva, P., Kelly, N., López, T., Marchán, P., & Padula, B. (2024). The emotional side of teaching conceptions: Exploring the relationship between conceptions of teaching and teacher burnout, well-being, and resilience. *Australian Journal of Teacher Education*, 49(12). https://doi.org/10.14221/1835-517X.6328

Clarà, M., Vallés, A., Coiduras, J., Silva, P., Justiniano, B., López, T., Padula, B., Barril, J. P., Cavalcante, S., Chávez, J., Donoso, D., Marchán, P., Ramos, F. S., & Uribe, C. P. (2022). Unpacking the role of work demands in teacher burnout: Cognitive effort as a protective factor. *Electronic Journal of Research in Educational Psychology*, 20(22), 245–266. https://doi.org/10.25115/ejrep.v20i57.4374

Clarà, M., Vallés, A., Franch, A., Coiduras, J., Silva, P., & Cavalcante, S. (2023). How teachers' appraisals predict their emotional experience: Identifying protective and risk structures in natural appraisals. *Teaching and Teacher Education*, 130, Article 104166. https://doi.org/10.1016/j.tate.2023.104166

Clarà, M., Vallés, A., Franch, A., Coiduras, J., Silva, P., & Cavalcante, S. (2025). Developing teacher resilience by modifying cognitive appraisals: What is reappraised in teacher reappraisal? *Contemporary Educational Psychology*, 81, Article 102354. https://doi.org/10.1016/j.cedpsych.2025.102354

Frenzel, A. C., Daniels, L., & Burić, I. (2021). Teacher emotions in the classroom and their implications for students. *Educational Psychologist*, 56(4), 250–264. https://doi.org/10.1080/00461520.2021.1985501

Klusmann, U., Richter, D., & Lüdtke, O. (2016). Teachers' emotional exhaustion is negatively related to students' achievement: Evidence from a large-scale assessment study. *Journal of Educational Psychology*, *108*(8), 1193–1203. https://doi.org/10.1037/edu0000125

Madigan, D. J., & Kim, L. E. (2021). Does teacher burnout affect students? A systematic review of its association with academic achievement and student-reported outcomes. *International Journal of Educational Research*, *105*, Article 101714. https://doi.org/10.1016/j.ijer.2020.101714

Oberle, E., & Schonert-Reichl, K. A. (2016). Stress contagion in the classroom? The link between classroom teacher burnout and morning cortisol in elementary school students. *Social Science & Medicine*, *159*, 30–37. http://dx.doi.org/10.1016/j.socscimed.2016.04.031

OECD. (2018). *TALIS 2018 database* [Data set]. OECD. https://www.oecd.org/en/data/datasets/talis-2018-database.html (accessed July 22, 2025).

Redín, C. I., & Erro-Garcés, A. (2020). Stress in teaching professionals across Europe. *International Journal of Educational Research*, *103*, Article 101623. https://doi.org/10.1016/j.ijer.2020.101623

Salvagioni, D. A. J., Mesas, A. E., Melanda, F. N., González, A. D., & de Andrade, S. M. (2022). Burnout and long-term sickness absence from the teaching function: A cohort study. *Safety and Health at Work*, *13*, 201–206. https://doi.org/10.1016/j.shaw.2022.01.006

Shen, B., McCaughtry, N., Martin, J., Garn, A., Kulik, N., & Fahlman, M. (2015). The relationship between teacher burnout and student motivation. *The British Psychological Society*, *85*, 519–532. http://dx.doi.org/10.1111/bjep.12089

Vallés, A., & Clarà, M. (2023). Conceptualizing teacher resilience: A comprehensive framework to articulate the research field. *Teachers and Teaching: Theory and Practice*, *29*(1), 105–117. https://doi.org/10.1080/13540602.2022.2149483

Acknowledgements

The authors are very grateful to the following groups and individuals, without whom this handbook would not have been published:

- The 42 Australian teachers who generously shared their experiences in the Australian research project
- Associate Professor Marc Clarà for creating and leading the international NARRES study, and for writing the Foreword to this book
- The other researchers in the international NARRES study, including Ms Alba Vallés, who contributed to the Australian research project's data analysis
- Ms Felicia Chan, Ms Khadijah Ebrahim, Ms Clare Midgley, Ms Vilija Stephens and their colleagues from Routledge who have been supportive and rigorous in equal measure
- Mr Prabhu Chinnasamy and his colleagues from KnowledgeWorks Global Ltd. for their expert typesetting and copyediting of the manuscript
- The four anonymous reviewers of the book proposal whose insightful feedback enhanced the quality of this volume
- Mr Emilio A. Anteliz for identifying literature for inclusion in some of the chapters
- Ms Anika Ferreira for transcribing some of the interviews
- Associate Professor Robert Kleinsasser and Associate Professor Glenda McGregor for writing endorsements of the book
- This study was funded by the Ministerio de Economa, Industria y Competitividad (the Spanish Government's Ministry of Economy, Industry and Competitiveness, Grant EDU2017-87406-P), with Associate Professor Marc Clarà as the Principal Investigator

List of Acronyms and Abbreviations

ACARA	Australian Curriculum Assessment and Reporting Authority
AITSL	Australian Institute for Teaching and School Leadership
COVID-19	Coronavirus Disease 2019
EALD	English as an Additional Language or Dialect
EdTech	Educational Technology
NARRES	La relación entre las narrativas y el desarrollo de la resiliencia en los profesores [The relationship between narratives and the development of resilience in teachers]
OECD	Office of Economic and Cultural Development
PISA	Program for International Student Assessment
SRL	Self-Regulated Learning
TPACK	Technological, Pedagogical and Content Knowledge
UNESCO	United National Educational, Scientific and Cultural Organization

Data Availability Statement

Owing to the nature of this research participants in the research agreed that their data would not be shared publicly, so supporting data are not available.

1 Conceptualising and Contextualising Australian Teachers' Success Strategies

Introduction

Globally, teachers are positioned at a number of intersections: between idealism and realism (Voss & Kunter, 2020), professionalisation and deprofessionalisation (Buchanan, 2020), policy and practice (Lemke et al., 2024), structure and agency (Giddens, 1984), economies of performance and ecologies of practice (Stronach et al., 2002), symbolic forms and material necessities (Fawns, 2008), and a host of other contrasting polarities. These intersections and polarities underscore both the challenges of the work and identities of teachers in the third decade of the 21st century and the opportunities arising from those challenges. It is against the backdrop of these broader international, regional, national and local factors and forces that individual teachers envision, enact and evaluate their teaching activities.

More specifically, this complex terrain frames the diverse ways in which teachers tell their stories about their success strategies, while acknowledging the constraints on such strategies. As we argue throughout this book, teachers' success strategies are fundamentally interwoven with their narratives of motivation, resilience and several other emotions (Peel et al., 2023, 2024). This is because, as we exemplify in the successive chapters, teachers' emotions influence how they apprehend the effectiveness or otherwise of their work, and how they perceive and navigate the multifaceted contexts with which they must engage.

Like the teachers whose experiences we portray in this book, we have sought to steer a path between a particular polarity: that of an uncritically celebrationist discourse pertaining to teachers, on the one hand (Kelly et al., 2016), and capture by the opposing narrative of teaching being in a state of irredeemable crisis, on the other hand (Giroux, 2010)—neither of which discourse was prominent in the interviews with the participants in this research project. From this "middle ground" perspective, the book's title and subtitle have been carefully chosen. The focus is on *Understanding Australian Teachers' Success Strategies*—that is, not accepting such strategies uncritically, but rather analysing them through the prism of the international La relación entre las narrativas y el desarrollo de la resiliencia en los profesores (NARRES) study's goals and the Australian research project's aim and objectives, as well as comprehending

DOI: 10.4324/9781003564850-1

them through the "give and take" of our conversations with the participating teachers. Relatedly, the book's evocation of *Narratives of Motivation and Resilience* highlights the crucial connection between the participants' identified success strategies and the emotional domain of their work, which is vital to explaining why and how the teachers saw these strategies as being successful.

In this way, the book reflects our conviction of the relevance to these teachers' interviews of constrained agency (Coe & Jordhus-Lier, 2010; Damman & Henkens, 2017; Gulati & Srivastava, 2014; Herndl & Licona, 2007) as one among several powerful concepts that afford compelling insights into those narratives. As a consequence of their professional roles, teachers are assigned considerable occupational autonomy, such as often being the sole adult working with a group of children in the case of early childhood educators and primary/elementary and secondary school teachers. At the same time, teachers (including the participants in this research project) have identified significant and seemingly increasing incursions into that autonomy, such as through centralised curricula and high-stakes assessment of their students' learning (and by implication equally high-stakes evaluation of their teaching). For teachers, this is an example of constrained agency—what Lassalle and Shaw (2021) referred to as "a lack of choice due to structural constraints" (p. 1509). These structural constraints explain why the participants' success strategies were neither automatic nor easy, but instead needed to be negotiated against the grain of highly complex organisations and large systems not necessarily sympathetic to the teachers' intentions. Intriguingly for this analysis, Porter (2023) referred explicitly to the links between teachers' constrained agency and their emotions: "… more adaptability in agency may result from experiencing permutations of emotions that create recognisable opportunities to act in novel ways" (p. 67).

In other words, we are interested in elaborating in the following chapters how the participants, working in highly diverse contexts and with varied access to resources, were able "to act in novel ways" (Porter, 2023, p. 67) in order to achieve their success strategies despite the constraints that they variously identified. More particularly, we are attentive to the ways in which the teachers' emotions both facilitated and constrained that ability and those strategies, as key elements of their motivation and resilience. In this regard, we have intentionally entitled and conceived the ten data chapters constituting this book as a series of declarative propositions: "Teachers as … designers for learning, emotional labourers, narrative constructors and deconstructors, pandemic navigators" and so on, that is, rather than starting each chapter from the deficit perspective of what teachers are not able to do, we focus on what the participants in this research project demonstrated that they were able to achieve—on what they did and why they did it, the inevitable constraints on their capacity to do so notwithstanding. We see these declarative propositions as functioning simultaneously at three levels: conceptually, by emphasising the participants' constrained agency (Porter, 2023); methodologically, by framing our approach to data analysis across the ten chapters with reference to each proposition in turn; and ethically, by mobilising the propositions as concrete reflections of our sincere regard for the integrity, intellect and professionalism of every participant in the project.

It is with these features of the asserted distinctiveness of this volume in mind that we see *Understanding Australian Teachers' Success Strategies* taking its place in a succession of books that have explored teachers' work and identities from multiple perspectives. The subsequent chapters examine relevant literature related to such work and identities in other countries as well as in Australia; here we refer to selected volumes about Australian teachers, to provide an impression of the array of topics traversed in this country to date (but see also Bascia [2023], Bascia & Maton [2026/forthcoming] and Griffiths [2025] as current and recent accounts of equivalent research in other countries). From that standpoint, Connell's *Teachers' Work* (1985) remains seminal, linking what teachers do in classrooms with deeper social structures of gender and class. Hayes et al. (2006) elicited the lessons gleaned from research conducted in 1,000 Australian primary and secondary classrooms related to the Productive Pedagogies framework. Mayer et al. (2017) reported on the Studying the Effectiveness of Teacher Education (SETE) project that recorded workforce data with about 5,000 recently graduated teachers and 1,000 school principals in Australia to gauge their reflections on initial teacher education. Written in the style of an experientially grounded memoir, Stroud's *Teacher* (2018) presented a highly personalised account of what brought her to teaching and what took her away from it. Larsen and Allen (2021) elaborated several aspects of the notion of teachers as professional learners (including apprehending professional learning as purposeful, work intensive and an act of compliance). Most recently, Karnovsky and Kelly (2025a) assembled accounts of Australian teachers' work, including selected analyses taken from the research project framing this book (although drawing on different data from those presented here), that highlighted those teachers' emotional experiences. In doing so, Karnovsky and Kelly (2025b) argued strongly for "a new emotional discourse in education" (p. 1) in which "… the lived experiences of teacher practitioners must be elevated, so that policy makers and broader communities can attend to critical issues facing the profession such as workload intensification, low professional status and precarious workplace wellbeing" (p. 8). Accordingly, this volume's emphasis on Australian teachers' success strategies understood through the prism of motivation and resilience narratives both aligns with and builds on these and other earlier accounts of teachers' work and identities.

With the book's conceptualisation and contextualisation having been introduced in this way, this first chapter has been clustered around the following four sections:

- The international NARRES study
- The Australian research project
- The research project's research design
- The book's structure

The International NARRES Study

This book is one outcome of the Australian research project that we elaborate in the next section of this chapter, and that in turn is part of the international NARRES study, which was created and is led by Dr Marc Clarà, Serra Húnter Fellow and Associate Professor in the Department of Psychology, Sociology and Social Work at the Universitat de Lleida, Spain. The NARRES study title, expressed originally in Spanish as "La relación entre las narrativas y el desarrollo de la resiliencia en los profesores", translates into English as "The relationship between narratives and the development of resilience in teachers". Drawing on Associate Professor Clarà's seminal scholarship over many years pertaining to the connections among representation, emotion and action, discursive constructions of joint activity and processes of learning, and the mediation of digital media in processes of learning (see, for example, Clarà, 2013, 2015a, 2017, 2019, 2021), NARRES has four goals:

- "We study the structure of the teachers' narratives".
- "We look for relationships between certain aspects of the narratives and teacher resilience".
- "We study the transformation processes of teachers' narratives".
- "We compare the narratives of teachers in different socio-cultural communities" (http://www.erims.udl.cat/index.php/2021/11/03/narres-2/).

Currently, NARRES includes researchers from five countries: Spain, Ecuador, Chile, Brazil and Australia. In addition to recent and continuing publications (http://www.erims.udl.cat/index.php/publications/; see for example Chávez Rojas et al., 2024; Clarà et al., 2023; Vallés & Clarà, 2023), the study has included the development of a website (http://www.erims.udl.cat/index.php/research-projects/), videos (http://www.erims.udl.cat/index.php/video-results/), free online training modules (http://www.erims.udl.cat/index.php/training-and-transfer/) and analysis protocols and instruments (http://www.erims.udl.cat/index.php/analysis-protocols-and-instruments/).

The beginning of the "Abstract" on the NARRES study website is worth quoting in full, partly because it provides a concise synthesis of the conceptualisation of the study and also because it resonates strongly with the more specific concerns of the Australian research project framing this book:

> The NARRES project has studied the emotional experience of teachers in the kindergarten, primary and secondary education levels. The project has focused on the way in which teachers make sense of the situations in their practice, based on the hypothesis that the way in which these situations are narrated is related to the way in which these situations "feel." It is assumed, therefore, that the same events can generate different emotional experiences in the teacher depending on how the teacher narrates them. Understanding this narrativization process

and its implications for teachers' emotions is important for the development of teacher resilience, understood as the functional adaptation to adverse situations of teaching practice, and that allows teachers to maintain their emotional well-being and their teaching commitment despite the adversities, intrinsic, in part, in the current educational systems.

(http://www.erims.udl.cat/index.php/2021/11/03/narres-2/)

We contend that the NARRES study's emphasis on teachers' emotional experiences, teachers' narratives of those experiences and their impact on teachers' resilience aligns closely with, and adds a crucial psychosocial element to, the notion of teachers' constrained agency (Porter, 2023) introduced earlier in this chapter. Furthermore, this tripartite emphasis is taken up extensively in the successive chapters, which deepen the discussion of the relationship among teachers' emotional experiences, narratives and resilience with particular reference to each chapter's respective focus.

Similarly, the NARRES study website's first-named major finding has another important connection with this book:

The NARRES project has shown that the narrativization of events in terms of students, colleagues or families "know how to do" and "can do", and in terms of "I (the teacher) do it", is related to a better emotional experience of the teacher.

(http://www.erims.udl.cat/index.php/2021/11/03/narres-2/)

This significant outcome affords a timely justification of the declarative propositions guiding the following chapters, in the sense that, for example, the notion of "Teachers as self-regulated learners" (Chapter 8) associates with more positive assertions such as "I know how to do", "I can do" and "I do it" much more directly than it does with more negative statements like "They don't want to do it", "They can't do it", "They don't do it" and "I don't do it" (http://www.erims.udl.cat/index.php/2021/11/03/narres-2/)

The Australian Research Project

Against the backdrop of the international NARRES study introduced in the preceding section, the Australian research project was entitled "Studying Resilience in Australian Teachers", and its focus was distilled as follows: "The aim of this research is to understand and describe the emotional experiences of teachers in their professional lives" (Australian research project participant information sheet). Likewise, the hypothesis at the project's commencement was articulated thus: "... a crucial element of resilience is how teachers explain to themselves what happens to them; i.e., the narratives that they elaborate to make meaning of the situations of their teaching practice" (Australian research project human ethics approval application). From this perspective, the following objectives were proposed for the project:

1 "Establishing the extent to which the level of modal contradictions in the teachers' narratives predict their level of resilience, controlling for working conditions"
2 "Comparing the narratives, resilience and working conditions of teachers in different socio-cultural contexts"
3 "Identifying the changes in the semantic structure of narratives which are associated with improvements in teachers' resilience, and the semantic operations which make these changes possible" (Australian research project human ethics approval application).

This aim and these objectives were pursued by means of two concurrent research instruments whose details are provided in the next section. It is noteworthy that, as the data gathering progressed and preliminary findings began to emerge, the enacted research project added experiential depth to the inevitably more theoretical character of the project's initially stated purpose:

> The continuing impact of the Covid-19 pandemic on learning and teaching has highlighted starkly the crucial roles conducted by teachers, as well as the complexity and diversity of their work and identity. This research project has focused on the emotional element of that work and identity, including the metaphors that teachers use to describe their working lives and the strategies that they enact to enhance their resilience.
>
> The Australian [data gathering] highlighted teachers as engaging with an increasing number of challenges and pressures that manifested as emotional stressors in very diverse ways in the participants' lives, yet these same teachers emerged also as highly professional, as engaging in innovative classroom strategies and as continuing to derive considerable personal pleasure from their work.
>
> (Australian research project summary, 23 August 2021)

The following chapters take up these preliminary findings and extend their experiential depth and analytical complexity by detailed reference to the respective declarative proposition elaborated in each data chapter, as well as through accounts of the particular intersections and polarities introduced at the beginning of this chapter that participants were required to navigate.

The Research Design

Data Collection

As we noted above, the Australian research project's data collection was pursued through two concurrent research instruments that in most cases were combined in a single session of approximately one and a half hours. The first instrument was a single survey instrument that was administered to participating teachers in all five countries involved in the international NARRES study after being translated into the respective national language of each country. After canvassing appropriate demographic questions such as gender, age, employment status, years of experience in teaching and age range of the participant's students, this instrument combined four previously separate surveys, as follows:

1 The Brief Resilience Scale (BRS) (Smith et al., 2008) is a six-question Likert scale instrument for assessing resilience.
2 The Short Warwick–Edinburgh Mental Well-being Scale (SWEMWBS) (https://www.corc.uk.net/outcome-experience-measures/short-warwick-edinburgh-mental-wellbeing-scale-swemwbs/) is a seven-question Likert scale instrument for assessing mental well-being.
3 The Copenhagen Psychosocial Questionnaire, 2nd edition short version (COPSOQ-II) (https://nfa.dk/media/fmqgl5nq/1_copsoq-ii-short-questionnaire-english.pdf) is a 23-question Likert scale instrument for measuring the psychosocial environment in the workplace.
4 The Maslach Burnout Inventory for Educators (MBI-ES) (https://www.researchgate.net/publication/263809804_Maslach_Burnout_Inventory_-_Educators_Survey_ES) is a 23-question Likert scale instrument for assessing educators' propensity for burnout.

The second instrument was a semi-structured interview protocol (see Appendix) that asked participants to respond in particular ways to the topics traversed in the interview (for instance, by visualising a situation or by explaining what it was like to carry out a specific aspect of the participant's teaching role). The interview opened by asking participants to describe a good day of teaching and concluded by enquiring what it meant to the interviewee to be a teacher. In between, questions covered the participant's career as a teacher, situations experienced as a teacher, relationships with colleagues, students, parents and administrators, specific tasks, identified issues, continuity and change, and the distinctive circumstances of the COVID-19 pandemic. All interviews were conducted on the Zoom videoconferencing platform, and the audiorecording of each interview was professionally transcribed. As we elaborate below, 42 Australian teachers participated individually in the interviews. Most interviews were conducted by a single member of the research team; however, 12 interviews were conducted by two team members, and one interview was carried out with three team members interviewing a single participant. The intention of the multi-team member interviews was to introduce the research team more fully to those teachers who took part in such interviews and also to provide an informal "checking in" among team members that our approaches to interviewing were reasonably consistent, while allowing for the inevitable variability attendant on semi-structured interviews being conducted by multiple researchers.

Various strategies were mobilised to advertise the research project and to elicit interest from possible participants. Word of mouth and the researchers' respective networks were effective in generating interest. We also recruited participants by approaching relevant professional associations to include information about the project in their magazines and newsletters. In a few cases, a particular participant recommended the project to colleagues from the same school. We were very conscious of teachers' well-known exceedingly busy workloads, and we were grateful to all teachers who agreed to participate. Data gathering was undoubtedly affected significantly by the exigencies of COVID-19, with the first interview occurring on 9 March 2019 and the final interview being recorded on 22 December 2020.

Table 1.1 presents the 42 participants' assigned pseudonyms and selected information about them while still preserving their anonymity. The interviewees exhibited considerable diversity, being located in all six Australian states and the Northern Territory, and with a gender distribution of 33 females (78.5%) to 9 males (21.5%). They also traversed many year levels in primary school and varied subject areas in secondary school, as well as a wide range of years of teaching experience, and they worked in a blend of government, independent and religious schools, flexible learning centres and distance education schools. Many participants were classroom teachers, while others held varying kinds of leadership responsibilities. A few respondents had specialist roles, such as being special needs educators and itinerant teachers rotating among a number of schools. Moreover, participants manifested a variety of employment situations, ranging from permanent and contract to full- and part-time to casual and supply (relief) teaching.

Data Analysis

Our approach to analysing the nearly 300,000 words of transcripts yielded by the 42 semi-structured interviews needed to engage with the rich complexity of what the participants had generously and courageously shared with us, without being overwhelmed by the sheer volume of data. Consequently, our data analytic strategy exhibited the following features:

- *Collective*, in the sense that we remained attentive to one another's developing ideas about the direction and shape of the data analysis, and we worked towards a working consensus while still allowing for individual interests.
- *Deductive*, in the sense that a starting point for the data analysis was awareness of the international NARRES study's goals and the Australian research project's aim and objectives outlined above, and also of the distinctive strategy for analysing teachers' narratives championed by Associate Professor Marc Clarà (for example, applying the principles of semiotic analysis at the linguistic level of the speech act or utterance to explore semantic structures [Clarà, 2015b]).

Table 1.1 Interview Participants

Participant pseudonym	Participant information
1. Harriet	Female, primary school, Queensland
2. Katie	Female, secondary school, Queensland
3. Sally	Female, primary school, South Australia
4. Doug	Male, secondary school, South Australia
5. Ella	Female, secondary school, Queensland
6. Alexa	Female, secondary school, Victoria
7. Paul	Male, secondary school, Victoria
8. Diana	Female, secondary school, Queensland
9. Helen	Female, secondary school, Queensland
10. Jalena	Female, secondary school, Queensland
11. Chantelle	Female, secondary school, New South Wales
12. Serene	Female, secondary school, Queensland
13. Norman	Male, secondary school, Queensland
14. Erin	Female, secondary school, Queensland
15. Sylvia	Female, secondary school, Queensland
16. Anthea	Female, primary and secondary school, Queensland
17. Adriana	Female primary and secondary school, Tasmania
18. Dean	Male, primary school, New South Wales
19. Elspeth	Female, secondary school, Queensland
20. Stella	Female, primary and secondary school, Queensland
21. Rosalie	Female, secondary school, Queensland
22. Maurie	Male, secondary school, Queensland
23. Shirley	Female, secondary school, New South Wales
24. Arthur	Male, secondary school, Victoria
25. Kelly	Female, secondary school, Northern Territory
26. Marnie	Female, primary school, Queensland
27. Cindy	Female, primary school, Queensland
28. Viv	Female, primary school, Queensland
29. Kate	Female, primary school, Queensland
30. Alice	Female, primary school, Queensland
31. Keira	Female, primary school, Queensland
32. Sophie	Female, primary and secondary school, Queensland
33. Charlotte	Female, secondary school, Queensland
34. Kylie	Female, secondary school, Queensland
35. Gail	Female, secondary school, Queensland
36. Perry	Male, secondary school, Queensland
37. Audrey	Female, primary school, Queensland
38. Angela	Female, primary school, Victoria
39. Declan	Male, secondary school, New South Wales
40. Sharon	Female, secondary school, Queensland
41. George	Male, primary school, New South Wales
42. Ruth	Female, primary school, Western Australia

- *Individual,* in the sense that, while we worked as a research team and aspired to a collective sense of overall patterns in the analysed data, we were free to develop sub-analyses, and to write corresponding publications and presentations, related to our respective interests (for instance, while we were guided by the NARRES study's goals and the Australian research project's aim and objectives, as noted above, specific research questions were deployed in individual publications rather than in the project as a whole).

- *Inductive*, in the sense that we approached our reading and re-reading of individual interview transcripts as an opportunity to engage in new meaning-making, informed but not predetermined by our prior literature reviews and immersion in this scholarly field.
- *Interpretive*, in the sense that we sought to understand how the participants interpreted the emotions and experiences that they reported to us.
- *Narrative*, in the sense that we approached the transcripts as a story being told by the respective participants about their work and identities, with sense-making being co-constructed by participants and interviewer/s as the interviews unfolded.
- *Qualitative*, in the sense of using non-numerical data to gain an accurate and authentic understanding of the participants' lives as self-reported by the participants.

Moving from the principles to the processes and practices of our data analytic strategy, after concluding data gathering with the final interview on 22 December 2020, we held concentrated, day-long, face-to-face research meetings at the Queensland University of Technology (11 June 2021 and 17 December 2021) and at the University of Southern Queensland (3 September 2021 and 27 June 2022), interspersed by meetings held by videoconference. The purpose of the face-to-face meetings was to set aside our respective daily commitments long enough to allow us to focus exclusively on the rigours of data analysis, leavened by the genuine pleasure of reconnecting as a group of like-minded people with shared pleasures derived from research and publishing.

As part of this focus, we used the Miro software (https://miro.com/) to help us to visualise and evaluate connections and patterns as they emerged from our intensive reading of the transcripts and our associated lively discussions. We used this approach to articulate and clarify the sense that each of us made of particular utterances, to challenge and test out that emergent sense-making, and thereby to develop a provisional consensus about the data analysis, while accommodating variations on understanding specific data.

One outcome of these principles, processes and practices of data analysis was the generation of what we termed four **nodes** (see also Peel et al., 2024):

- Complexities (CY): Engaging with multifaceted events and issues
- Challenges (CE): Encounters with difficult and potentially stressful events and issues
- Contradictions (CN): Events and issues with at least two competing influences and pressures
- Comforts (CT): Sources of encouragement, motivation and pleasure

These four nodes have been interwoven in the following data chapters as they elaborate and exemplify their respective declarative propositions.

In addition to the four nodes, we elicited what we identified as five **dimensions** (see also Peel et al., 2024):

- Psychosocial: The interdependence of personal thoughts and behaviours with the contextual and relational influences of being a teacher
- Profession and professionalism: Teachers' ethical and partly autonomous enactment and dissemination of knowledge, and their interactions with other educational stakeholders
- Changes and continuities: Elements and experiences of teachers' work and lives that have been dynamic and constant
- Naming, framing and shaming: The social, cultural and political issues, tensions and changes that influence the public and sometimes politicised positioning of teachers' work and identities
- Teaching by design: Curriculum, pedagogy and assessment as intentions, outcomes and effects, and opportunities for teachers to engage in adaptive, innovative and sometimes transformative educational practice

These five dimensions have likewise been deployed to assist in framing the discussion in the following data chapters, with one and sometimes two dimensions being explicated in each chapter.

We developed and trialled a matrix that brought together these four nodes and five dimensions (see Table 1.2). The intention was to synthesise what we had discerned as highly significant patterns and themes in the data in an efficient way to inform our continuing data analysis, without unnecessarily constraining subsequent iterations of that analysis.

In addition to the macro level of these four nodes and five dimensions, and as an exemplification of how we enacted the micro level of data analysis, each of us assigned **codes**, and thereby created coded extracts and elicited emergent themes, for different samples of eight transcripts, then we conducted a collective review of the outcomes before entering the results in the Miro software. More specifically, we clustered the codes that we had created (for instance, "frustration not being heard by administration") in order to summarise the coded extracts from the transcripts in order to generate a number of emergent themes (such as "lack of power"). From this perspective, the code "enjoyment gained from helping" aligned with the emergent theme "psychological

Table 1.2 Data Analysis Matrix

	Psychosocial	*Profession and Professionalism*	*Changes and Continuities*	*Naming, Framing and Shaming*	*Teaching by Design*
Complexities					
Challenges					
Contradictions					
Comforts					

pleasure", the code "losing my temper with students" generated the emergent theme "emotional regulation" and the code "wanting to help students and not being able" led to the emergent theme "wanting to help students". The purpose of creating and discussing these codes, coded extracts and emergent themes was less about developing sets of definitive examples of each classification at the micro level than about demonstrating the relevance and rigour of the nodes and dimensions elicited at the macro level.

Research Ethics

Appropriate university human ethics approval was gained (H18REA161), and corresponding processes were observed, such as the participants' perusal of the research project information sheet and signing of the informed consent form, as well as the use of pseudonyms to refer to participants. Equally if not more importantly, we remain highly cognisant of the responsibilities of our continuing relationships with the participants, including the ethics and politics of issues of representation and vocality (Midgley et al., 2013, 2014). These responsibilities encompass how we write about the emotions and experiences that the participants shared with us, which in turn underpinned our selection of the declarative propositions outlined above and explicated in the subsequent data chapters as an intentionally respectful valuing of teachers' work and identities, while acknowledging the complex and challenging environments in which they conduct that work and enact those identities.

The Book

As we noted above, the book has been clustered around the selected declarative propositions about Australian teachers' work and identities, gleaned from the participants' interview transcripts and sequenced alphabetically. Furthermore, each data chapter has been structured around the following headings, in order to maximise clarity and coherence within and across the chapter:

1 Abstract
2 Introduction
3 Selected literature
4 Data analysis
5 Implications
6 Conclusion
7 References
8 Recommended further reading

There is some variation on the subheadings in the "Data Analysis" across the data chapters.

Moreover, although all five authors were integrally involved in conducting the Australian research project, in collecting and analysing the data, and in planning the writing of the book, particular responsibility for writing each

Table 1.3 Chapter Titles, Authors and Coverage of Data Dimensions

Chapter no	Chapter title	Chapter author/s	Chapter data dimension/s (if applicable)
1	Conceptualising and contextualising Australian teachers' success strategies	R. E. (Bobby) Harreveld and Patrick Alan Danaher	-
2	Teachers as designers for learning	Nick Kelly and Karen L. Peel	Dimension 5: Teaching by design
3	Teachers as emotional labourers	Deborah L. Mulligan	Dimension 1: Psychosocial Dimension 2: Profession and professionalism
4	Teachers as narrative constructors and deconstructors	Deborah L. Mulligan and Patrick Alan Danaher	Dimension 4: Naming, framing and shaming
5	Teachers as pandemic navigators	Patrick Alan Danaher and Karen L. Peel	Dimension 3: Changes and continuities
6	Teachers as policy refractors	R. E. (Bobby) Harreveld	Dimension 2: Profession and professionalism
7	Teachers as relationships brokers	R. E. (Bobby) Harreveld and Deborah L. Mulligan	Dimension 1: Psychosocial
8	Teachers as self-regulated learners	Karen L. Peel and Nick Kelly	Dimension 2: Profession and professionalism
9	Teachers as situated ethicists	R. E. (Bobby) Harreveld and Patrick Alan Danaher	Dimension 4: Naming, framing and shaming
10	Teachers as teaching idealists	Deborah L. Mulligan and Patrick Alan Danaher	Dimension 3: Changes and continuities
11	Teachers as technology reframers	Nick Kelly and Patrick Alan Danaher	Dimension 5: Teaching by design
12	Celebrating teachers: Lessons for teachers and teaching nationally and globally	Karen L. Peel and Nick Kelly	-

chapter reflected our specific research interests. Table 1.3 presents the details of the chapter titles, authors and coverage of the five dimensions of the data analysis identified earlier in this chapter.

In addition, Karen L. Peel composed the index.

Conclusion

This chapter has introduced this book, *Understanding Australian Teachers' Success Strategies: Narratives of Motivation and Resilience*, by conceptualising and contextualising those success stories. The conceptualisation highlighted the notion of constrained agency (Porter, 2023), which simultaneously emphasises teachers' capacity to act purposefully and productively and pays due attention to the environmental elements that both facilitate and hinder that capacity. The contextualisation entailed articulating the international NARRES study of which the Australian research project that framed and animated this book is a part. The project's research design and the book's structure, were also presented.

More broadly, we see this book as situating Australian teachers' success stories and their narratives of motivation and resilience against the backdrop of deeper and wider forces and structures that frame and inform their emotional experiences. Additionally, we see the declarative propositions underpinning the ten data chapters as constituting a distinctive and significant means of apprehending teachers' work and identities, by accentuating the diverse ways in which the participants manifested the key elements of each proposition, to which we now turn.

References

Bascia, N. (2023). *Teachers' work during the pandemic (critical perspectives on teaching and teachers' work)*. Routledge.

Bascia, N., & Maton, R. M. (Eds.) (2026/forthcoming). *Handbook on teachers' work: International perspectives on research and practice (critical perspectives on teaching and teachers' work)*. Routledge.

Buchanan, J. (2020). *Challenging the deprofessionalisation of teaching and teachers: Claiming and acclaiming the profession*. Springer.

Chávez Rojas, J., Barril, J. P., López Jiménez, T., Clarà, M., Silvestre Ramos, F., Peel, K. L., & Justiniano, B. (2024). Navigating burnout: A study of teacher identity in Chile, Ecuador, Brazil, Spain and Australia. *Pedagogy, Culture & Society*. Advance online publication. https://doi.org/10.1080/14681366.2024.2302314

Clarà, M. (2013). The concept of situation and the microgenesis of the conscious purpose in cultural psychology. *Human Development, 56*(2), 113–127. https://doi.org/10.1159/000346533

Clarà, M. (2015a). What is reflection? Looking for clarity in an ambiguous notion. *Journal of Teacher Education, 66*(3), 261e271. https://doi.org/10.1177/0022487114552028

Clarà, M. (2015b). Protocol of semiotic analysis of teachers' narratives on emotion and resilience. Retrieved from https://www.researchgate.net/profile/Marc_Clara/contributions

Clarà, M. (2017). Teacher resilience and meaning transformation: How teachers reappraise situations of adversity. *Teaching and Teacher Education, 63*, 82–89. http://dx.doi.org/10.1016/j.tate.2016.12.010

Clarà, M. (2019). Building on each other's ideas: A social mechanism of progressiveness in whole-class collective inquiry. *Journal of the Learning Sciences, 28*, 302–336. https://doi.org/10.1080/10508406.2018.1555756

Clarà, M. (2021). Conceptually driven inquiry: Addressing the tension between dialogicity and teleology in dialogic approaches to classroom talk. *Educational Review, 75*(3), 468–487. https://doi.org/10.1080/00131911.2021.1923462

Clarà, M., Vallés, A., Franch, A., Coiduras, J., Silva, P., & Cavalcante, S. (2023). How teachers' appraisals predict their emotional experience: Identifying protective and risk structures in natural appraisals. *Teaching and Teacher Education, 130*, 104166. https://doi.org/10.1016/j.tate.2023.104166

Coe, N. M., & Jordhus-Lier, D. C. (2010). Constrained agency? Re-evaluating the geographies of labour. *Progress in Human Geography, 35*(2), 211–233. https://doi.org/10.1177/0309132510366746

Connell, R. W. (1985). *Teachers' work*. Routledge.

Damman, M., & Henkens, K. (2017). Constrained agency in later working lives: Introduction to the special issue. *Work, Aging and Retirement, 3*(3), 225–230. https://doi.org/10.1093/workar/wax015

Fawns, R. (2008). Idealism and materialism in the culture of teacher education: The mythopoetic significance of things. In T. Leonard & P. Willis (Eds.), *Pedagogies of the imagination: Mythopoetic curriculum in educational practice* (pp. 157–167). Springer.

Giddens, A. (1984). *The constitution of society: Outline of the theory of structuration*. Polity Press.

Giroux, H. A. (2010). Dumbing down teachers: Rethinking the crisis of public education and the demise of the social state. *Review of Education, Pedagogy, and Cultural Studies, 32*(4–5), 339–381. https://doi.org/10.1080/10714413.2010.510346

Griffiths, C. (Ed.). (2025). *Teacher burnout from a complex systems perspective: Contributors, consequences, contexts and coping strategies*. Palgrave Macmillan.

Gulati, R., & Srivastava, S. B. (2014). Bringing agency back into network research: Constrained agency and network action. In D. J. Brass, G. Labianca, A. Mehra, D. S. Halgin, & S. P. Borgatti (Eds.), *Contemporary perspectives on organizational social networks (research in the sociology of organizations vol. 40)* (pp. 73–93). Emerald Group Publishing Limited.

Hayes, D., Mills, M., Christie, P., & Lingard, B. (2006). *Teachers & schooling making a difference: Productive pedagogies, assessment and performance*. Allen & Unwin.

Herndl, C. G., & Licona, A. C. (2007). Shifting agency: Agency, kairos, and the possibilities of social action. In M. Zachry & C. Thralls (Eds.), *Communicative practices in workplaces and the professions: Cultural perspectives on the regulation of discourse and organizations* (pp. 133–154). Routledge.

Karnovsky, S., & Kelly, N. P. (Eds.). (2025a). *Teachers' emotional experiences: Towards a new emotional discourse (Palgrave critical perspectives on schooling, teachers and teaching)*. Palgrave Macmillan.

Karnovsky, S., & Kelly, N. P. (2025b). Towards a new emotional discourse in education. In S. Karnovsky & N. P. Kelly (Eds.), *Teachers' emotional experiences: Towards a new emotional discourse (Palgrave critical perspectives on schooling, teachers and teaching)* (pp. 1–16). Palgrave Macmillan.

Kelly, N. P., Clarà, M., Kehrwald, B. A., & Danaher, P. A. (2016). *Online learning networks for pre-service and early career teachers*. Palgrave Macmillan/Palgrave Pivot.

Larsen, E., & Allen, J. M. (2021). *Teachers as professional learners: Contextualising identity across policy and practice*. Palgrave Macmillan.

Lassalle, P., & Shaw, E. (2021). Trailing wives and constrained agency among women migrant entrepreneurs: An intersectional perspective. *Entrepreneurship Theory and Practice, 45*(6), 1296–1521. https://doi.org/10.1177/1042258721990331

Lemke, M., Nickerson, A., & Saboda, J. (2024). Global displacement and local contexts: A case study of U.S. urban educational policy and practice. *International Journal of Leadership in Education, 27*(3), 471–494. https://doi.org/10.1080/13603124.2021.1884747

Mayer, D., Dixon, M., Kline, J., Kostogriz, A., Moss, J., Rowan, L., Walker-Gibbs, B., & White, S. (2017). *Studying the effectiveness of teacher education: Early career teachers in diverse settings*. Springer.

Midgley, W. J., Danaher, P. A., & Baguley, M. M. (Eds.). (2013). *The role of participants in education research: Ethics, epistemologies, and methods (Routledge research in education vol. 87)*. Routledge.

Midgley, W. J., Davies, A., Oliver, M. E., & Danaher, P. A. (Eds.). (2014). *Echoes: Ethics and issues of voice in education research*. Sense Publishers.

Peel, K. L., Kelly, N. P., & Danaher, P. A. (2024). Australian teachers' causal attributions along a motivational continuum in supporting their resilience. *Issues in Educational Research*, 34(1), 163–182. http://www.iier.org.au/iier34/peel.pdf

Peel, K. L., Kelly, N. P., Danaher, P. A., Harreveld, R. E., & Mulligan, D. L. (2023). Analysing teachers' figurative language to shed new light on teacher resilience. *Teaching and Teacher Education*, 130, 104175. https://doi.org/10.1016/j.tate.2023.104175

Porter, K. (2023). *As easy as ABC? A novel psychological approach to teacher agency: Exploring the influence of affect on behaviour and cognition* [Doctoral dissertation]. University of St Andrews, Scotland. https://research-repository.st-andrews.ac.uk/handle/10023/28376

Smith, B. W., Dalen, J., Wiggins, K., Tooley, E., Christopher, P., & Bernard, J. (2008). The brief resilience scale: Assessing the ability to bounce back. *International Journal of Behavioral Medicine*, 15(3), 194–200. https://doi.org/10.1080/10705500802222972

Stronach, I., Corbin, B., McNamara, O., Stark, S., & Warne, T. (2002). Towards an uncertain politics of professionalism: Teacher and nurse identities in flux. *Journal of Education Policy*, 17(1), 109–138. https://doi.org/10.1080/02680930110100081

Stroud, G. (2018). *Teacher: One woman's struggle to keep the heart in teaching*. Allen & Unwin.

Vallés., A., & Clarà, M. (2023). Conceptualizing teacher resilience: A comprehensive framework to articulate the research field. *Teachers and Teaching: Theory and Practice*, 29(1), 105–117. https://doi.org/10.1080/13540602.2022.2149483

Voss, T., & Kunter, M. (2020). "Reality shock" of beginning teachers? Changes in teacher candidates' emotional exhaustion and constructivist-oriented beliefs. *Journal of Teacher Education*, 71(3), 292–306. https://doi.org/10.1177/0022487119839700

Recommended Further Reading

Chen, J. (2021). Refining the teacher emotion model: Evidence from a review of literature published between 1985 and 2019. *Cambridge Journal of Education*, 51(3), 327–357. https://doi.org/10.1080/0305764X.2020.1831440

Mansfield, C. F. (Eds.). (2021). *Cultivating teacher resilience: International approaches, applications and impact*. Springer.

Onyefulu, C., Madalinska-Michalak, J., & Bavli, B. (2023). Teachers' motivation to choose teaching and remain in the profession: A comparative mixed methods study in Jamaica, Poland and Turkey. *Power and Education*, 15(1), 37–65. https://doi.org/10.1177/17577438221109907

Søreide, G. E. (2006). Narrative construction of teacher identity: Positioning and negotiation. *Teachers and Teaching: Theory and Practice*, 12(5), 527–547. https://doi.org/10.1080/13540600600832247

Thorburn, E. K. (1999). *Success stories: A means of enhancing the personal–professional development of teachers* [Doctoral dissertation]. Edith Cowan University, Australia.

2 Teachers as Designers for Learning

Introduction

It is useful to consider the dual roles that a teacher takes on, one at "learntime", when they are in the classroom with students, and another prior to this: the act of "designing for learning" (Goodyear & Dimitriadis, 2013). The two are very much entangled, yet the role of teacher as a *designer of learning experiences*, the latter of the two, has been made salient only in recent decades (Goodyear & Carvalho, 2014; Laurillard, 2013). The design capabilities of a teacher are critical for enabling teachers to achieve the aspirations that they set for themselves in the classroom. Yet, despite this significance of design capabilities, teachers rarely self-identify as designers, even though many teachers are indeed expert designers.

The consequences of recognising teachers as educational designers remain contested territory. One interpretation, that taken by the authors, is to suggest that teachers should be therefore empowered to develop as designers and to model designerly ways of knowing, acting and thinking (Kelly, 2025). A contrasting viewpoint is that teachers ought to be given "ready-to-teach" packages so that they can focus more fully on their role at learntime. An example of these contested ideas playing out can be found in discussions around the statewide *curriculum into the classroom* (C2C) programme introduced in Queensland, Australia in 2012 (Bradfield & Exley, 2020; Hardy, 2015). What is generally agreed upon is that teachers' reflective practice enables them to gain a deeper understanding of the complex learning designing processes that are involved in working with diverse learners and materials (Bosch et al., 2025).

From our perspective, it is vital that teachers be respected as designers of learning and supported in their development as expert designers. Good design is recognised as responding to context. An apt analogy is the difference between an architecturally designed house—one that responds to research into the site, the surrounds and the needs of the inhabitants—and a "stock home", where an off-the-shelf plan is reused over and over on sites that are levelled, cleared and treated as interchangeable units of land (Kelly & Gero, 2021). In a similar way, good design for learning needs to respond to the learners,

DOI: 10.4324/9781003564850-2

the learning space, the school community, the teachers' abilities, the context for the class and so on. Many teachers are indeed expert designers of learning and for these teachers their design capabilities form a vital part of their success strategies.

This chapter aims to provide some clarity around this relationship between teacher design expertise and teacher success strategies. Firstly, we clarify what is meant by terms like "design expertise" and "design capabilities" in the context of teachers. Secondly, we suggest that developing and using design capabilities support teachers in meeting their basic psychological needs of relatedness, autonomy and competence. We adopt a *self-determination theory* perspective in framing this relationship (Ryan & Deci, 2000). We then draw upon quotations from a range of different teachers in the La relación entre las narrativas y el desarrollo de la resiliencia en los profesores (NARRES) project to exemplify this relationship between teachers' success strategies and their design capabilities, based upon teachers' own words. The chapter can be read as an appreciation of the virtuous cycles that arise when teachers are internally motivated to produce high-quality learning experiences by catering for the needs of learners in front of them, supporting the satisfaction of basic psychological needs.

Selected Literature

Design and Teaching

Teachers operate at the intersection of pedagogy, general knowledge and specific content knowledge (Shulman, 1986). Expert teachers need to know their students, know how they learn, know how to teach them, know the content that they are teaching and know how all of this fits into the broader field of knowledge. Designing for learning in schools is a complex cognitive task that involves understanding and navigating multifaceted and interconnected systems.

Decades of design theory provide a basis for understanding what it means for teachers to be experts at designing for learning. It is useful to begin with a definition of design, as a verb, to understand better what we mean when we talk about teachers as expert designers. Competing definitions of what it means to *design* have three elements in common:

1. Design is a goal-driven activity, which distinguishes it from activities driven by self-expression such as art (Gero, 1990; Lawson, 2006). It involves imagining the world differently from how it is found (the goal) and finding ways to achieve this goal (where the output may be documentation rather than successful achievement of that goal).
2. Design responds to a specific sociocultural context and requires cognitive processes of interpretation and exploration (Gero, 1990; Simon, 1969). This distinguishes design from activities like solving a mathematical equation in which all variables are known at the outset. In this respect, design often

involves "wicked problems" in which overlapping systems, diverse stakeholders and competing variables must all be managed (Buchanan, 1992).
3 Design is an iterative process of drawing on resources and organising elements into a way of achieving the goal (Alexander, 1964; Buchanan, 1992; Norman, 2013). In design there is no "one solution" but rather a set of possible responses, one or some of which a designer may find to be satisfactory.

We can summarise these three parts, following Simon (1969), by suggesting that design is about changing situations into preferred situations through an iterative process that involves exploration. Teachers thus design every time that they plan any kind of learning experiences for their students.

In designing, teachers make use of design capabilities. These can be generally understood as creativity, critical thinking, communication and collaboration—general capabilities that are referred to in other contexts as 21st-century skills (Koh et al., 2015); and it is important for educators to have these capabilities if they are to model them for student (Kickbusch et al. 2020; Wrigley & Straker, 2017). For our purposes, we can link these three parts of the definition of design to teachers' design capabilities.

Design is a goal-driven activity, but the goal shifts as teachers learn more about a problem. Design is distinct from problem-solving—tasks like solving a Rubik's cube or a mathematical equation—in which all necessary information is present at the outset. Teachers have the ability to "solve the right problem" in designing learning experiences by trying out different ways of framing the problem until a satisfactory way of thinking about the issue is found (Dorst, 2011; Kelly & Gero, 2022).

As a part of framing, teachers conduct activities, like testing out ideas (e.g., sketching them, mapping them, writing them, discussing them), that shift their understanding of the problem. They expand their knowledge of the sociocultural context of the problem by considering their students and doing research. In conducting these activities, a designer draws upon resources, such as other people, knowledge objects and technology.

Finally, teachers have the ability to iterate in developing a response to a design problem. They can frame a problem, but this is not sufficient; expert designers know how to avoid fixation upon initial ideas (Lawson & Dorst, 2013). They can work with the frame to change it through design activities. They can continue doing this until a frame is found in which a solution "suffices" to address the design problem. This model of the core cognitive capabilities for design is the *frame-activity model of design* (Kelly & Grace, 2025), and here we apply this model to the world of a teacher.

Design Cycles, Frames and Activities

Good design for learning requires that teachers respond to reality as they find it: *this* particular class of students, *this* learning environment, *this* curriculum, *these* resources, *this* much time and so on. One formulation for the way that

Figure 2.1 Design as cycles of learning and creating (adapted from Berkun, 2020)

teachers achieve the complex integration of these overlapping (and often competing) considerations is to recognise that teachers as designers go through *cycles of design* in which they create things and then learn from what they have done, in ongoing cycles, as presented in Figure 2.1. This notion of cycles of design has been formalised in *design thinking* frameworks for teachers, most notably the *double diamond* (Kochanowska & Gagliardi, 2022) and the *d.school framework* (Stanford d.School, n.d.).

In these frameworks, cycles of learning and creating involve teachers defining problems, empathising with students, ideating possible learning experiences, creating lessons and materials, trying their designs out and iterating over this until the design is satisfactory (Henriksen et al., 2020; Koh et al., 2015). Design thinking frameworks provide a list of phases of design and suggest potential activities within each of those phases.

Critiques of design thinking frameworks focus upon their linear and limited nature and implicit claims to be expressing the totality of design activity (Cross, 2023; Kelly & Gero, 2021; Kimbell, 2011). A consequence is that one can be an expert in using design thinking frameworks without having the design expertise of knowing how to use activities to work with a frame in the context of a problem. A response has been a description of design expertise based on designers working with a frame—a conception of the problem and how to address it—through design activities (Kelly & Grace, 2025), following the *frame innovation* theory of Dorst (2015) (see Figure 2.2).

The frame-activity perspective recognises that the expertise of a designer (a teacher in this case) lies in knowing *which* activities are needed within *this* design cycle in the context of *this* particular problem. Design expertise in this view involves understanding and framing a problem. The role of activities—whether empathising, researching, prototyping or testing, etc.—is to change the frame in a useful way. A *design frame* is the way that a teacher understands a particular design problem (Dorst, 2011; Kelly & Gero, 2022). A useful way to think about a design frame is that it is the way a designer would respond to the question, "What are you doing now?" Their response is an externalisation

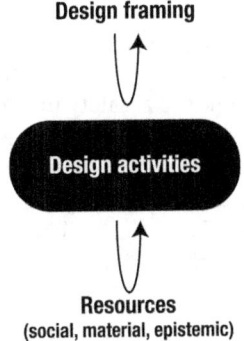

Figure 2.2 Teachers design by framing a problem, conducting activities and drawing on resources (adapted from Kelly & Grace, 2025)

of the frame (Clancey, 1999; Kelly & Gero, 2022). As designers learn more about a problem, the frame changes.

For teachers, having this kind of design expertise is valuable for meeting their basic psychological needs, as is discussed later in the chapter. To explain these concepts of design frames and design activities, we use a running example of a high school mathematics teacher wishing to commence a series of classes about trigonometry. Our (fictional) mathematics teacher commences designing their first lesson with an idea that perhaps they will get students to discuss ideas for how they might measure a tall tree without climbing it. The teacher discovers when using this idea in the classroom that the students are reluctant to speak up at all; perhaps, the teacher thinks, "I need to begin by creating a safe and communal learning environment before starting the discussion". The teacher has changed their framing of *what they think they are doing* in their designing for this lesson.

A design frame changes through *design activities*, where the term "activity" is drawn from the literature on activity theory (Engeström, 2000; Zahedi et al., 2017). Here, activities involve anything from formal design methods (e.g., brainstorming, sketching, prototyping, interviewing someone, etc.) through to informal activities that indirectly relate to the design problem (e.g., "chatting about my ideas with a colleague" or "going for a walk to let my subconscious work on things").

In the frame-activity model, design expertise is about knowing which activities are likely to shift the design frame in a useful direction. In our running example, the mathematics teacher tried out their idea with a class of students (a design activity) and this shifted their frame (they realised that they needed to evoke feelings of safety and community in the classroom). This in turn shifted future design actions and they then altered the lesson plan to, say, introduce an "ice-breaker" activity.

A further part of design expertise is having the capability to draw on resources in the service of design activities. Activities require some combination of social, material and epistemic resources (Goodyear & Carvalho, 2014). For example, our mathematics teacher might ask other teachers for advice (social), use funds to create physical teaching resources (material) and look up the literature on how to create psychosocial safety in a learning context (epistemic).

The value of the frame-activity model of design is to recognise that the design capabilities required of teachers run deep. Being an expert designer has at least as much to do with general capabilities (e.g., creativity, critical thinking, collaboration, communication) and experience (knowing how frames and activities relate to problems) as it does with "design thinking" as it is commonly framed.

Design Expertise and the Basic Psychological Needs of Teachers

Self-determination theory originated within psychology (Ryan & Deci, 2000) as a basis for understanding "the relation of basic psychological needs to wellbeing, psychological flourishing, and high quality of life" (Ryan & Deci, 2024, p. 6230). Its essence is that humans have their basic psychological needs met and maintain internal motivation for tasks when three features are present: autonomy, relatedness and competence. Autonomy refers to the ability to do a task in a way that is in harmony with the individual's understanding of the world. Relatedness refers to connections with other humans through a task, either directly or indirectly. Competence refers to a feeling that one's abilities are being utilised, expanded or appreciated. The theory has been validated through empirical studies in many ways over the past three decades (Deci & Ryan, 2012; Ryan & Deci, 2024) and widely applied in the context of students and teachers (Ahmadi et al., 2023; Eyal & Roth, 2011; Niemiec & Ryan, 2009). Self-determination theory confirms that there is increased internalisation towards intrinsic motivation when these psychological needs are satisfied, as all humans contain an intrinsic need to be self-determining, feel competent and be connected to others.

Many Australian teachers bring their design expertise into their professional life. They teach in a way that is in harmony with their own values by embedding their own educational philosophy (beyond what is written in the curriculum) into their design for learning—an example of autonomy. They develop meaningful relationships with other teachers and with their students through collaboration and communication as examples of relatedness. They see repeatedly their own effectiveness as teachers through this process of designing and teaching and recognise their own competence. In this way, the use of design capabilities helps teachers to meet their own basic psychological needs. The link between design expertise and self-determination has been recognised by others (Chiu et al., 2021). We represent this relationship in schematic form in Figure 2.3 with explicit mapping between the constructs of self-determination theory and teachers' design cycles.

Design, understood as a way of satisfying psychological needs, plays an important role in Australian teachers' success strategies. It enables them to deal with realities as they find them (Kelly, 2025). It allows them to internalise their

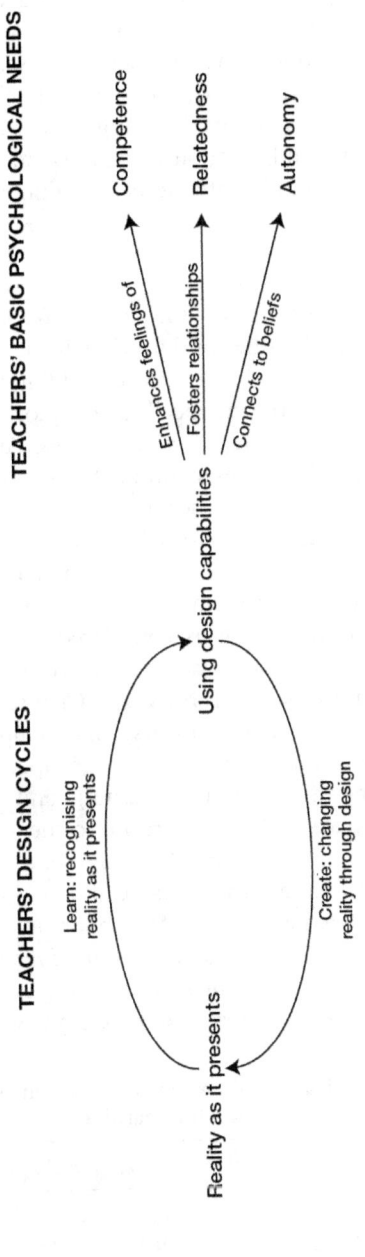

Figure 2.3 How design capabilities lead to satisfaction of basic psychological needs

own interests, values and competencies through their work. In this way, it makes their work more intrinsically motivating and self-determining. It is evident that the frame-activity model of design (Kelly & Grace, 2025) and self-determination theory (Ryan & Deci, 2000) combine to provide a fitting lens through which to investigate the teachers' multiple and varied strategies for success in designing effective and transformative educational experiences for their students.

Teachers seemed, in our interviews, to take great pleasure in designing learning experiences for their students. We suggest that this might be due to the relatedness, competence and autonomy that is found through this activity, and we provide examples from our interviews to highlight where this occurs.

Data Analysis

This chapter focuses on the dimension of *teachers as designers* from the five aspects of teachers' work and identities outlined in Chapter 1. The data analysis strategy, also detailed in Chapter 1, involved examining interview transcripts from the Australian research project, specifically exploring references to design that could be found within teachers' narratives. Analysis drew on the four nodes of complexities, challenges, contradictions and comforts. The *complexities* address the intricate issues teachers faced; *challenges* highlight difficult and potentially stressful experiences; *contradictions* reflect the tensions arising from competing demands; and *comforts* identify the sources of support and motivation that fostered encouragement and satisfaction.

Seven participants' narratives that were considered useful for understanding teachers as designers for learning were selected, listed in Table 2.1 with their respective assigned pseudonyms (see Table 1.1 in Chapter 1 for demographic information about the project's participants). Based upon our conceptual framework, the extracts from the narratives were grouped into two categories of: (1) how teachers frame their design for learning; and (2) cycles of designing for learning. These cycles of designing relate to the arc of "what happens at learntime", through to "reflection on the design and outcomes", and into the next design cycle with changes to the frame and new activities proposed.

The notion of "success" (as per the title of this book) in relation to teachers as designers for learning is construed as maintaining *intrinsic motivation*, the willingness to keep on "doing the work" through recurring cycles of design. As has been described, we adopt the *self-determination theory* perspective that intrinsic

Table 2.1 Data Analysis Matrix for Teachers as Designers for Learning

	Teaching by design
Complexities	Alexa, Ella
Challenges	Sharon, Charlotte
Contradictions	Katie
Comforts	Ella, Alexa

motivation is maintained when teachers have autonomy to do work in a way that feels true to them, relatedness through connection with other humans through the work and a sense of their competence being valued (Ryan & Deci, 2000).

Teachers Framing Their Design for Learning

Teachers have agency to bring their own values into their designing for learning. For example, teachers can choose to bring their own personal teaching philosophies into their preparation, in addition to achieving the minimum standards for professionalism that are expected of them. Teachers create their own design problems. They are given a basic brief of what they need to achieve (curriculum, students, reporting, etc.) but within this they bring their own educational philosophy and their own sense of teacher identity, and they construct their own frame for the challenge of designing for learning. In this way, all teachers should see themselves as educational designers.

Teachers' motivation for framing their design for learning impacts on their decision-making as they draw on resources to achieve a goal. Within the complex environment of a school, the conditions present to support and sustain motivation to meet the teachers' psychological needs (Ryan & Deci, 2020) determine the multifaceted interplay between teachers' intrinsic and extrinsic motivations (Arthur & Bradley, 2023). Understanding the varying sources of motivation that provide teachers with the reasons for their performances is integral to providing clarity around the relationship between teacher design expertise and teacher success strategies.

Against this backdrop, Katie describes her feeling that, for her, what matters is students becoming "the best they can be" and learning to become good learners. She brings this priority into her designing for learning:

> It's not about the content. I shouldn't say that because it is, but you always want your kids [students] to learn. At the end of the day, if you teach them to be the best person that they can be, then you're making a difference, and that's what we're about.
>
> (Katie, contradictions)

Katie recognises that teachers should value curriculum content learning. Yet, Katie's motivation is fulfilled by the realities of her work whereby she perceives she has the autonomy to design for learning that holistically meets the students' physical, social, emotional and academic needs.

Other teachers bring their educational philosophies into their teaching in different ways. For example, Alexa describes that, for her, students learning to collaborate well is important:

> I think that, for so many young people [teachers], they come in [to the school] and, for some of them, they think that somebody else is going to give them all the resources. It's [about] teaching them how to work with

someone else or work with the team of teachers to develop something together.

(Alexa, complexities)

Alexa expresses her frustration that, while she values the satisfaction from relatedness that is gained from connecting and collaborating to design something with others, she has observed this is something that needs to be explicitly shown and taught to some less experienced teachers. Although the design processes of interpretation and exploration can be conducted independently, a team approach to design framing draws on different perspectives and strengths to meet the common goal. From this perspective, design challenges can be internally motivating when they involve working together to define a problem and create a design solution.

The following extract from Sharon's interview transcript is specific to the design challenges of a language teacher, having the added burden of needing students to *choose* the language programme, thereby having a challenge of "design for marketing her subject area" on top of the responsibility of design for learning. Yet we can hear the pride in the way that Sharon takes on this design challenge of responding to the reality as it presents:

Every kid [student] has to do English, so their curriculum can be as boring as they want it to be. The kids have to do it. Ours is different, so we have to make sure our…programs [languages] are dynamic. They're exciting, they're relatable, they change with the cohort. Uhm… a Japanese program I would have had 10 years ago looks completely different to what I have now; 10 years ago we might have looked at…I don't know, Samurais, and temples and castles. Now we're looking at Pokémon Design and robots in everyday Japanese life, so you've got to keep up with your subject area …. It's got to be relevant and interesting. So we're doing constant promotional teaching, if I can put it that way. Our students have to like us, because, if they don't like us, they won't do our subject.

(Sharon, challenges)

Sharon shared that she felt capable of shifting the design frame to meet the needs and interests of the changing cohorts of students. Knowing that she has done this in the past, and has the competency to do so again, provides a source of internalised motivation. Clearly, this challenge of responding to reality as it presents is there for all teachers in designing for learning. Even English teachers who supposedly do not have the burden of maintaining relevance often take on this challenge of staying relevant because they care about their students being engaged with their learning.

However, for some teachers, finding the motivation for change year after year in the face of others who do not appreciate or value change can be challenging. Charlotte found herself in an environment where autonomy to be innovative in designing for learning was constrained:

> When you start out, you feel very positive and you feel like you have a lot of good ideas, and you really want to make a difference and make changes and be very innovative. That's how I felt. I really wanted to do these things. Then I feel what's hard is you don't really have a say and you're constantly told, "There's no need for that, don't do this, don't do that". You get to the point where you're not allowed to do anything; you are not allowed to make changes to a program or plan. Then I think that's where it's very limiting. I think that's where we are not innovative at all; complete opposite and that's pretty much in most places [schools].
>
> (Charlotte, challenges)

Clearly, Charlotte's motivation to design innovative learning had been thwarted by the lack of autonomy that she experienced in her teaching contexts, even though her self-perception as a competent, innovative designer was obvious. Her autonomy frustration comes from the externally imposed resistance to change. Charlotte laments the loss of her source of control to "make a difference and make changes and be very innovative". In this case, Charlotte's engagement in her work is controlled by demands external to her, thereby challenging her internal motivation and perception of teachers as design experts.

Teachers bring many different kinds of expertise and understanding into their framing of design for learning. Their positive competence and capacity to influence students' outcomes rely on their continuous reflection about their personal beliefs in their abilities to design learning to meet students' learning needs (Pendergast, 2020). For example, Alexa really cares about making things more "hands on" and interactive for students:

> In my teaching, we often include little animations or things that I might've found on the internet to enhance that explanation of things, especially some of the concepts in biology that are out there and how the cells talk to each other and stuff. If you can find a little animation of "Here is my hormone joining to a receptor" and things, those are things that you can find these days to help you out, but I'm very much that students are kinaesthetic learners. You've got to have hands-on stuff. You've got to have something that they can actually do to that end.
>
> (Alexa, complexities)

Alexa identifies that she seeks to provide structures for her students with varying degrees of support to clarify the expectations and ways of achieving success in learning (Jang et al., 2010). She also emphasises the need for the learning design to provide an awareness of the tasks as smaller unit by offering scaffolded, step-by-step instructions:

> Helping them [students] plan things that aren't all the same just by PowerPoint is a problem. It's getting teachers to realise if you've done PowerPoint for one topic, for the next topic you've got to have notes or have it some other way you're doing things. If you've had a poster or assessment task for one thing, the next thing can't be a poster assessment task. You've got to think of something else, but have some things scaffolded for them.
>
> (Alexa, complexities)

Alexa recognises that keeping things varied and framing learning at different levels of abstraction are capabilities that teachers need in order to form their learning design in a way to achieve the goal.

To summarise, as teachers talked about framing their design for learning, a number of key success strategies emerged. Firstly, having the competency and autonomy to design learning to teach students holistically in order to meet their needs beyond what is stated in the curriculum is motivationally enhancing. Secondly, teachers' design competency extends to being able to overcome challenges that will always be part of the complexities of educational settings. Thirdly, framing learning requires teachers to respond to the context in which they are teaching, so building relationships with students provides them with a knowledge of their students' interests and needs essential to learning design. Furthermore, a sense of relatedness is linked to internal motivation that can be inspired by collaborating as a learning design team.

Cycles of Design for Learning

Teachers frame their understanding of designing for learning, and then they work within that framing to prepare their lessons. It can bring great joy to teachers to enact their hard work as designers in the classroom and to be appreciated for it, and then to continue to improve their designs over time. For example, Ella recognises this enjoyment explicitly:

> I had [a] PE [Physical Education] theory lesson at the start of last term with my Year Sevens. It just went really well. It wasn't a one-on-one experience. It was just watching everybody get really into a topic and just working together and talking to each other and really getting into it. I really, really, really enjoyed watching that. It was just the setup of an activity that just allowed them to think and critique and discuss. It was just a really nice activity that made them think and question basic assumptions. I don't know. That comes to mind. That was pretty cool. Also they had a pre-service teacher doing observations. She was like, "Woe, you're the best teacher." I was like, "That's not the best lesson I've taught all

year." That was really good. That lesson took bloody hours to plan and like cut everything up and stuff. It just worked and it was a really nice stepping stone, but it was more about like watching the kids just get into it and ask awesome questions.

(Ella, comforts)

This kind of joy arises for teachers from their sustained effort to improve their design for learning over time. Further, teachers do the metacognitive work of reflecting upon their design processes and improving them, with Ella recognising that she was perhaps overpreparing in the past and changing her process as a result:

I am teaching stuff that I've done before. So my Year Sevens – my Year Seven HPE [Health and Physical Education] classes are doing the stuff that they did last year, so the hours and hours of prep[aration] I did last year is paying off now. Rather than having to spend three hours on creating a one hour lesson, I spend 20 minutes, 30 minutes, sometimes even just in the spare [lesson] before the [teaching] lesson, just fixing up the little things that I remember, making it better. So my Year Sevens are the same; my Year 12s are just a bit more relaxed. I've taught a lot of this stuff as well before. I know them, the kids, better as well, I know the kids, I know how the school works. Last year, starting in a new school, starting in a new school was just horrible. Working out the new systems, working out just how everything works, it's horrible. The same with my Year Nines: I've done that twice before, because there's semesters. My Year Seven IT [Information Technology] stuff I had to write from scratch, but there was already a backbone for stuff and it was just fine-tuning, so I think it's just luck. I'm also starting to feel more confident with winging it. I can get up, and I know what I'm going to do, I don't have to have every single word written down, which is what I used to do.

(Ella, complexities)

Teachers are informed by their experiences, professional discussions and theoretical understandings to adjust their existing practices and to apply new practices in different contexts (Peel, 2021). Ella's feelings of competency when enacting the designed learning enable her to uncover her tacit knowledge and professional beliefs during learntime. As a part of these ongoing cycles of reflection and designing, teachers come to see how the time that they spend designing serves them in unexpected ways. In this quotation, Alexa describes her hope that "young teachers" can come to appreciate that doing the work in "planning" (designing) is a kindness to their future selves and can save them time in the long run:

I have developed much more work–life balance these days, and this year I'm actually working part-time, which is a change for me. Also, because I've taught for so long, I've got resources that I can then pull up and just use that. I tend to adapt stuff every year and make it a bit updated or whatever, but you use things that you've already got. Then you know more how to work with other people in your school. I share an office at Academy with the head of science, and he and I both teach Year 8 together. The person on the level below us teaches Year 8 with us, so we often get together, [the] three of us, and plan what we're doing. We're all experienced teachers, so we can all jump in there and we'll get in there because we know that's what it takes and it'll be easier for all of us, but we're also writing to, "How are we going to assess this; what are we doing?" Plan it all out ahead of time. Put a bit more time into planning, then everything else doesn't take as much time at all. That's something that's probably really important to teach young teachers. Put the time into your planning because everything else becomes much easier because you've planned everything out.

(Alexa, comforts)

Implications

This chapter has recognised the importance of teachers as *professional designers of learning experiences*, with a primary theoretical contribution of suggesting that teachers' design capabilities are an undervalued basis of teachers' success. Specifically, we have suggested that *design capabilities provide a basis for teachers being able to meet their basic psychological needs*. The chapter has discussed quotations from teacher interviews that support this claim, although these provide merely anecdotal support for what is primarily a theoretical suggestion.

In framing the chapter, we have suggested that self-determination theory (Ryan & Deci, 2000), with its constructs of relatedness, competence and autonomy, is a useful and well-studied way to understand teachers' basic psychological needs. We have referred to notions of 21st-century skills and the metacognitive skills implied by the frame-activity model (Kelly & Grace, 2025) as our basis for articulating teachers' design capabilities.

An implication of the work for educational leaders, teacher educators and administrators is to suggest that supporting teachers to become stronger designers could be a way to address concerns around teacher retention by providing a basis for them to have more internal motivation. Such support would involve recognising the time and professionalism required to design for learning with appropriate care. An implication is that more emphasis might be placed upon what happens in design for learning to rectify a perceived imbalance, with a tendency to prioritise what happens in learntime. As such, considering the dual roles of teachers as professional designers of learning experiences extends their work beyond the duration of their direct contact with students. With the many competing demands for their time and energy, they often become the silent voices during the processes that lead to educational change (Peel, 2021). This chapter, like all the other chapters in this book, appreciates the knowledgeable voices of teachers who design learning from conceptually aligned curriculum learning areas and distinctive contexts to engage students in meaningful learning experiences.

Conclusion

This chapter positions teachers as designers whose success strategies are grounded in their ability to engage in reflexive, situated and collaborative design practice. The recognition of design as central to teaching opens a pathway for more robust professional development frameworks that respect and nurture design expertise. Such recognition has profound implications for educational leadership, policy and teacher education: it necessitates systemic support for teacher autonomy, structured opportunities for design collaboration and sustained investment in the cultivation of design capabilities. Ultimately, to support teacher motivation, resilience and effectiveness, we must engage seriously with the proposition that teaching is a design profession.

References

Ahmadi, A., Noetel, M., Parker, P., Ryan, R. M., Ntoumanis, N., Reeve, J., Beauchamp, M., Dicke, T., Yeung, A., & Ahmadi, M. (2023). A classification system for teachers' motivational behaviors recommended in self-determination theory interventions. *Journal of Educational Psychology*. https://doi.org/10.1037/edu0000783

Alexander, C. (1964). *Notes on the synthesis of form*. Harvard University Press.

Arthur, L., & Bradley, S. (2023). Teacher retention in challenging schools: Please don't say goodbye! *Teachers and Teaching*, 29(7–8), 753–771. https://doi.org/10.1080/13540602.2023.2201423

Berkun, S. (2020). *How design makes the world*. Berkun Media LLC.

Bosch, N., Härkki, T., & Seitamaa-Hakkarainen, P. (2025). Teachers as reflective learning experience designers: Bringing design thinking into school-based design and maker education. *International Journal of Child-Computer Interaction*, 43, 100695. https://doi.org/10.1016/j.ijcci.2024.100695

Bradfield, K. Z., & Exley, B. (2020). Teachers' accounts of their curriculum use: External contextual influences during times of curriculum reform. *The Curriculum Journal*, 31(4), 757–774. https://doi.org/10.1002/curj.56

Buchanan, R. (1992). Wicked problems in design thinking. *Design Issues*, 8(2), 5–21. https://doi.org/10.2307/1511637

Chiu, T. K., Chai, C. S., Williams, P. J., & Lin, T.-J. (2021). Teacher professional development on self-determination theory–based design thinking in STEM education. *Educational Technology & Society*, 24(4), 153–165.

Clancey, W. J. (1999). *Conceptual coordination: How the mind orders experience in time*. Psychology Press.

Cross, N. (2023). Design thinking: What just happened? *Design Studies*, 86, 101187. https://doi.org/10.1016/j.destud.2023.101187

Deci, E. L., & Ryan, R. M. (2012). Self-determination theory. In P. A. M. Van Lange, A. W. Kruglanski, & E. T. Higgins (Eds.), *Handbook of theories of social psychology* (Vol. 1, pp. 416–437). Sage Publications.

Dorst, K. (2011). The core of 'design thinking' and its application. *Design Studies*, 32(6), 521–532. https://doi.org/10.1016/j.destud.2011.07.006

Dorst, K. (2015). *Frame innovation: Create new thinking by design*. MIT Press.

Engeström, Y. (2000). Activity theory as a framework for analyzing and redesigning work. *Ergonomics, 43*(7), 960–974. https://doi.org/10.1080/001401300409143

Eyal, O., & Roth, G. (2011). Principals' leadership and teachers' motivation: Self-determination theory analysis. *Journal of Educational Administration, 49*(3), 256–275. https://doi.org/10.1108/09578231111129055

Gero, J. S. (1990). Design prototypes: A knowledge representation schema for design. *AI Magazine, 11*(4), 26–26.

Goodyear, P., & Carvalho, L. (2014). Framing the analysis of learning network architectures. In P. Goodyear & L. Carvalho (Eds.), *The architecture of productive learning networks* (pp. 66–88). Routledge.

Goodyear, P., & Dimitriadis, Y. (2013). In medias res: Reframing design for learning. *Research in Learning Technology, 21*. https://doi.org/10.3402/rlt.v21i0.19909

Hardy, I. (2015). Curriculum reform as contested: An analysis of curriculum policy enactment in Queensland, Australia. *International Journal of Educational Research, 74*, 70–81. https://doi.org/10.1016/j.ijer.2015.09.010

Henriksen, D., Gretter, S., & Richardson, C. (2020). Design thinking and the practicing teacher: Addressing problems of practice in teacher education. *Teaching Education, 31*(2), 209–229. https://doi.org/10.1080/10476210.2018.1531841

Jang, H., Reeve, J., & Deci, E. L. (2010). Engaging students in learning activities: It is not autonomy support or structure but autonomy support and structure. *Journal of Educational Psychology, 102*(3), 588–600. https://doi.org/10.1037/a0019682

Kelly, N. (2025). Four golden rules for designerly leadership in schools. *Australian Educational Leader, 47*(2), 25–28.

Kelly, N., & Gero, J. S. (2021). Design thinking and computational thinking: A dual process model for addressing design problems. *Design Science, 7*, e8. https://doi.org/10.1017/dsj.2021.7

Kelly, N., & Gero, J. S. (2022). Reviewing the concept of design frames towards a cognitive model. *Design Science, 8*, e30. https://doi.org/10.1017/dsj.2022.25

Kelly, N., & Grace, K. (2025). Design thinking and artificial intelligence: A framework for analysis. In E. Pei & K. Becker (Eds.), *Design thinking: Theory and practice*. CRC Press.

Kickbusch, S., Wright, N., Sternberg, J., & Dawes, L. (2020). Rethinking learning design: Reconceptualizing the role of the learning designer in pre-service teacher preparation through a design-led approach. *International Journal of Design Education, 14*(4), 29–45. https://doi.org/10.18848/2325-128X/CGP/v14i04/29-45

Kimbell, L. (2011). Rethinking design thinking: Part I. *Design and Culture, 3*(3), 285–306. https://doi.org/10.2752/175470811X13071166525216

Kochanowska, M., & Gagliardi, W. R. (2022). The double diamond model: In pursuit of simplicity and flexibility. *Perspectives on Design II: Research, Education and Practice*, 19–32. https://doi.org/10.1007/978-3-030-79879-6_2

Koh, J. H. L., Chai, C. S., Wong, B., Hong, H.-Y., Koh, J. H. L., Chai, C. S., Wong, B., & Hong, H.-Y. (2015). *Design thinking and education*. Springer.

Laurillard, D. (2013). *Teaching as a design science: Building pedagogical patterns for learning and technology*. Routledge.

Lawson, B. (2006). *How designers think*. https://doi.org/10.4324/9780080454979

Lawson, B., & Dorst, K. (2013). *Design expertise*. Routledge.

Niemiec, C. P., & Ryan, R. M. (2009). Autonomy, competence, and relatedness in the classroom: Applying self-determination theory to educational practice. *Theory and Research in Education, 7*(2), 133–144. https://doi.org/10.1177/1477878509104318

Norman, D. (2013). *The design of everyday things* (Revised and expanded edition). Basic books.

Peel, K. L. (2021). Professional dialogue in researcher-teacher collaborations: Exploring practices for effective student learning. *Journal of Education for Teaching, 47*(2), 201–219. https://doi.org/10.1080/02607476.2020.1855061

Pendergast, D. (2020). Middle years education. In D. Pendergast, K. Main, & N. Bahr (Eds.), *Teaching middle years* (pp. 3–20). Routledge.

Ryan, R. M., & Deci, E. L. (2000). Self-determination theory and the facilitation of intrinsic motivation, social development, and well-being. *American Psychologist, 55*(1), 68. https://doi.org/10.1037/0003-066X.55.1.68

Ryan, R. M., & Deci, E. L. (2024). Self-determination theory. In F. Maggino (Ed.), *Encyclopedia of quality of life and well-being research* (pp. 6229–6235). Springer.

Shulman, L. S. (1986). Those who understand: Knowledge growth in teaching. *Educational Researcher, 15*(2), 4–14.

Simon, H. A. (1969). *The sciences of the artificial.* MIT Press Books.

Stanford d.School. (n.d.). *An introduction to design thinking: Facilitator's guide.* Stanford University. https://dschool.stanford.edu/resources/getting-started-with-design-thinking

Wrigley, C., & Straker, K. (2017). Design Thinking pedagogy: The Educational Design Ladder. *Innovations in Education and Teaching International, 54*(4), 374–385. https://doi.org/10.1080/14703297.2015.1108214

Zahedi, M., Tessier, V., & Hawey, D. (2017). Understanding collaborative design through activity theory. *The Design Journal, 20*(sup1), S4611–S4620. https://doi.org/10.1080/14606925.2017.1352958

Recommended Further Reading

Kimbell, L. (2011). Rethinking design thinking: Part I. *Design and Culture, 3*(3), 285–306. https://doi.org/10.2752/175470811X13071166525216

Koh, J. H. L., Chai, C. S., Wong, B., & Hong, H.-Y. (2015). *Design thinking for education: Conceptions and applications in teaching and learning.* Springer. https://link.springer.com/book/10.1007/978-981-287-444-3

Lawson, B., & Dorst, K. (2013). *Design expertise.* Routledge. https://doi.org/10.4324/9781315072043

Niemiec, C. P., & Ryan, R. M. (2009). Autonomy, competence, and relatedness in the classroom: Applying self-determination theory to educational practice. *Theory and Research in Education, 7*(2), 133–144. https://doi.org/10.1177/1477878509104318

3 Teachers as Emotional Labourers

Introduction

"Emotion" refers to nonverbals such as facial expression, body language and tone of voice. Careful and considered usage of language and terminology is employed. "Labour" refers to the work the individual must engage in to achieve a deliberate result, even though the person's true feelings may differ from those that are visually and verbally apparent.

An important aspect of teachers' lives at their workplace is managing emotions. It is up to the teacher as a leader/role model to regulate the feelings of others and themselves in the learning environment for effective and meaningful learning to occur. At any given time of the day, a teacher may be called upon to calm/pacify/appease a student/colleague/parent or a member of the wider community. This emotional landscape is convoluted and unpredictable, and can be traversed successfully only when the teacher has assessed the circumstance(s) and decided on an appropriate reaction, even when their true feelings may have to remain suppressed. In other words, emotional labour is reflected in an individual's management of the ebb and flow of emotional exchanges between themselves and the people they interact with at their paid employment.

At this point, it is timely to differentiate between the terms "emotion work" and "emotional labour". Emotion work occurs in an individual's personal life. It is exhibited when engaging and maintaining relationships with friends/family/acquaintances. For example, it may manifest during a disagreement where the person accedes to another in order that the circumstances do not escalate. Emotion work is characterised by an unpaid "interpersonal task" (Grandey, 2024, n.p.).

Like emotion work, emotional labour can be referred to as "the hiding or changing of true feelings in an effort to display a more acceptable emotional front" (Jarzabkowski, 2001, p. 133). In the case of paid employment, however, the term may further be defined as "... the management of feeling to create a publicly observable facial and bodily display [that is] sold for a wage ..." (Hochschild, 1983, p. 7). In her seminal research into the hidden emotions of flight attendants, Hochschild (1983) referred to emotional labour as a

DOI: 10.4324/9781003564850-3

workplace construct where (in that context) the participants were obligated to conceal/disguise their real emotions behind a mask of friendliness and compliance with their clients' multiple and diverse requests. Gabriel et al. (2015) defined emotional labour as "… the management of emotions as part of the work role …" (p. 2).

In summary, emotion work is dependent on social norms where emotions are managed to enhance/maintain relationships with valued others such as family members, whereas emotional labour is performed professionally as a part of the roles and responsibilities of employment. "Expectations are explicitly stated in handbooks, training, financial gains" (Grandey, 2024, n.p.).

Selected Literature

Each of the three elements of a profession that requires emotional labour (Walsh & Baker, 2022) can be applied to teaching. These consist of jobs that necessitate:

- "face to face or voice to voice contact with the public
- the worker to produce an emotional state in another person" (n.p.)
- The ability of the employer to exert some control over the "emotional activity" (n.p.) of the employee.

Face-to-face or voice-to-voice contact has historically been a standard communicative practice between teacher and parent, and between teacher and the wider community. However, it was generally acknowledged that teachers were professionals and as such worked at specific times confined to the daylight hours. Throughout the COVID-19 pandemic, teachers were required to offer themselves as an online face-to-face/voice-to-voice resource for students and parents/wider school community, and the traditional practices were deemed obsolete by leadership and government. Most schools in Australia provided both the physical classroom for students who were the children of essential service workers and the online component of lesson delivery for others. In the contemporary post-pandemic world, the pandemic has been downgraded, but teachers are faced with the additional pressure to provide both the traditional physical environment and an after hours online component (such as email and text messages). Both prior to and after the classroom face-to-face working day, teachers are often required to provide unlimited email/phone/face-to-face access to the school administration/community, as well as attention to curriculum matters and planning.

Fostering a student's emotional development is an unspoken requirement of the teaching profession. Whether the student is a child, young adult or older adult, establishing a positive, safe and authentic relationship is an essential element of good practice. This type of association affords favourable learning outcomes (Carey & Sutton, 2024). Not everyone who enters a classroom environment is predisposed to learn. Students enter the teaching space with emotional landscapes—both overt and hidden—that can be tricky for teachers to navigate. Optimal learning can occur only when both parties have similar expectations for skill and knowledge growth. When this notion breaks down, teachers are required to strategise in order to produce emotional states in their students that, at the very least, open them up to the idea of learning. As students are individuals, this may require the teacher to attend to the separate emotional needs and wants of each student all day, every day. Generating a positive academic outlook in students can be a tiring and complicated process, particularly when the teacher has their own mental health/wellness concerns to contend with.

The feeling of employers' rights to manipulate their employees' emotional sensibilities is not a new concept. Turnbull (1999) interrogated the demands of emotional labour in middle management. She discussed "the trend towards more 'normative' organisation, demanding 'moral' psychological contracts" (p. 127). The applicability of these demands to the role of the teacher resonates. The author posited that employers require that their managers are disciplined and situationally dominant and are able to ignore their personal problems while in the workplace. Furthermore, employees are also required to be passionate, able to influence subordinates emotionally and able to elicit enthusiasm when applying new workplace initiatives (such as the case of teachers striving to navigate an overcrowded curriculum). Turnbull argued that this complex paradox leaves the manager (teacher) no choice but to enact a role play that reflects emotional labour.

Kendrick (2019) denoted "organizational feeling rules" (n.p.) as the suitable and unsuitable protocols imposed by workplace administrators. The author argued that fulfilling the obligations of these codes of behaviour may lead to a rendering by employees of "superficial acting" (Kendrick, 2019, n.p.) in order to hide their true feelings. This surface acting is akin to mask wearing where the actor (teacher) pays lip service to an imposed expectation and speaks the corporate lexis. The mask is then removed when out of the sphere of the organisational environment and the actor is free to speak their own truth. Ultimately, the stress and unrelenting pressure of this enforced situation may impact on the actor's state of mental health and lead to emotional toxicity, resulting in long-term physical and mental exhaustion—i.e., burnout. Engagement with performative "deep acting" requires the actor to "manipulate [their] internal thoughts and feelings" (Näring et al., 2012, p. 63) and obliges the actor (teacher) actually to alter their own beliefs to align with those of the management. The current pressure on teachers to treat their students as commodities or customers has been exacerbated (and even promoted) by policymakers and other associated stakeholders who target and monitor national rankings. Thus, teachers are required to enforce unhealthy and insidious emotional management upon their students and themselves.

Data Analysis

As noted in Chapter 1, our data analytic strategy for engaging with the nearly 300,000 words of interview transcripts related to the Australian research project on which this book focuses included the elicitation of four "nodes":

- Complexities (CY): Engaging with multifaceted events and issues
- Challenges (CE): Encounters with difficult and potentially stressful events and issues
- Contradictions (CN): Events and issues with at least two competing influences and pressures
- Comforts (CT): Sources of encouragement, motivation and pleasure

Five "dimensions" were then applied to each of these nodes. These included psychosocial; profession and professionalism; changes and continuities; naming, framing and shaming; and teaching by design. This chapter focuses on the two dimensions referencing "psychosocial" and "profession and professionalism". In Chapter 1, we defined the former dimension as "The interdependence of personal thoughts and behaviours with the contextual and relational influences of being a teacher". The latter dimension, "Profession and professionalism", was identified as "Teachers' ethical and partly autonomous enactment of dissemination of knowledge, and their interactions with other educational stakeholders".

Teachers are susceptible to daily psychosocial hazards owing to their interactions with multiple actors. An adverse or hostile link between behavioural and social elements can negatively affect teacher mental health if left unmanaged or unregulated. Safe Work Australia (2024) listed the multiple forms of psychosocial harm that may affect an individual's ability to carry out the requirements of their job effectively. Specific teacher workplace examples have been cited. These include:

- Sustained high job demands that include:
  - Physical (overloaded work expectations—e.g., overcrowded curriculum);
  - Mental (skill deficits owing to a lack of training—e.g., being assigned to work with a disabled student without instruction regarding the particular disability);
  - Emotional (exposure to harassment—e.g., gender/power imbalances)
- Low job control—e.g., minimal agency, enforcement of expectations from administration
- Lack of role clarity— e.g., uninformed/blurry lines between societal expectations and the educative environment
- Inadequate organisational change management or no consultation around change—e.g., variation of staff meeting dates and times
- Inadequate reward and recognition—e.g., zero/limited feedback/guidance from administration
- Poor organisational justice—e.g., lack of effective behaviour management for unruly students or threatening parents

- Traumatic events—e.g., lack of counselling after being subjected to workplace bullying/violence
- Remote or isolated work—e.g., working alone on campus after hours
- Poor physical environment—e.g., asbestos in classroom walls, threatening/uncontrollable student/parent behaviour.

Teacher professionalism consists of a code of conduct employed by the teacher when interacting with others that is consistent with best practice and is considered and appropriate. There is a foundational linkage between professionalism and teacher identity. Sachs (2005) posited that:

> Teacher professional identity then stands at the core of the teaching profession. It provides a framework for teachers to construct their own ideas of 'how to be', 'how to act' and 'how to understand' their work and their place in society. Importantly, teacher identity is not something that is fixed nor is it imposed; rather it is negotiated through experience and the sense that is made of that experience. (p. 15)

Thus, professionalism and opinions around teaching as a profession are formed through an individual's interactions with others both inside and outside the workplace. These interactions are influenced by the degree of emotional labour that the teacher is prepared to engage in.

Table 1.1 in Chapter 1 presented applicable demographic information about the participants, who are represented by their respective assigned pseudonyms and whose lived emotional experiences are investigated in this exploration. Building on the data analysis matrix presented in Table 1.2 in Chapter 1, Table 3.1 illustrates the approach taken to data analysis in this chapter, referencing teachers as emotional labourers. The data are separated into the two dimensions of psychosocial, and profession and professionalism. These are

Table 3.1 Data Analysis Matrix for Teachers as Emotional Labourers

Nodes		*Psychosocial*	*Profession and professionalism*
Complexities	Participants	Angela; Keira	Keira
	Focal point/s	Interpersonal/ Organisational dynamics	Interpersonal/ Organisational dynamics
Challenges	Participants	Dean; Stella; Alice	Sharon; Rosalie
	Focal point/s	Lack of agency Emotional exhaustion	Commodification and corporatisation
Contradictions	Participants	Rosalie; Arthur	Rosalie
	Focal point/s	Management	Reduced professional acknowledgements
Comforts	Participants	Stella; Ruth	Kate; Maurie; Keira
	Focal point/s	Personal growth	Moral value

further categorised within the four nodes—i.e., complexities, challenges, contradictions and comforts. Focal points are then extrapolated from the data.

Emotional labour can be viewed through both a negative and a positive lens. This chapter highlights a number of elements that are fundamental to the employment of emotional labour as teachers' lived experience. In order to illustrate this application of emotionality, the following quotations are divided into the respective subheadings of psychosocial, and profession and professionalism.

Complexities

Psychosocial

INTERPERSONAL/ORGANISATIONAL DYNAMICS

Playing on the emotional connection between teacher and student was often reframed by the organisational leadership as part of the teacher's duty to their students. This was highlighted by Angela, who, when asked, "Can you think of any situation that you've experienced during your career or that you're currently experiencing that's had some important emotional charge associated with it?", replies:

> I think the biggest one that I can think of is students who are suicidal. I had a student in one of my classes where I was expected to basically look out for her the whole time that she was at school. It was just so draining on me because I just thought that is not like what the job of a teacher is to make sure that this child is not doing things to herself. I know that there's child safety rules and all that sort of stuff, but I thought it was just stepping beyond what my job was.

This comment illustrates the complexities of teaching impinging on the psychosocial dimension in such a way that teachers mobilise their emotions as a crucial part of their strategies for success in this challenging environment. This type of psychosocial hazard—i.e., being on suicide watch—reflects a lack of role clarity combined with poor organisational justice for both Angela and the student. The emotional labour involved was obviously quite traumatising for Angela.

Keira reflects on the lack of emotional and practical care taken by organisations and on the fact that grassroots teachers were treated poorly. This was reflected in minimal job control:

> I think for many people, it's a broken system; for some of us, it's disjointed and we have the resilience to pull ourselves through most of the time. I think any system where you've got employees who feel it's broken, then it's broken. The organisation is big enough and powerful

enough to put teachers first, but they choose not to [do so]. We are top-heavy with upper management and middle management at a departmental level, and we are experience-poor in the schools.

Profession and Professionalism

INTERPERSONAL/ORGANISATIONAL DYNAMICS

The relationships that teachers have with their students and colleagues and the organisation in which they work have a significant impact on their emotional well-being. The emotional investment teachers have in the well-being of their students impacts on both their professional and their personal lives.

Efforts to work within the constraints of the COVID-19 pandemic led some teachers to the brink of emotional exhaustion and burnout. Keira comments on the sustained high job demands coupled with the lack of agency for her staff:

> Throughout this whole pandemic, those lead principals ... all of those people who say, "We worked really hard". Yes, they did, but they accumulated many hours that they could have off and have a rest and a break. My teaching staff had no school holidays at all after Term One, there was not a day ..., and it was expected by the Department [of Education] that they wouldn't. Then we've got a department that, as an example of bullying, they play on a teacher's emotional connection to their students.

Keira also references the complexities involved around inadequate change management and the lack of administrative thought around teaching practicalities during the COVID-19 phenomenon:

> So this crap—and it is bullshit to give teachers two extra days off at the end of the year to make up for all the time that they've put in. [That] is rubbish because we all know that school is going to finish on a Wednesday, so what?
>
> We're going to be at school for the rest of the week, we're going to be working, we're going to be doing the same things that we would have done because all they've done is shorten the amount of time that we've got to get things completed for the end of the year, so that's bullshit.
>
> What they've played on is the emotional insecurity of younger teachers and new graduates and people who are afraid to rock the boat. That guilt: "We're in a pandemic, you don't deserve a pay-rise because you're in a pandemic, you don't deserve to have holidays, we're in a pandemic, you are expected to work extra hours, you're expected to teach full-time in a classroom and online and prepare external work for the kids that can't make it".

Keira's most potent comment was based on the unreasonable and excessive teaching demands with no support structures in place:

> "You're expected to do three full-time jobs but we're going to give you two days off"; that's bullying. That's a broken system when they're not recognising that, when the people above are forgetting that they have got options and the people below don't have options. That's broken; there's no two ways about it. When you're saying you've got these helplines for teachers to go to, you can ring the crisis centres and all that, they record. They don't record your conversation, but they make a record of who's [rung]. How is that anonymous for a start, and how is that secure? How do you feel secure about that? That's really not a good support for teachers, and I personally wouldn't use it.

Challenges

Psychosocial

LACK OF AGENCY

The role of teacher agency is a convoluted and contested concept. Many organisations are policy driven and leave no space for teacher discussion around the implementation of educational practice (see intext workplace examples). This is detrimental to teachers' well-being and emotional investment as values and experience are negated.

When decisions are made without teacher consultation, teachers are left to come to terms emotionally with the situation. This feeling of imposed emotional isolation is reflected by Dean, who had learnt to come to terms with his lack of agency or control in certain situations:

> I guess really, for the most part, I feel like I do everything I can and what happens is, by and large, out of my control. Probably the biggest thing to navigate is really the things that I can't control and being okay with what does and doesn't happen, especially when it doesn't go the way I hope it would go.

Dean continues in a similar vein: "In a lot of situations, I felt the best thing to do is just to put up and shut up".

EMOTIONAL EXHAUSTION

Generally, emotional exhaustion is not a phenomenon that occurs spontaneously. It is a condition that manifests over a period of time. Repeated adverse or challenging circumstances, where emotional labour is a burden, result in feelings of heightened fatigue and professional ineptitude (Hanson, 2024).

Stella reflects upon her emotional exhaustion when confronted with the experience of teaching traumatised refugee children from Cambodia and Vietnam. She describes the manner in which she responded to these feelings of exhaustion brought on by her emotional labour:

> I think that what I notice is that I need to actually be more aware of my own exhaustion and things with teaching. Whether that's a generalised thing or just because I'm getting older, I don't know. I just can't keep going flat out in one setting either. I find that I'll just get burnt out.

Alice's experience was physically and mentally distressing owing to a lack of support from colleagues and leadership, and adverse conditions in her personal life. She acknowledges the toll of combined negative emotional experiences and the labour involved in order to keep going professionally:

> I had students in Grade Two throwing desks at me, and I was not supported. Emotionally, it was pretty hard. I don't know, it was extremely hard, to be honest, because at that stage I was already away from my family. I had actually missed out on my daughter's birthday, on her 16th birthday.

This perceived lack of support from leadership coupled with the distress of missing an important family celebration compounded an emotionally fraught situation. When asked if she met any of the local parents/children, Alice replies:

> Yes, I did, but it was hard to form a connection because I felt like an outsider from the start. It was just so hard to connect with, not just the staff because I couldn't connect with the staff at the new school I went to. One of the staff members, her son was in my class.
> That itself was hard enough, let alone anything to try and connect to parents. That principal wasn't even on my side or supportive. That within itself didn't help either.

This highlights the emotional fatigue that is generated by poor organisational justice in the form of lack of effective behaviour management and the isolation that occurs when a teacher cannot make positive emotional connections in the workplace.

Profession and Professionalism

COMMODIFICATION AND CORPORATISATION

Sharon refers to the challenging amount of emotional labour required when working in the private schooling system, and the fact that she felt highly visible to parents, students and other stakeholders at all times. She felt pressure to dress and act in a certain way because of the nature of privatisation and the privilege of parents who pay for that system. This type of emotional responsibility reflected sustained high job demands physically (general presentation such as dress), mentally (continually worrying about a perceived mis-step that could lead to job loss) and emotionally (attempting to live up to the school's expectations).

> You really have to watch what you say [and] what you do in a class. Kids could have devices recording; every kid has a laptop; they could have their camera on, so all your lesson plans, all your assessment outlines and course overviews are now visible to parents through our online learning system. So parents can sit and go through your lesson plans—they're very, very visible. The stress of that, and it's highly emphasis[ed in] an independent school because they're a business as well.
>
> Parents are paying [a] minimum [of] $10,000 a year to have their children in that school, so they've purchased that product. And often they want their money's worth, and your job is to teach them well, keep them happy, take care of their pastoral needs and keep the parents happy. They need to pay their fees and you're visible to them and the competition, particularly in that price bracket of the schools that I've worked at. You're a billboard for the school in the way you dress, in the way you are behaving, the way you run your lessons. You've got to be a professional 24/7.

Rosalie mentions the commercialisation of curriculum programming and its negative effect on teacher performance. The emotional labour involved in working for a system that did not value her creativity and work ethic was an anathema:

> What was disheartening for me was that I felt that I was doing quite innovative stuff with the kids and getting a really good reaction and engagement, and yet there was zero interest in that. It was so corporatised that it was just like, "We only are interested in what we've spent a lot of money on because we've got to justify why we've got this program".

Contradictions

Psychosocial

MANAGEMENT

Relationships are influenced by the amount of power imposed over the teaching cohort by the school leadership. Contradictions occur when teaches are successfully fulfilling their roles in the classroom, but management does not recognise the value and success of their work and the effort expended by teaches to achieve academic progress and to keep students engaged (see intext workplace examples). The imposition of more tasks provides yet another layer of stress.

When asked her opinion about the manner in which other teachers coped with imposed, unnecessary meetings, Rosalie details the emotional labour involved in superficial acting enacted by teachers. By wearing a mask of compliance, Rosalie believes that she had dealt with the unsavoury situation of a meeting that she felt wasted her time:

> They just don't give a fuck. They say, "You know what? This is a load of rubbish. Just sit here smile, participate. Don't give a shit." Because we know it's a waste of time. Let them do what they need to do, but look like you care.

This situation illustrated that teachers may momentarily engage in the superficiality of looking like they are interested, in order to return to what they consider as core business as soon as possible. This is also demonstrated by Arthur when he describes his coping mechanism when confronted with a perceived contradiction between management and teachers: "What I've gotten a little bit better at is nodding and smiling, [then] going back and doing whatever I want".

Profession and Professionalism

REDUCED PROFESSIONAL ACKNOWLEDGEMENT

Affirmative professional acknowledgement fosters a productive and motivational environment. Boosting the morale of workers should be seen as one of the primary principles of a healthy workplace. When this obligation is ignored, teachers may become disillusioned and unenthusiastic. This situation can create increased stress and pressure in the form of emotional labour to assure students (and colleagues) that striving for academic and personal success is a worthwhile achievement. Contradictions occur when teachers make a great effort to engage students and this goes unrecognised and unrewarded by school management.

Rosalie cites the lack of professional affirmation and celebration as a discouraging and potentially injurious circumstance, especially in the light of an overcrowded curriculum that demanded more policy implementation by teachers:

> There was no celebration of teacher innovation. It was more just like, "Okay, guys, we've paid $100,000 for this latest acronym and now we want you all to have PD [professional development] in this latest acronym and you're just going to teach it this way. If you teach these seven steps, they're going to know how to do really well in that plan, and then la, la, la."

Comforts

Psychosocial

PERSONAL GROWTH

Isenbarger and Zembylas (2006) cited the caring role that teachers may willingly adopt for the emotional benefit of both themselves and their students. Many teachers recognise the value of their societal role and acknowledge the rewarding professional and personal outcomes from the emotional labour expended in order to be an effective teacher.

Stella relates how she grew to love the job that she had initially found exceedingly stressful. In doing so, she transformed her attitude and discovered an emotional investment that was rewarding and emotionally nurturing. Stella strategically assessed the elements of her job that were playing on her mental health and identified distressing episodes involving negative experiences of emotional labour. She then transformed her approach to emotional interactions that had a positive effective on her professionalism and willingness to engage in the workplace:

> I think my first year, I just thought—I cried every morning on the way to school and every day on the way home for that first year. It was just traumatic. That really made me think, "Why on earth am I doing this to myself when I don't even like this?" I think it was that first year, then I just—teaching is about people, I think, and that's what I realised somewhere in that first year. I just fell in love with those kids as people. I think I spent all my lunch hours. I did this right from my teaching degree, teaching career, really. I rarely went to the staff room, not because I didn't like the teachers, [but] because I just wanted to be with my students. We would spend the whole time talking, and I'd ask questions and I'd learn about their culture, and that changed it for me.

Ruth ponders the emotional involvement that teachers assume when dealing with students in crisis. She refers to the significant role a teacher can play in the life of a student, and to her satisfaction in building up positive long-term relationships:

> Well, those are my happy days and when I look back and I think so, you know you were dealing with some very difficult children in those times. Okay, you know, children who come up to you and say, "My mum died this morning" and you'd say, "Aah, ah. I'm very sorry to hear that", and then you have a little chat and he'd say, "Do you mind if I don't join the choir at the moment?" I'll just say, "No, you just sit out there and when you're ready …". So some of those children we had them from Year One to Year Seven or Year Six, every week, so we were really significant

people in their lives and they would—they would talk, they would talk to us ... because we were very significant. Can I just tell you that this was really, really special? You get the boys to sing, and the whole class to sing. I love hearing children sing.

Profession and Professionalism

MORAL VALUE

Kate describes her passion for teaching and the potential it had for her personal and professional development. This is illustrated in her feelings of agency when opportunities for growth emerged:

> I love my job. When you're a graduate and you think about what schools are supposed to be like and what teaching is supposed to be like, that is what [name of school] is like .... I really, really, really, love my job, and I can see so much potential for growth. You know, they say that in a whole lifetime you couldn't learn everything there is to know about teaching; I definitely feel that.

The positive emotional labour that a teacher employs can lead to personal benefits for both teacher and student. Maurie communicates his thoughts on the true value of being a teacher and the ongoing rewards this had for students, particularly those in adolescence:

> A teacher is someone that's willing to persevere with and putting [in] time to reasonable levels with a student, with a young person to help them get through some challenging parts of life, especially the teenage years, with the adolescence years. There's so much going on, so that they're able to look back and see this was not just some lessons in terms of content, but some life lessons that perseverance—that they can be forgiven for mistakes made and being able to see how they've grown and developed as a person and to be proud of that.

Finally, Keira demonstrates the beating heart of teaching as a profession and the act of professionalism when she reflects on her role as a teacher and the part she played in the personal and academic development of herself and others: "I think teaching is about accepting who you are and accepting who others are and helping them be the best that they can be".

Implications

Elements to do with the healthy application of emotional labour and of a resilient professional attitude encompass a range of personal strategies. Many of these were signposted within the interview extracts discussed previously. Self-awareness and the capacity to self-regulate are paramount. Many of the teachers interviewed adhered to the following processes: they utilised a judicious application of empathy; they managed their emotions with a view to a contextually positive outcome; they employed effective communicative approaches; and they were courageous in their efforts to confront challenges in order to shift mindsets, either their own or those of others. Feelings of agency or control were listed by the interviewees as fundamental when realising strategies that managed the phenomenon of emotional labour.

Agentic practices and strategies included the following:

- Being able to project into the future and conceiving a vision of the professional self in the immediate or long-term future enable a feeling of control and goal setting.
- Effective communication and collaboration with others afford sharing the burdens of teaching with colleagues and lessen the weight of internal conflict. Similarly, sharing the joys of teaching moments enriches the soul and lightens the daily grind.
- Learning from mistakes—one's own and others'—enables and opens pathways to effective praxis.
- Practising a flexible mindset releases constrained emotional tension and develops emotional resilience. Challenges can be reframed and dealt with in a more constructive manner.
- Consciously practising an optimistic outlook changes attitudes and expectations for the better. Recognising that certain situations are temporary and will evolve provides a sense of emotional fortitude.
- Developing healthy self-care and self-esteem knowledge ensures that stress can be dealt with so that it does not permanently negatively impact on resilience.
- Increasing decision-making skills and problem-solving capabilities improves the likelihood of successful interactions.
- Accepting support from others as well as providing support to others leads to feelings of emotional connectedness and belonging.

Conclusion

In summary, emotional labour consists of the management of feelings while in paid employment. These emotions may be negative or positive. Generally, overburdening teachers with intensive emotional labour owing to a negative workplace is reflected in diminished or non-existent positive interpersonal/organisational dynamics, a lack of agency, emotional exhaustion, commodification and corporatisation, reduced professional acknowledgement and uneven power dynamics. When emotional labour is utilised by the teacher as a positive, beneficial relationships are developed. These are signposted in beliefs around personal growth and moral values. From that perspective, Carey and Sutton (2024) noted the wider importance of facilitating teachers' positive emotional labour: "Promoting teachers' well-being at work is not only important for the profession, but also to sustainably provide good quality care and education for children, families, and communities" (p. 1).

References

Carey, S., & Sutton, A. (2024). Early childhood teachers' emotional labour: The role of job and personal resources in protecting well-being. *Teaching and Teacher Education, 148*. https://doi.org/10.1016/j.tate.2024.104699

Gabriel, A. S., Daniels, M. A., Diefendorff, J. M., & Greguras, G. J. (2015). Emotional labor actors: A latent profile analysis of emotional labor strategies. *Journal of Applied Psychology, 100*(3), 863–879. https://doi.org/10.1037/a0037408

Grandey, A. (2024). What is emotional labor? WELD LAB. PennState College of the Liberal Arts. https://weld.la.psu.edu/what-is-emotional-labor/

Hanson, A. (2024). Managing chaos by sacrificing self: Experiences of ICU nurse managers: A classic grounded theory study. https://utmb-ir.tdl.org/items/91f36870-227a-4b45-a531-3d18a84a2649

Hochschild, A. (1983). *The managed heart: Commercialization of human feeling*. University of California Press.

Isenbarger, L., & Zembylas, M. (2006). The emotional labour of caring in teaching. *Teaching and Teacher Education, 22*, 120–134. https://doi.org/10.1016/j.tate.2005.07.002

Jarzabkowski, L. (2001). Emotional labour in educational research. *Queensland Journal of Educational Research, 17*(2), 123–137. http://www.iier.org.au/qjer/qjer17/jarzabkowski.html

Kendrick, A. (2019). *Love, heartbreak, and teacher emotional well-being*. https://www.edcan.ca/articles/teacher-emotional-well-being/

Näring, G., Vlerick, P., & Van de Ven, B. (2012). Emotion work and emotional exhaustion in teachers: The job and individual perspective. *Educational Studies, 38*(1), 63–72. http://dx.doi.org/10.1080/03055698.2011.567026

Sachs, J. (2005). Teacher education and the development of professional identity: Learning to be a teacher. In P. Denicolo & M. Kompf (Eds.), *Connecting policy and practice: Challenges for teaching and learning in schools and universities* (pp. 5–21). Routledge.

Safe Work Australia. (2024). *Psychosocial hazards*. https://www.safeworkaustralia.gov.au/safety-topic/managing-health-and-safety/mental-health/psychosocial-hazards

Turnbull, S. (1999). Emotional labour in corporate change programs: The effects of organizational feeling rules on middle managers. *Human Resource Development International, 2*(2), 125–146.

Walsh, M. J., & Baker, S. A. (2022, July 11). What is emotional labour – and how do we get it wrong? *The Conversation*. https://theconversation.com/what-is-emotional-labour-and-how-do-we-get-it-wrong-185773

Recommended Further Reading

Bodenheimer, G., & Shuster, S. M. (2019). Emotional labour, teaching and burnout: Investigating complex relationships. *Educational Research, 62*(1), 63–76. https://doi.org/10.1080/00131881.2019.1705868

Burić, I., & Frenzel, A. C. (2020). Teacher emotional labour, instructional strategies, and students' academic engagement: A multilevel analysis. *Teachers and Teaching, 27*(5), 335–352. https://doi.org/10.1080/13540602.2020.1740194

Clark, M., Robertson, M., & Young, S. (2018). "I feel your pain": A critical review of organizational research on empathy. *Journal of Organizational Behavior, 40*(2), 166–192. https://doi.org/10.1002/job.2348

Vial, A. C., & Cowgill, C. M. (2022). Heavier lies her crown: Gendered patterns of leader emotional labor and their downstream effects. *Frontiers in Psychology, 13.* https://doi.org/10.3389/fpsyg.2022.849566

4 Teachers as Narrative Constructors and Deconstructors

Introduction

Narratives (personal accounts or stories) are an important facet of professional and personal life. They are a significant conduit to communication with the self and with others. The creation of narratives helps set the contextual and ideological understandings to be extrapolated from life episodes that may have had successful or unsuccessful outcomes for the individual. As such, the fluid nature of the narrative allows for an investigation that may provide clarity or redirection for both the audience and the speaker. Narratives are multifaceted, nuanced and fundamentally subjective. Most narratives are emotion-driven or possess a significant level of feelings (both positive and negative) that increase the degree to which a person is committed to the story they are telling. In fact, these accounts are framed by a certain amount of emotional labour (please refer to Chapter 3) and are deemed an important aspect of the life of the teller.

Work that is inherently complex, such as teaching, requires equally complex narratives. These stories allow practitioners to communicate professional and personal issues effectively among themselves as well as with other participants and stakeholders (Brown, 2022; Veenswijk & Berendse, 2008). Importantly for the concerns of this book, a major result of Scott's (2022) research using life story interviews with 119 adults was that "... people made sense of their work lives most often by constructing themes about personal agency" (p. 1057). Such a finding resonated with this volume's focus on Australian teachers' success strategies as gleaned from their motivation and resilience narratives. At the same time, and as we highlighted in the introductory chapter, that agency is constrained in significant ways by the teachers' multifaceted and challenging occupational environments (Porter, 2023). Accordingly, and as we explicate in the implications section of this chapter, the narratives that the participants constructed and deconstructed in the semi-structured interviews conducted for this research project encapsulate crucial lessons for their understandings of their success strategies and of how those strategies are facilitated by their self-reported motivation and resilience.

As explained above, narrative construction involves individuals who create stories based on their lived professional and/or personal experience. These

DOI: 10.4324/9781003564850-4

stories, once shared, may then undergo a process of deconstruction where the stories are disassembled and reflected upon to reinforce actions or to include different or alternative perspectives. After examining relevant literature about the meanings and significance of teachers' narratives, this chapter elaborates the declarative proposition of "Teachers as narrative constructors and deconstructors" by analysing selected participants' utterances about their success strategies through the prism of their statements about their motivation and resilience, informed by our understandings of their narrative work. We then distil specific wider implications for apprehending teachers' emotional experiences against the backdrop of that work.

Selected Literature

It is fortunate, given the focus of this chapter, that literature abounds focusing on teachers' narratives about their work and identities. A useful starting point in that regard is the study by Estola et al. (2003) of perhaps the most vital element of such identities: their sense of vocation, which is further developed in Chapter 10, where we explicate the declarative proposition of "Teachers as teaching idealists". For Estola et al., "the teachers' vocation" was presented "… as a moral voice and its manifestation in the form of caring in teachers' descriptions of their own practices" (p. 239). Relatedly, Altan and Lane (2018) posited teachers' narratives as an accurate and authoritative means of "… exploring the influences of teachers' significant life experiences on their dispositions and teaching practices" (p. 238). Moreover, Ho (2005) demonstrated how Hong Kong secondary school teachers used their narratives to enact a metaphorical construction of themselves, although tellingly she found that construction to be "… largely paradoxical", manifested in the "co-creation of a negative self and a positive self" (p. 359): the negative self was concentrated on such matters as students' disciplinary problems and poor interpersonal relationships in the school, while the positive self emphasised an abiding sense of "… commitment, care and a great sense of responsibility" (p. 359).

Much of the scholarly literature related to teachers' narratives has analysed the themes and topics of those narratives. These themes and topics traverse curriculum application (Shkedi, 2009) and pedagogical design capacity (Davis et al., 2011), the dynamic character of teachers' work (Lutovac et al., 2024), relationships with students (Stuhlman & Pianta, 2002) and supposedly disruptive versus non-disruptive students (Spilt & Koomen, 2009), and partial school reopenings during the COVID-19 pandemic (Kim et al., 2021), among many others. Despite this diversity of focus, these stories all exhibited the complex structure and metaphorical significance common to consciously constructed and communicated narratives intended to share fundamental elements of teachers' experiences and identities.

Like the variety of issues canvassed in the teacher narrative literature, there is considerable diversity evident over the past few decades in the manner in which narratives, including those of teachers, are constructed and deconstructed (see for example Panday, 2003; Parker, 1998; Pino Gavidia & Adu, 2022; Prior & Talmy, 2021). Again, despite this laudable variation, we apprehend both construction and deconstruction as agential and purposeful processes in which the participants engaged as their contribution to shared meaning-making in the context of the interviews. In this chapter, we posit narrative construction as careful and creative composition of often disparate experiences into a generally clear and consistent form for communicating with us in the study's semi-structured interviews. Similarly, rather than necessarily approaching narrative deconstruction "... as a radical *perplexity* in the face of narrative" (Gilbert-Walsh, 2007, p. 317; *italics in the original*), we envisage deconstruction in the setting of the interviews as an equally careful and creative activity of self-examination and reflexivity, prompted by the developing conversation as the interview unfolded. Sometimes, this deconstruction can be used to identify and explain, if not to resolve, particular complexities and contradictions related to the construction. Mostly, deconstruction serves to clarify and deepen understanding of construction as they pertain to teachers' work and identities and to their motivation and resilience narratives. Relatedly, it is important to acknowledge that teachers' narratives are not automatically or necessarily consistent or in concert with one another; a key stressor for many teachers is that their narratives mobilise oppositional ideas and contradictory forces (Clarà, 2017).

A timely exposition of this account of teachers' narrative construction, deconstruction and reconstruction was provided by Clarà et al. (2025), who analysed these processes as "narrative mechanisms of reappraisal", or more specifically "modifying cognitive appraisals". The authors demonstrated the profound personal impact of these mechanisms occurring over a considerable time period, and entailing an authentic transformation in understanding of specific incidents experienced by the participating teacher. Moreover, this dramatic change in perception occurred in sync with the participant's ongoing development of "her teacher resilience", which in turn resonates strongly with this book's focus on maximising Australian teachers' success strategies.

From the perspective of this selected literature review, teachers' narratives are a powerful component of their professional and personal lives and have the ability to influence—both positively and negatively—the lives of those with whom they interact on a daily basis. Narratives contain knowledge and, by listening to the multidimensional voices of teachers articulated through their narratives, more consideration could be given to issues involving organisational best practice, concepts of self and identity (for all stakeholders), social justice and future educational direction. Generally, it would appear teacher narratives are an under-represented aspect of organisational leadership; however, education systems as a whole would benefit as much as individual teachers from foregrounding the importance of teacher narratives. Such an approach would make it more likely that teachers' personal narratives and systemic discourses were working in alignment rather than in opposition to each other.

Data Analysis

As we noted in Chapter 1, our data analytic strategy for engaging with the nearly 300,000 words of interview transcripts related to the Australian research project on which this book focuses included the elicitation of four "nodes":

- Complexities (CY): Engaging with multifaceted events and issues
- Challenges (CE): Encounters with difficult and potentially stressful events and issues
- Contradictions (CN): Events and issues with at least two competing influences and pressures
- Comforts (CT): Sources of encouragement, motivation and pleasure

Furthermore, that strategy entailed the elicitation of five "dimensions": psychosocial; profession and professionalism; changes and continuities, naming, framing and shaming; and teaching by design. As we mooted in the introductory chapter, each data chapter elaborates one or two dimensions; in this chapter, the emphasis is on naming, framing and shaming. In Chapter 1, we defined "naming, framing and shaming" as "The social, cultural and political issues, tensions and changes that influence the public and sometimes politicised positioning of teachers' work and identities" (see also Danaher et al., 2013). More specifically, we draw on the following conceptualisation of the first two of these three processes, as articulated by Cook et al. (2013). Firstly, "... naming is a key element of identification ..." (p. 141). Secondly, framing is:

> ... the ideological positioning of specific communities and individuals in certain kinds of ways .... [Sometimes, framing] might be considered to be politically neutral or even empowering. However, we see framing as inevitably ideological and as needing to be scrutinized for its intended and unintended effects. (pp. 141–142)

When applied to Australian teachers, these three intertwined processes can be understood as follows. Firstly, naming individuals as "teachers" can be a positive and/or neutral discursive practice, but it can also be redolent of scepticism, verging on contempt, on the part of some parents/caregivers and community members. Secondly, framing individuals as "teachers" generally involves linking them with organisations such as schools and with broader education systems, again in ways that can be positive, neutral or negative. Thirdly, shaming individuals as "teachers" occurs when excessive emotional investment is made in denigrating those individuals on the basis of their occupational

Table 4.1 Data Analysis Matrix for Teachers as Narrative Constructors and Deconstructors

	Naming, framing and shaming
Complexities	Dean; Anthea; Katie
Challenges	Declan; Ella; Kylie; Arthur
Contradictions	Rosalie; Audrey; George
Comforts	Stella; Alexa; Sophie

status, and also when the recipients of that investment similarly experience it in emotionally negative ways.

Building on Table 1.2 in Chapter 1, Table 4.1 illustrates the approach taken to data analysis in this chapter about teachers as narrative constructors and deconstructors, clustered around the naming, framing and shaming dimension, and organised around the four aforementioned nodes. Table 1.1 in Chapter 1 presents relevant demographic information about the participants, represented by their respective assigned pseudonyms, whose emotional experiences are canvassed in this analysis.

Complexities

Dean highlights certain complexities of teaching that derived from the specific characteristics and needs of particular groups of students. Consequentially, those complexities could easily change when he started working with a different set of children. Thus he constructs a positive, forward-looking narrative to assuage his present feelings of professional uncertainty:

> I think next year I might feel a bit differently because I might have a different caseload of children with [a] different set of needs and complexities, which will be new for me and therefore give me new challenges. I guess it is, perhaps, a matter of time, plus perhaps looking into more conversations with people who are further ahead than me and have similar values to mine.

In this regard, Dean's narrative construction can be seen simultaneously as a discursively successful strategy designed to "think himself forwards" in a new and hopefully more engaging teaching scenario and also as a contribution to (re-imagining) teaching as a purposeful, positively challenging profession, in implicit contrast to teachers being named and framed (and potentially shamed) by others in a less positive light.

Similarly, Anthea reflects on her unexpectedly positive experience of being assigned a middle management role with an informal leadership dimension working with other teachers, thereby demonstrating that the complexities of teaching are not inherently negative but instead can generate unanticipated long-term professional learning. Anthea had now deconstructed the narrative she had built around remaining in the classroom and, upon reflection, she created a new professional ambition:

> That was a really great opportunity. It opened my eyes to what I wanted to do post classroom. I thought I'd never want to leave the classroom, but looking after other teachers and helping them to become better teachers is something that I'd like to do more of. That position really allowed me the opportunity to do that.

Here Anthea deconstructs and then reconstructs a potentially stressful experience in a much more productive way. In doing so, her success strategy entails her mobilisation of her capacity to allow the experience to enable "[her] eyes" to be "opened", which in turn facilitates her reframing of her self-narrative about what "teaching" could involve for her. This example suggests that, when circumstances are favourable, teachers can benefit significantly from opportunity for learning that can strengthen their own naming and framing of who they are as teachers, leaders and persons.

Continuing this theme of participating teachers' narratives reflecting constructions and reconstructions of complex situations and (re)framing those situations in a positive light, rather than responding reactively to naming, framing and sometimes shaming of teachers by others, Katie responds as follows to the interviewers' opening question about what makes teaching a satisfying day for her:

> You still had your behavioural concerns [but] they got less and less, and they got more minor as the days went on, so, for me, it's hard because I don't look for a success in just one day. Sometimes I look at it over a week because one day for some classes isn't enough, if that makes sense. To be honest, over the day, it'd be mainly, you might get two students or even just that one student who finally clicks in that one lesson and you're like, "Oh, thank God." [chuckles] [Mine] is just that little success that you find in your students, and you've just got to look for that every day. That's pretty much how I see my days being really good. If I go through a [day] where I can't find a success, to me, that's a bad day.

Here Katie reframes the complexity of student learning by acknowledging the longer-term perspective needed to facilitate and experience success by her students and hence by herself. Implicitly, less experienced teachers might feel frustrated if they expected to see student learning as an incremental, progressive process, with students consistently moving forwards in their understanding of complex material. By contrast, Katie implies that some students might indeed move forwards while others were treading water or even regressing in their understanding until "one student ... finally clicks in that one lesson". This analysis also functions as a counternarrative to educational stakeholders who expect instant results and/or permanent improvement in learning outcomes.

Challenges

Declan elaborates what he sees as the deleterious effects of a fundamental disjuncture between effective teaching and effective school leadership, which he identifies as being a challenge simultaneously for individual teachers who had been promoted and an education system striving to promote sustainable succession planning. Declan's narrative is constructed around reasons why this is so, thus clarifying for himself the situations he had witnessed in his profession:

> There are a number of things which are challenging about education today …. I do think that you end up with teachers being promoted beyond their capabilities in many … areas. Now … that's with good intentions, and because people see, "Okay, you're a really good classroom teacher, so we'll promote you", but there's not necessarily that managerial skill, and that managerial training that happens as part of someone's teaching—teaching education, and, without those managerial skills, you're not going to be that effective … unless you['re] naturally gifted …. I think you do learn a lot on the job and … along the way in terms of management as well, but it's a skill set … that's not generally part of a teacher's remit.

From one perspective, Declan's narrative segment presented here can be read as a lament for school leaders not being sufficiently trained or well equipped to function in that role. From a different perspective, his words can be interpreted as constructing and perhaps reconstructing effective school leadership as a specialist "skill set" with distinctive characteristics that need to be developed and honed "on the job". Accordingly, Declan frames teaching and school leadership as separate yet interdependent domains of crucial professional practice with their respective success strategies.

Ella recalls a highly challenging interaction with her student's mother who Ella feels had deliberately shamed her publicly:

> The parent, she was so bad. There needed to be a notification when you clicked on that student, saying, "Do not discuss student behaviour with the mum; she's crazy." Her surname became a verb, like "You got so-and-so-ed", because she attacked you, she was horrible. Horrible, horrible, horrible woman. She did do that to me at parent–teacher interviews one year, and so we had a follow-up meeting with the Head of [Subject] when I was teaching [Subject] at the time. I was extremely [in]experienced then, and I only had a year of teaching behind me before I was introduced to her son, who was generally fine. Meeting with the [Head of Department] helped sort that out, long story short. [laughs]

Ella's narrative repays careful attention because it encapsulates broader, systemic issues that influence teachers' self-efficacy and constrain their agency. The incident conveyed by Ella is one of the most overt instances in the interview transcripts of a teacher being named, framed and shamed by the mother of Ella's student. On the one hand, Ella's raw emotional response to an extremely confrontational situation could still be felt in her words as she recounts the situation some years later. On the other hand, Ella's strategy for success in learning from an experience that could have derailed her teaching career includes reconstructing what had occurred as a learning opportunity from which she had grown professionally. From a wider perspective, while Ella feels that the Head of Department had been supportive of her, the incident prompts questions about the school's and the Department of Education's capacity to deal with a parent who engaged in such a behaviour. While acknowledging that such situations are complex, one reading of Ella's narrative is that she was one of a number of inexperienced teachers who had undergone stressful interactions with a parent who was consistently hostile in her dealings with her son's teachers.

For Kylie, "challenge" in the context of her teaching work seems to operate in at least two alternative ways. On the one hand, the term has a positive valence when it refers to the interest and excitement of planning and implementing a new syllabus. On the other hand, the word has a less positive resonance as a consequence of the countervailing negative impact of other aspects of her work:

> I find working with teachers that building their understanding is in a time frame, and in the complexity the school processes, environment and compliance [are] very tricky, but certainly it's my classroom practice that is most emotionally draining, working with those students. It's part of the reason why I've requested that I need a break next year that I don't want to teach [subject]. Next year I need out of the senior [secondary] syllabus for a year. I've implemented it; [now] I need a rest, something new, something different, a new challenge.

Kylie's narrative segment here illustrates her mindful mobilisation of critical self-reflection as an effective success strategy designed to sustain her in the next academic year. In doing so, she deconstructs and then reconstructs her initial construction whereby she identifies her "classroom practice" as the element of her workload "that is most emotionally draining" and then reframes her work as follows: "[Now] I need a rest, something new, something different, a new challenge". This carefully articulated utterance constitutes a powerful statement of Kylie's constrained agency (Coe & Jordhus-Lier, 2010; Damman & Henkens, 2017; Gulati & Srivastava, 2014; Herndl & Licona, 2007), in that she asserts her capacity to contribute productively to her school, while acknowledging her need for strategic self-care in order to prepare herself for the next "challenge".

Arthur emphasises the particular challenge of teaching in an area of artistic practice where excelling as a practitioner results from individual hard work and perseverance that the individual can control to a large extent, while teaching successfully in the corresponding subject area depended considerably on active support from the school leadership:

> I want to feel the same kind of emotional engagement with my teaching that I feel with my artistic practice and with [my] artistic discipline. I don't think that that's been a good perspective to base my teaching practice on ....
>
> We're only going to be able to grow the program if the principal and the principal's lieutenants allow [it]. When you hit up against that, you're going to tie yourself up in knots if your personal emotional self-image is dependent on what you're doing as part of your teaching practice.
>
> For music teachers and for drama teachers, we want to have that same kind of feeling of commitment and teaching that we have in our artistic practice. In my experience, and in looking at other people over 20+ years teaching, that's a really, really dangerous position to teach from because it's just so fraught. You cannot control that scope that you're given to teach in. If you try and push up against it, it's just constant frustration.

Like the other selected quotations presented in this chapter and throughout this book, Arthur's narrative can be interpreted through a variety of lenses. For the chapter authors, what stands out clearly is Arthur's discursive movement between two domains of practice with highly varied and potentially conflicting values. On the one hand, he refers to his colleagues and his "artistic practice" and "artistic discipline", with a distinctive frame of reference about teachers as specialist practitioners with accompanying expertise as well as awareness of the pedagogical implications of such expertise (e.g., the importance of sufficient flow and time being devoted to creating an artistic work). On the other hand, Arthur identifies a different domain led by "the principal and the principal's lieutenants", implicitly positioned as needing to oversee the wider school budget of which the arts formed a potentially small part, which in turn significantly curtails the extent and potentially the effectiveness of the arts programmes: "You cannot control that scope that you're given to teach in". We note the negative impact of the collision between these two domains: "If you try and push against it, it's just constant frustration". Yet we note also Arthur's determined self-framing of his colleagues and his work and hence of the value of that work, which represents a counternarrative centred on articulating "your personal emotional self-image", in implicit contrast to "being framed" otherwise by school leaders and colleagues without that same artistic background.

Contradictions

Rosalie recognises that she was framed contradictorily as a teacher striving to enact her role with purpose and intentionality in a much larger system of educational policy and provision:

> ... I definitely saw that I was working within a system. That sometimes the problems that you saw about you were the creation of that system. You're only one person, so you're always trying to work out what's the way that you can be most effective with the least amount of damage to yourself in terms of your own emotional wellbeing.

Here we observe Rosalie reflecting at length on her teaching environment and constructing her reflection in terms of systemic contradictions, encapsulated in her insightful assertion: "That sometimes the problems that you saw about you were the creation of that system". Instead of being named, framed and potentially shamed for her supposed incapacity to achieve more against the backdrop of those contradictions, Rosalie elects to deconstruct and reconstruct the situation as one in which she did her best, but also in which she recognises, "You're only one person", with the corollary that she needs to "work out what's the way that you can be most effective with the least amount of damage to yourself in terms of your own emotional wellbeing". We consider this a powerful statement of a long-term success strategy that other teachers could do well to emulate.

Audrey provides a heartfelt account of how she experiences a crucial contradiction in relation to her relationships with her students that in her view result directly from the demands of her school leadership:

> I said to my [school] admin[istration] a couple of years ago back ..., "Do you want a robot in the room or do you want me? If you want a robot, why have you hired us? Just put a screen in front of these kids and they can teach the kids." They go on and on and on about relationships with the children: "Have a relationship, have a relationship. Make sure your relationship is strong, and then you'll have behaviour management and everything else will fall into place."

In this narrative segment, Audrey reacts powerfully to the self-identified contradiction between a hypothetical emphasis on teachers developing strong relationships with their students and the reality of unrelenting demands on teachers that rendered such relationships unviable or meaningless. In this regard, Audrey's posing of the powerfully rhetorical questions, "Do you want a robot in the room or do you want me? If you want a robot, why have you hired us?" can be interpreted as her rejection of being named and framed (and potentially shamed) by the education system in ways that are profoundly uncongenial to her sense of teacher self.

George refers to the negative emotional impact of a systemic contradiction centred on the person of his school principal, who, on the one hand, seeks to encourage George and his colleagues, and who, on the other hand, is perceived as placing unrelenting pressure on them to go further in their work:

> ... I think here's the contradiction .... there's some disconnect. On the one hand, [the principal] does [recognise George's contributions] but on the other hand he wants more—more—more, and ...I don't know how to deal with that any more.

Here George analyses a different kind of contradiction, but one with similarly deleterious long-term effects on his well-being and his capacity to sustain his enthusiasm for his work. As George expresses the situation, "On the one hand," he feels that the principal recognises George's contributions to the school, yet, "on the other hand", the principal "wants more—more—more". The twofold repetition of "more" is concerning, as is George's stark admission, "I don't know how to deal with that any more". More positively, as a possible success strategy, George's identification of the personal and systemic contradiction contains the potential for George to contest future impositions from the principal. In terms of the naming, framing and shaming dimension helping to organise this chapter, George's analysis represents an example of that same dimension being used by teachers like George to "speak back to" a sometimes unheeding system that can be seen as complicit with the naming, framing and shaming of teachers in the first place. This is potentially constructive for George and likeminded teachers as a success strategy, in that it gives them the analytical tools needed to move beyond individual responsibility—"It's my fault if I can't make these systemic contradictions work effectively for me"—to the more empowered standpoint of recognising those contradictions and seeking to hold them to account—"I am willing to support a contradictory system if it supports my work".

Comforts

Stella recalls deriving considerable comfort from learning informally from the dispositions of highly experienced teachers working in the same school as herself:

> There was that kind of really tough school but the teachers had been there for years, most of them. I remember asking them ..., "What keeps you here? .... I don't understand how you could stay here? It's just demoralising". He said, "Oh, would you like to have another Friday afternoon?" [laughs]. He was joking, but I think in the really toughest schools the teachers—one or two teachers would just debrief and keep you sane and offer to help with behaviour support. Those were the things that kept you going, and you keep those friendships over the years.

By contrast with the preceding examples of complexities, challenges and contradictions that tended to evoke narrative constructions and reconstructions about more negative naming and framing (and sometimes shaming) of teachers, even when some participants used their narratives to distil success strategies for their colleagues and them, this subsection highlights the comforts identified by some teachers that shine a more positive light on the naming and framing experienced by participants. Here Stella's narrative evokes her surprise that in a "really tough school" that she found "just demoralising" a number of experienced teachers "had been there for years", and appeared to enjoy doing so. In this way, Stella deconstructs and then reconstructs her initial construction of a "really tough school" through her own reframing of the teachers' relationships in that particular school. More specifically, Stella refers to the generosity whereby "one or two teachers would just debrief and keep you sane and offer to help with behaviour support", implicitly transforming teaching from an individualised and potentially lonely profession to one predicated on community and collegiality, and the outcome is certainly a strategy for success and a narrative of motivation and resilience: "Those were the things that kept you going, and you keep those friendships over the years".

Relatedly, Alexa, who is an experienced scientist, derives considerable comfort from working with younger and less academically successful science students:

> That's exciting stuff. That's why I love teaching Year 7. They're still a little excited, and they want to learn. They want to use the Bunsen burner and, "Oh, Miss, what are we doing today?" It's not …, "Oh, Miss, how am I going to get the highest marks so I get into medicine?" ….
>
> They're the ones that are going to do it anyway. They don't need your absolute energy and your expertise to help them drive along, because they've already got that goal in mind. They just need you to push them along. It's the ones that are scared or the ones that think science is the worst subject ever, you know?

Here Alexa's narrative segment "speaks back to" the dominant discourse privileging academic success and senior secondary schooling being fixated on facilitating graduating students' entrance into highly competitive university degrees. Instead, she (re)constructs and (re)frames what generates continuing fulfilment for her as a teacher in terms of "why [she loves] teaching Year 7" with her evocative encapsulation: "They're still a little excited, and they want to learn".

Finally in this section of the chapter, Sophie relishes the complexity of what in different circumstances might induce negative emotions related to perceived excessive challenges and contradictions. Her response to the interviewer's question, "What does a good day in your current role look like for you?" is worth quoting at length because of both the breadth and depth of her various responsibilities and the character of her emotional response to those responsibilities:

> It's probably my highlight of my day if you go back into the classroom, still working with the kids, having that open discussion and that going into having that collaborative talking and stuff like that.
>
> So that's probably my highlight when I go into my teaching role. My highlight with working with my team is really about being able to facilitate and engage and coach them and to support them in all their different roles. As you can imagine, just the complexity of their different roles that they have and different things that they have to all address and stuff like that ....
>
> Having my hands in the new senior [secondary school] system, but then also looking ... right back at our Grade Sevens and actually working with our primaries as well. I'm still working very closely with these schools. A good day for me is actually being able to see kids learning and engaging in schools. That is certainly [the] highlight of my work.
>
> Just to see all the pieces fit together .... I like to have that overview, and I think that's what my role does. I get to have that big overall picture, and at times it can be a bit daunting because you've got so many buckets you're juggling because I'm also in charge of facilitat[ing] the Indigenous budget and working with our Indigenous teams .... There's always so many buckets to juggle, I guess. Every time there's a new focus with our region, it's all of a sudden [a] case of them get[ting] to hit around this really quickly. "What do we need to know? What do we –?" It's fast-paced, but I love that in a way. I wouldn't be in the job if I didn't love the fast pace ...

In her narrative segment presented here, Sophie combines a number of elements being canvassed in this chapter. Firstly, we have the impression that Sophie's currently expressed fulfilment and excitement about what would otherwise be a daunting set of responsibilities have been burnished over a considerable period of time, with associated narrative construction, deconstruction and reconstruction likely to be in evidence as she engages with overall effectiveness with a series of important commitments. Secondly, in this segment Sophie articulates her professional identity, and her affective dimension of that identity, in a proactively agential manner; she has control of the naming and framing of teachers and teaching from her empirically grounded perspective, and certainly no shaming is to be permitted. Thirdly, the modestly expressed "I like to have that overview, and I think that's what my role does" belies her role as a school leader with a dynamic and insightful "system view" that enables her to support and sustain large numbers of teachers in her school. That kind of productive leadership entails enacting a succession of strategies for success for Sophie and her colleagues alike.

Implications

Teachers navigate their professional world and enact their individual narratives within their professional and personal boundaries. Thus, identities (fashioned from lived experience) are constructed and deconstructed as contextualised narratives form, unfold and reform. As is so often described within the chapters of this book (e.g. Chapter 3), resilience or the act of being resilient often depends upon a teacher's sense of agency and feelings of personal and professional identity. Here the authors have drawn upon the interviewees who have profoundly and eloquently related the ways in which they have fulfilled their individual roles as both narrative constructors and narrative deconstructors—and where possible narrative reconstructors. Their professional and personal stories reflect strategies that can shape professional identities and that can provide lessons for personal motivation and resilience.

Agentic practices and strategies included the following:

- Recognising the power of narratives in framing the work and identities of teachers is crucial.
- Analysing how teachers construct, deconstruct and reconstruct their own narratives and those of their colleagues helps to identify opportunities for success strategies to be enacted.
- Motivation and resilience as explicitly developed narratives can guide and encourage teachers in implementing and evaluating their success strategies.
- The idea of looking to the future when the present is static and professionally devoid of challenges is a restorative concept.
- Seeking out colleagues with similar value systems and whose careers are more advanced can promote avenues for professional wisdom and insight. Highlighting the importance of communicating with more experienced colleagues and the support that they can give should be factored into professional life.
- Consciously upskilling in order to be effective in a managerial role provides awareness of the manner in which educational leadership may be enhanced.
- The notion that not all complexities are necessarily a negative occurrence affords the individual a wider and more variable lens through which to gain perspective. Some seemingly complex circumstances may deliver opportunity for professional development that may not have consciously manifested previously.
- Challenging situations can be remediated when support is sourced from responsive and approachable administration.
- Self-care should be prioritised and acted upon, especially when a particularly stressful teaching/student load creates tension and pressure in the workplace. Focusing on one's own mental and physical well-being and recognising that individuals are part of a larger system that has shaped (and perhaps at times promoted?) professional issues that are beyond one's control afford avenues for reflective practice.

- The role of hard work and perseverance and the recognition of elements over which one has control, as well as those over which one has little or no control, should be acknowledged.
- Reflecting upon contradictory messages sent by leadership around teacher/student relationship building can lead to a pathway of clarification around professional values.
- Embracing the "fast-paced" nature of the classroom and professional life in general, while experiencing the enjoyment of working in the classroom and interacting with students, can be gratifying.

Conclusion

Professional identity is a complex, multidimensional and dynamic entity. It is a crucial factor in a teacher's success or failure in the workplace. It spills over into an individual's personal self-concept. Through constant reflective negotiation constructing and deconstructing narratives both in and out of the educative environment, teachers form and reform values and ideals that are then showcased within their best practice. "Teachers are change agents in societies. Class size, administration, and resources are important, but it is teachers who have the most influence on student achievement …" (Altan & Lane, 2018, p. 238). Positive student outcomes are reliant upon the manner in which teachers question and respond to the educative climate of their work environment. Indeed, the very culture and health of our society are dependent upon the effectiveness of our teachers and their ability to navigate social, professional and personal challenges in a way that is best practice for productive learning. The specific success strategies elicited above from the selected teachers' constructed and deconstructed narratives are crucial to facilitating such learning for students and teachers alike.

References

Altan, S., & Lane, J. F. (2018). Teachers' narratives: A source for exploring the influences of teachers' significant life experiences on their dispositions and teaching practices. *Teaching and Teacher Education, 74*, 238–248. https://doi.org/10.1016/j.tate.2018.05.012

Brown, A. D. (2022). Identities in and around organizations: Towards an identity work perspective. *Human Relations, 75*(7), 1205–1237. https://doi.org/10.1177/0018726721993910

Clarà, M. (2017). Teacher resilience and meaning transformation: How teachers reappraise situations of adversity. *Teaching and Teacher Education, 63*, 82–91. http://dx.doi.org/10.1016/j.tate.2016.12.010

Clarà, M., Vallés, A., Franch, A., Coiduras, J., Silva, P., & Cavalcante, S. (2025). Developing teacher resilience by modifying cognitive appraisals: What is reappraised in teacher reappraisal? *Contemporary Educational Psychology, 81*, 102354. https://doi.org/10.1016/j.cedpsych.2025.102354

Coe, N. M., & Jordhus-Lier, D. C. (2010). Constrained agency? Re-evaluating the geographies of labour. *Progress in Human Geography, 35*(2), 211–233. https://doi.org/10.1177/0309132510366746

Cook, J. R., Danaher, M. J. M., Danaher, G. R., & Danaher, P. A. (2013). Naming, framing, and sometimes shaming: Reimagining relationships with education research participants. In W. J. Midgley, P. A. Danaher, & M. M. Baguley (Eds.), *The role of participants in education research: Ethics, epistemologies, and methods (Routledge research in education vol. 87)* (pp. 140–154). Routledge.

Damman, M., & Henkens, K. (2017). Constrained agency in later working lives: Introduction to the special issue. *Work, Aging and Retirement, 3*(3), 225–230. https://doi.org/10.1093/workar/wax015

Danaher, M. J. M., Cook, J. R., Danaher, G. R., Coombes, P. N., & Danaher, P. A. (2013). *Research education with marginalized communities*. Palgrave Macmillan.

Davis, E. A., Beyer, C., Forbes, C. T., & Stevens, S. (2011). Understanding pedagogical design capacity through teachers' narratives. *Teaching and Teacher Education, 27*(4), 797–810. https://doi.org/10.1016/j.tate.2011.01.005

Estola, E., Erkkila, R., & Syrja, L. (2003). A moral voice of vocation in teachers' narratives. *Teachers and Teaching: Theory and Practice, 9*(3), 239–256. https://doi.org/10.1080/13540600309381

Gilbert-Walsh, J. (2007). Deconstruction as narrative interruption. *Interchange, 38*, 317–333. https://doi.org/10.1007/s10780-007-9034-z

Gulati, R., & Srivastava, S. B. (2014). Bringing agency back into network research: Constrained agency and network action. In D. J. Brass, G. Labianca, A. Mehra, D. S. Halgin, & S. P. Borgatti (Eds.), *Contemporary perspectives on organizational social networks (research in the sociology of organizations vol. 40)* (pp. 73–93). Emerald Group Publishing Limited.

Herndl, C. G., & Licona, A. C. (2007). Shifting agency: Agency, kairos, and the possibilities of social action. In M. Zachry & C. Thralls (Eds.), *Communicative practices in workplaces and the professions: Cultural perspectives on the regulation of discourse and organizations* (pp. 133–154). Routledge.

Ho, J. W. Y. (2005). Metaphorical construction of self in teachers' narratives. *Language and Education, 19*(5), 359–379. https://doi.org/10.1080/09500780508668691

Kim, L. E., Leary, R., & Ashbury, K. (2021). Teachers' narratives during COVID-19 partial school reopenings: An exploratory study. *Educational Research, 63*(2), 244–260. https://doi.org/10.1080/00131881.2021.1918014

Lutovac, S., Uitto, M., Keränen, V., Kettunen, A., & Flores, M. A. (2024). Teachers' work today: Exploring Finnish teachers' narratives. *Teaching and Teacher Education, 137*, 104378. https://doi.org/10.1016/j.tate.2023.104378

Panday, P. (2003). *Narrative after deconstruction*. State University of New York Press.

Parker, I. (1998). Constructing and deconstructing psychotherapeutic discourse. *European Journal of Psychotherapy & Counselling, 1*(1), 65–78. https://doi.org/10.1080/13642539808400506

Pino Gavidia, L. A., & Adu, J. (2022). Critical narrative inquiry: An examination of a methodological approach. *International Journal of Qualitative Methods, 21*. https://doi.org/10.1177/16094069221081594

Porter, K. (2023). *As easy as ABC? A novel psychological approach to teacher agency: Exploring the influence of affect on behaviour and cognition* [Doctoral dissertation]. University of St Andrews, Scotland. https://research-repository.st-andrews.ac.uk/handle/10023/28376

Prior, M. T., & Talmy, S. (2021). A discursive constructionist approach to narrative in language teaching and learning research. *System, 102*, 102595. https://doi.org/10.1016/j.system.2021.102595

Scott, K. S. (2022). Making sense of work: Finding meaning in work narratives. *Journal of Management & Organisation, 28*(5), 1057–1077. https://doi.org/10.1017/jmo.2019.43

Shkedi, A. (2009). From curriculum guide to classroom practice: Teachers' narratives of curriculum application. *Journal of Curriculum Studies*, 41(6), 833–854. https://doi.org/10.1080/00220270902927030

Spilt, J. L., & Koomen, H. M. Y. (2009). Widening the view on teacher–child relationships: Teachers' narratives concerning disruptive versus nondisruptive children. *School Psychology Review*, 38(1), 86–101. https://doi.org/10.1080/02796015.2009.12087851

Stuhlman, M. W., & Pianta, R. C. (2002). Teachers' narratives about their relationships with children: Associations with behavior in classrooms. *School Psychology Review*, 31(2), 148–163. https://doi.org/10.1080/02796015.2002.12086148

Veenswijk, M., & Berendse, M. (2008). Constructing new working practices through project narratives. *International Journal of Project Organisation and Management*, 1(1), 65–85. https://doi.org/10.1504/IJPOM.2008.020029

Recommended Further Reading

Baker, N. J., & Boykin, H. (2024). *Real teacher talk: A collection of narratives by real teachers with recommendations to improve a broken education system*. Wheatmark.

Chaaban, Y., Al-Thani, H., & Du, X. (2021). A narrative inquiry of teacher educators' professional agency, identity negotiations, and emotional responses amid educational disruption. *Teaching and Teacher Education*, 108, 103522. https://doi.org/10.1016/j.tate.2021.103522

Gholami, K., Faraji, S., Meijer, P. C., & Tirri, K. (2021). Construction and deconstruction of student teachers' professional identity: A narrative study. *Teaching and Teacher Education*, 97, 103142. https://doi.org/10.1016/j.tate.2020.103142

Søreid, G. S. (2006). Narrative construction of teacher identity: Positioning and negotiation. *Teachers and Teaching: Theory and Practice*, 12(5), 527–547. https://doi.org/10.1080/13540600600832247

Zhu, G., Rice, M., Rivera, H., Mena, J., & Van Der Want, A. (2020). "I did not feel any passion for my teaching": A narrative inquiry of beginning teacher attrition in China. *Cambridge Journal of Education*, 50(6), 771–791. https://doi.org/10.1080/0305764X.2020.1773763

5   Teachers as Pandemic Navigators

Introduction

The Coronavirus Disease 2019 (COVID-19) quickly became a global pandemic as the rapid transmission of the infection was recognised throughout the world (Ozamiz-Etxebarria et al., 2021). As a consequence, one measure widely used for decreasing the spread of the disease was to maintain social distancing. Globally, this necessitated the closure of many services, industries and schools that in turn resulted in health, social, psychological, economic and educational consequences. The COVID-19 pandemic affected life on an unprecedented scale, in every nation and potentially every profession. For instance, intermittent lockdowns and school closures mandated by the governments disrupted 90% of the global student population in 2020 (Psacharopoulos et al., 2020).

There is little doubt that the COVID-19 global crisis intensified the demands on the teaching workforce, placing unprecedented pressure on teachers. Many teachers reported a high level of stress and burnout (Aiello et al., 2023). The severity of COVID-19 transitioned the educational world into cyberspace to support the continuity of teaching and learning (Hindun et al., 2021). The rapid shift from traditional face-to-face classroom teaching to online delivery compelled teachers to adapt quickly to ensure the continuity of learning for their students. As teachers confronted the challenges of the digital platform, they were required, in many cases, to learn new pedagogies and technologies (Dempsey & Mestry, 2023). With severely limited preparation time and professional learning opportunities, the teachers had to adapt and manage the unexpected changes impacting their professional role, as well as having to cope with the personal stressors and uncertainties of COVID-19.

This chapter elaborates and exemplifies the declarative proposition "Teachers as pandemic navigators", which is intended to evoke the full spectrum of attributes, knowledge and skills demanded of full-scale change agents and managers. Despite the undoubted difficulties in individual classrooms and across education systems generated by COVID-19, the study participants whose experiences and voices are canvassed in the chapter demonstrated considerable professional agency in engaging in such navigation. Their success strategies

DOI: 10.4324/9781003564850-5

in being and becoming pandemic navigators are well worth recounting, not least because they reveal much about teachers' motivation and resilience under globally extraordinary circumstances. From this perspective, pandemic navigation is a carefully chosen metaphor that is envisioned to convey the experience of charting a course over unfamiliar and potentially hostile terrain, conducted at a time of widespread communal and individual fear and uncertainty.

At the same time, the pandemic explicated many paradoxes about contemporary schooling practices that will take longer to analyse and apprehend, as well as generating unprecedented opportunities for reviewing and transforming those practices if there is sufficient political will—and goodwill—to do so. Or as Bascia (2023) expressed the situation succinctly in her analysis of Canadian public school teachers' accounts of teaching during the pandemic: "The pandemic-era [teaching experiences] … show the top-down, hierarchical structure of school systems and demonstrate how educators' and governmental discursive practices maintain and reinforce—and sometimes challenge—these structural relations" (p. 2).

Selected Literature

Across many countries, teachers reported feeling overwhelmed and uncertain about the sudden suspension of face-to-face classroom interactions with their students (Aiello et al., 2023). Research has revealed the significant negative impacts on teachers' well-being associated with changes to schooling arising from the pandemic (Alves et al., 2020; Fray et al., 2023). Certainly, Australian teachers were challenged when they were required to move teaching and learning to online educational platforms and to both synchronous and asynchronous environments. A direct outcome of preparing teaching and learning that could be accessed from students' homes was the intensification of the teachers' workloads (Fray et al., 2023). Lessons were created using new or unfamiliar technologies as they simultaneously learned how to deliver teaching effectively through online and offline strategies (Aiello et al., 2023). Teachers' confidence in their capabilities to transform their teaching practices and to engage students in the learning varied considerably, with findings highlighting the ongoing impact on teacher self-efficacy to deliver quality teaching. For example, Fray et al. (2023) reported, "Declining teacher self-efficacy, underpinned by feelings of inadequacy, frustration, exhaustion and poor student engagement impacted significantly on teachers during COVID" (p. 716).

In what was a de facto testament to the breadth and depth of teachers' work during "normal times", the literature about COVID-19 highlighted the pandemic's impact on almost every aspect of that work, which was thereby thrown into sharp relief, including for education stakeholders who would not usually be familiar with what teachers do (Bascia, 2023). Thus, COVID-19 spawned empirical accounts—several of them coincidentally mobilising the navigation metaphor—of novice teachers (Mecham et al., 2021), school leadership (Netolicky, 2020), teacher–student relationships (Newberry & Hinchcliff, 2024), teachers' adaptations of curriculum and instruction (Nerlino, 2022), teachers' professional development (Dempsey & Mestry, 2023; West & Bautista, 2022) and more broadly education when juxtaposed with other elements of contemporary life unprecedently disrupted by COVID-19 (Lim, in press; Nosike & Nosike, 2024), including the ongoing effects of social inequities (Ismail et al., 2021).

Against this backdrop, it is unsurprising that much of the literature has articulated many of the difficulties attending teachers' work throughout the COVID-19 pandemic. In that vein, in a study of continuing professional development for South African teachers during this period, "… findings revealed that lack of guidance and support from educational authorities and school management teams negatively infringed on teachers' practice and professional development" (p. 1). On the other hand, the authors also found that "… teachers collaborated with peers and community members, engaged in knowledge-sharing, and adopted a trial-and-error approach to finding solutions" (p. 1). Moreover, Robinson et al. (2023) reported in their phenomenological research about the lived experiences of 52 teachers in 11 elementary schools across the Great Plains region of the United States in the 2020–2021 school year the need for support for and inclusion of teacher voice and teachers' perspectives in decision-making: "Findings suggest that[,] during the academic year, teachers experienced stressors related to their personal and professional roles, concerns for students' well-being which extended beyond academics, and frustrations with administration and other institutional entities around COVID safety measures" (p. 78).

In the Australian context, as COVID-19 required teachers to pivot in managing their amplified workloads, contradictions in government decision-making and the constantly changing rules about whether teachers were to be working from home created flagging morale (Fray et al., 2023). Billett et al. (2023) examined the interplay among Australian teachers' stress, well-being and safety during the pandemic, as evidenced by 534 teachers around Australia responding to a survey questionnaire administered in June and July 2020. The researchers found that:

> … most teachers … reported that they were not feeling anxious in their teaching role, teachers' responses indicated that they were experiencing high levels of stress and low levels of positive feelings such as joy, positivity, and contentment in their work during the COVID-19 pandemic[,] negatively impacting their well-being and self-efficacy. (p. 1394)

Likewise, Beames et al. (2021) contended that "Australian school teachers … have had to face relentless and challenging working conditions, take on new roles and responsibilities, and embrace new ways of working" and accordingly depicted them "… as the forgotten frontline of Covid-19 …" (p. 420). At the same time, some research reported positive aspects of this extraordinary change in working conditions being conveyed by Australian teachers. In that regard, their self-reported success strategies included "... enjoying learning new online skills and integrating IT in new ways" (Van Bergen & Daniel, 2023, p. 1457), with individual teachers referring to productive outcomes such as "... improved formative assessments" (Van Bergen & Daniel, 2023, p. 1469), "... learning new technical skills to pass onto students" (p. 1469), "... the ease of adding links and assistive technologies, such as text-to-read videos that assist in explaining concepts and topics" (p. 1470) and "... the online apps and resources that I am learning about that we could use if we return to our previous teaching methods ..." (p. 1470), as well as not having to commute to and from work (p. 1470). Van Bergen and Daniel (2023) synthesised the situation clearly: "Disruption brings with it both challenges and opportunities, with the potential to catalyse new efficient or effective approaches ..." (p. 1472).

Given the almost immediate shifts in teachers' work generated by COVID-19, and given also the ongoing debate about what should be altered and what should be retained in that work in view of the learnings from the pandemic (see for instance Lepp et al., 2021; Marshall et al., 2020; Trust & Whalen, 2020), it is appropriate that this chapter is aligned with the "Changes and continuities" dimension of the study's data analysis identified in Chapter 1 (see also Chapter 10), which we elaborate below. The chapter also presents a particular deployment of the book's recurring focus on teachers' overarching success strategies and on their narratives of motivation and resilience as viewed through the pandemic's distinctive, even unique, lens. This alignment also resonates with Bascia's (2023) extended investigation of Canadian teachers' experiences of teaching during COVID-19:

> These characteristics—the diversity of the student population and the sheer size of the teaching work force—enable this particularly robust and broadly relevant account and analysis of changes and continuities in teachers' educational practices during the COVID pandemic and beyond. (p. 2)

Data Analysis

As we noted above, this chapter aligns with "changes and continuities" as the third dimension of the study's data analytic strategy, which we defined in Chapter 1 as "Elements and experiences of teachers' work and lives that have been dynamic and constant" (see also Chapter 10).

As we also noted in Chapter 1, our data analytic strategy also elicited four "nodes" that help to organise the data analysis in this section of the chapter:

- Complexities (CY): Engaging with multifaceted events and issues
- Challenges (CE): Encounters with difficult and potentially stressful events and issues

Table 5.1 Data Analysis Matrix for Teachers as Pandemic Navigators

	Changes and Continuities
Complexities	Kylie; Sophie
Challenges	Viv; Declan
Contradictions	George; Audrey
Comforts	Kate; Gail

- Contradictions (CN): Events and issues with at least two competing influences and pressures
- Comforts (CT): Sources of encouragement, motivation and pleasure

Building on Table 1.2 in Chapter 1, Table 5.1 illustrates the approach taken to data analysis in this chapter about teachers as pandemic navigators, clustered around the changes and continuities dimension, and organised around the four aforementioned nodes.

Complexities

Kylie's experience of engaging with the COVID-19 pandemic highlight the underlying complexities associated with contemporary teaching, as well as demonstrating both significant changes and continuities in her colleagues' and her work. Despite these complexities, Kylie is able to enact a success strategy that represents her individual pandemic navigation that in turn enhanced her motivation and resilience:

> I definitely think that our school was not prepared in terms of technology to support teachers to move on to online [teaching and learning]. I was one of only two teachers in the school that provided the professional learning for teachers because I was quite confident because I've taught students across the state online before. It's that experience and understanding ... which is the technology model that helps teachers integrate. Supporting that technology enabled learning with our teachers.

For Kylie, the pandemic afforded her the opportunity to deploy and extend her existing technological expertise teaching in the online environment and also to embrace a productive change centred on helping to provide professional development for her teaching colleagues. A similarly welcome change was related to a rapid reduction in her work stress owing to not teaching students face-to-face and a concomitant reinforcement of her feeling valued because her specialist knowledge was directly helpful to other people, thereby highlighting the complexity in non-pandemic times of striving to impart information to non-responsive students. In an explicit counterpoint to the experiences of stress and burnout being exacerbated by the pandemic as reported in the introduction to this chapter, Kylie reports a very different kind of experience:

> Personally, I felt that [COVID-19] was a great opportunity. I got the most amazing sleep, [and I] could breathe and catch up. It was the least stressful period of my teaching career. That's what I would say. Those five weeks, I could breathe. I was only needed by teachers for my technical ability, like, "How do I enrol this kid?" Or "How do I teach this class online?". Everyone actually needed me because I had a skill set that I could give them right then and there rather than strategically leading them forward. I was satisfied. I was busy every day, but I loved it because people needed me and I could help them instantaneously .... It was certainly a struggle for other teachers who weren't confident in the use of technology, but I was. Like I said, I've caught up on my sleep and I could develop some professional and personal boundaries. I went home on time, and I looked after myself during that time. I certainly welcomed that experience.

Additionally, Kylie reveals another aspect of her success strategy as a pandemic navigator in her interactions with her students during COVID-19 that also accentuated the complexity of diverse student responses to the pandemic, as well as the positive outcome of a significant change to classroom dynamics:

> My students, however, they stopped; they were lazy and didn't engage. In terms of the technology, I found that teaching younger grades, like Grade Eight, that students that were on the autism spectrum were often more engaged in the learning, and that everyone has a voice. Everyone has an even playing field, and ... dominant personalities don't dominate the classroom because you can meet them or you can kick them out, really, but it was such an opportunity.

Sophie expresses a similar view to Kylie regarding the positive affordances of the rapid and radical changes—and the associated success strategies—generated by COVID-19. On the other hand, she laments the equally rapid reversion to the continuities of "... old practice ..." and "... our old traps ..." that she sees as old-fashioned and ineffective for enhancing students' learning. In that vein, her reference to "... education [being] a little bit funny ..." can be seen as reflecting the complexities of teachers as pandemic navigators:

> Look, I find education a little bit funny .... We were quick to make changes and with online programs, and we're all doing that, but we're also very quick when [pre-pandemic schooling resumed] ..., which is

disappointing. I don't speak for all the staff here, but there's many staff [who have] ... gone back to the old practice ... from the classroom rather than using their [online] platforms. There are certainly teachers that are still using their [online] platforms, and ... we have to have learned from it. I think COVID has done that well, that we've got our older teachers ... - not necessarily older, but other teachers who have never experienced that have actually gone on and used that to enhance their teaching, but we fell back into our old traps a little bit.

Challenges

In reflecting on the challenges attending teachers as pandemic navigators, Viv identifies both changes to and continuities in teachers' workloads that constrained their capacity to implement success strategies and that in turn diminished their motivation and resilience narratives. For instance, Viv expresses surprise about the relationship between COVID-19 and teachers' stress levels that she had observed:

... [COVID] certainly did add to it [teachers' stress]. I thought that that would reduce stress because you got rid of some of the students out of the school. You think that would make it easier, [with] less numbers in school. Actually, to my surprise teachers were more stressed.

Viv explains this surprising outcome by referring to various examples of differences among schools in how the pandemic was addressed at school level:

Well, there is some variation across schools because ... I've been in different schools, and they handled it slightly differently. Just the stress of there not being a blanket approach across schools, and this might be neighbouring schools, for example .... [The principals are] in the same situation where day by day they were getting information and having to act on it.

Viv shares a particular inconsistency of this school-by-school variation (and consequent lack of continuity across schools) on a significant change to teachers' work that augmented already existing teacher stress:

I think the department directive was that teachers had to be in touch with each household, so each student's [household] once a week .... Then one school, from the principal, they were told, "No, you will contact the household three times a week". I also know of another school where it was daily, and that was quite [a] stressful start to the day, perhaps.

Viv elaborates with further details of these cross-school differences that teachers experienced as challenges to their practice:

> I know of one way one school handled it was the teacher had to contact every single household while another teacher—I think they were put in pairs—would handle any students who were fronting up [at]. Then I think they'd swap, and the other teacher would bring her students [into class with] his students. Also, one school was not getting any supply [relieving] teachers in during lockdown, because, if somebody ... called [in] sick, they just said, "No, the other teacher of the partnership would have to pick up the [ill teacher's work]".

Viv explains the challenges arising from teachers being pandemic navigators, including having a continuity of expectation of facilitating students' learning despite significantly changed circumstances and learning locations, and needing to depend on parents/caregivers also taking on changed roles with regard to their children's learning:

> Just maybe the stress of teachers having to play these different roles [and to] take on these extra tasks, being told to be responsible for the education of each student in your class, which is a little tricky to do when they are off site. For example, they might contact the household and be told, "Yes, the student is doing their lessons". Then, when the students all return to school, they could see from the book work ... [that [other students weren't doing it. Some [students] threw the book in the bin. Perhaps the household was not up front with what was really happening, and then [when] all the students returned [to school], some had done all the work and others had not, so they were at all different stages.

Viv elaborates the exacerbated teacher stress resulting from school leadership teams' varied reactions to this unprecedented situation. While teachers responded to these significant educational changes by focusing on facilitating students' engagement with assessment tasks, some leadership teams insisted on re-establishing the continuity of leadership team members observing teachers' lessons, which in turn created considerable challenges for the teachers concerned:

> ... [Teachers] came back [to school after lockdowns had ended], and then they had—let's say six weeks of the rest of the term. They knew that they were heading into assessment, and they just had to really focus on what [was] needed in order for assessment to be effective without trying to teach to the assessment .... Some teachers trying to get all the children on the same page, leading into assessment, really focusing on what has to be done, and then being asked straightaway, "Oh, we want you to start making your bookings for when you're

having your observation lessons". Also, other sort[s] of meeting that required other things from the teachers, perhaps administrative tasks. A lot of teachers that I know [objected] to that. It caused friction and tears in the school.

Viv elaborates unfortunate consequences of this apparent inability or unwillingness by some school leadership teams to exercise flexibility in not delaying the resumption of lesson observations as a continuity in school practice, rather than seizing return to school as an opportunity to enact appropriate changes to that practice:

Well, ... [teachers] would be saying, "No" to some requests of them, some demands, but that would cause some trouble [with the school administration]. Also, they'd lean on each other, and give each other support, just some comforting [of] each other. They really would just think, "Well, I've got to ignore certain things and just focus on what has to be done". It is stressful .... [Teachers] just feel like it doesn't matter what they say, and they're trying to be reasonable, they're trying to communicate effectively, but basically, they think, "It doesn't matter what I say. We're still going to have to tick all these boxes [related] to the main job, the teaching, the assessing, the reporting" ...., which is the feeling they're being controlled. That's the term that I've been hearing more than once now.

Viv concludes this segment of her narrative by musing on the pandemic's role as an accelerant of challenges as negative changes to teachers' work that had been evident for some time before the pandemic began:

I think it's gradually occurring in the last few years. I think what COVID did, it stressed everyone. Perhaps a principal feeling stressed might become a little bit more OCD [obsessive-compulsive disorder], and then push that stress onto the staff. I really think that is a common thing. Principals are being given a lot to do .... Then they [are] pushing it onto teachers, and it's just becoming too much for some.

Declan perceives the pandemic from a different perspective, as at once a reflection of and an expediter of broader structural changes to the teaching profession that pose significant challenges to both teachers and students:

I think COVID this year has given us a snapshot into maybe ... the jobs market [for teaching] in five to 10 years' time .... [I]t's created a lot of other jobs, but then ... it's automated other jobs ... and it's really been a [shake] up that ... is very challenging for students and ... for everyone alike.

Contradictions

In presenting his reflection on teachers as pandemic navigators, and on the associated changes and continuities in teachers' work, George explicates a significant and unprecedented contradiction that impacted directly on the effectiveness of his colleagues' and his success strategies during COVID-19, and consequently on their and his motivation and resilience:

> Now, technology wise, because of our community, we've tried for .... years now to be as technologically advanced as we could to the point where we give every child ... Years Five and Six an iPad .... We replaced most of their exercise books, ... textbooks and so forth with an iPad, and that iPad is used to research, and it's used for ... collaborative working, [and] it's used to communicate .... It's all that stuff, so, when COVID happened, technologic[ally] our kids were in a great place to deal with it. The big problem we had was that, when you take that to [the] community, they weren't at the same level as their own students, their own children. So lots of homes ... didn't have [the] Internet, or they just had enough Internet [so that] they could do their emails and so forth, but you couldn't make a continuous video interaction with anyone. They didn't have enough [Internet connection] for that, or they didn't have devices at home, and we were happy to lend devices, but very few people wanted to borrow [them]. So ..., despite our advantage that our students had in using technology, when [it] actually came to the crunch, we ended up printing a whole bunch of booklets and sending them home, then it's [their] choice [about what] they did. We found that very few students actually participated in the work ... very few. It's like it was a holiday.

George concludes his reflection on what COVID-19 threw into sharp relief in terms of the changes and continuities, and an accompanying contradiction, framing teachers' work:

> ... [W]hen we came back to school [after the pandemic lockdown], we tried to continue with that concept [of students being technologically literate in using their iPads for learning] that ... we've put in place, continuing to teach like that because it was quite good. But ... I can see this gradually reverting to exactly where we were before COVID .... That is quite normal human behaviour .... You know that any ... change that you put in place in a school, and probably anywhere, for that matter, needs someone who's constantly driving it. If you don't have that, it will always revert back to what ... that norm was.

Audrey communicates in strongly expressed terms what she sees as a fundamental contradiction in the current education system that was illuminated starkly by the pandemic and that implicitly impacted on her self-efficacy as a pandemic navigator: the perceived differential treatment of individual professionals working in that system:

> That's not fair at all. I don't like the fact ... [that] they get to sit in their office, and during COVID they sat at home .... They told us they weren't visiting us, though ... normally we have inclusion coaches, we have learning support people visit ... A couple of times a term, we have people from the head office come in. During COVID, they got to stay in their homes because it was considered safe for them to be in their homes, but the underground staff had to be amongst the virus, and that's the system['s] fault. That shouldn't have occurred. If we have to be on the ground, then so should you.

This clearly articulated sense of inequity and hence of injustice derived from systemic power or its absence is felt keenly by Audrey, who also identifies what she sees as another inequity arising from a fundamental contradiction related to systemic power:

> I actually ended up, in the last three weeks of COVID, having half of my class there. I went back to pretty much normal teaching, and the ones who weren't there were nearly forgotten because they weren't there in front of me asking for my attention. That was another element.

For Audrey, systemic power mobilised effectively would have given her colleagues and her the appropriate resources to be successful pandemic navigators by developing sustainable success strategies with both attending and non-attending students simultaneously. Instead, from Audrey's perspective, there was a significant contradiction between students' and teachers' needs, on the one hand, and systemic priorities, on the other hand:

> I think in the system, when we think about these high needs students, when we think about the data collection, the PD [professional development] we've been given, they're not actually with us saying, "What do you need?". At the moment, we've got this wellbeing coach who's being paid to work 40 hours a week. Apparently, he's meant to be helping our wellbeing, but all he's been doing is saying, "Why don't we participate in the 10,000 step challenge?" .... If you're going to be a wellbeing coach, you [should be able to] take something away from ... [our workloads]. You give me some time to be with my family. You give me my weekend back.

Comforts

While not downplaying the complexities, challenges and contradictions associated with being a pandemic navigator engaging with the resultant changes and continuities in teachers' work, Kate uses her school leadership role to reflect on some unexpected but very welcome comforts related to her experiences during COVID-19:

> What helps the development of the team? That's actually a really easy [question to] answer. We get leadership coaching every week; we've got a HOD [Head of Department] whose … job is leadership coaching for year level leaders and other leaders in the school. I've been really well-supported to build that culture in my time …. Now I think it's true for a lot of our teams across the school …, and that's nice. Particularly during COVID, when we saw a lot of growth, actually …. They repurpose[d] the specialists to cover the kids that came in so that we could work together as a team on what we needed to be doing …. [E]xactly what we were sending out was a big deal. Also, what it was going to look like when we had to shorten reporting timelines. When we had to scratch the curriculum down into a smaller bundle for Semester Two and that sort of thing, we could have those conversations.

Kate distils the essence of the comfort that her colleagues and she experienced as pandemic navigators, engaging collegially and wholeheartedly with multifaceted educational changes and continuities:

> I think there's something about going through something dramatic with a group of people that pulls you together a little bit …. A lot of teams felt that growth during COVID when we got to [work together] because that's not something you ever do. You never get to stay in a room with your team colleagues and talk about what we're doing. We're always teaching.

For Gail, the comfort of being a pandemic navigator derived from considerable continuity between the exigency of pivoting to teaching students at home during lockdown and practices that she had already established with her students:

> I don't think I am probably the best person to talk about the COVID [pandemic] personally, just because I didn't feel like it … had such a significant impact on me personally …. [M]y classes were out of school for about five weeks, and most of that … [time], because they are senior students, we were doing some face-to-face work online, and then they would go away and they would complete some activities, [they] would come back, we'd do feedback, start the process again. So … I had already had a tiny bit of experience of doing some face-to-face teaching already, and I already had set up … online platforms for my students to place their work in to collaborate online, so I don't think that it had such a significant impact on me personally.

Implications

The eight study participants whose narratives have been analysed through the posited "teachers as pandemic navigators" prism exhibited highly diverse experiences that revealed different combinations of complexities, challenges, contradictions and comforts pertaining to distinctive changes and continuities in their work arising from COVID-19. Similarly, their efforts at implementing success strategies against the backdrop of the pandemic manifested considerable motivation and resilience, at the same time that varied responses to the pandemic severely tested the limits and limitations of that motivation and resilience.

From one perspective, the globally unprecedented character of COVID-19 tested students, families, teachers, school leaders and education systems as never before. In many instances, these stakeholders in the schooling enterprise rose to the occasion, pivoted swiftly and engaged in innovative practices, even if they were not recognised as such as the time. In other ways, however, they failed to do so—for instance, with students not completing their assigned work at home, with parents and caregivers not always having the space and time to supervise their children's home-based learning, with teachers overwhelmed by a new and unexpected array of responsibilities, by education systems proving themselves insufficiently agile and flexible in the face of changing circumstances.

From a different perspective, the pandemic generated potentially timely, even long overdue, opportunities for education reform. Certainly, the chance to contest taken for granted assumptions about why, how, where, when and with whom teaching and learning are undertaken should have been welcomed, and no doubt some policymakers and researchers (some of them represented in the selected literature section of this chapter) are considering such a contestation. By contrast, several of the participants highlighted specific and sometimes surprising continuities between the "before COVID-19" and "after COVID-19" iterations of schooling. In some cases, those continuities were appropriate, centred as they were on underlying pedagogical principles and educational values. In other cases, however, the participants regarded a return to "business as usual" in contemporary schooling as a wasted opportunity.

All of this suggests that teachers as pandemic navigators exhibited the same kind of constrained agency that was canvassed in Chapter 1, that is, they did their utmost to continue the essence of their work in facilitating their students' learning despite the extraordinary disruption to nearly all aspects of life that COVID-19 wrought. Depending on their students' and their contexts, they mobilised new ways of teaching and assessing, and/or they continued or adapted their previous practices in those domains. Furthermore, they did so against the backdrop of their personal concerns and fears about their family members' and their own health and well-being, and also of broader shifts in government policymaking, social attitudes and community behaviours. That teachers' success strategies persisted and transformed, along with their motivation and resilience, remains an enduring testament to their ongoing endurance and professionalism. Moreover, their accounts of their varied engagements with the pandemic reflected the starkly differentiated character of those accounts, with some teachers experiencing exacerbated pressure and stress, while others found comfort in unexpected opportunities for educational innovation and renewal.

Conclusion

The COVID-19 pandemic tested and transformed many aspects of contemporary life around the world, including educational provision. The pandemic extended the location and range of specific responsibilities assigned to teachers, and stretched even further the complexity and diversity of what it means to be a teacher in the first quarter of the 21st century.

In responding to this globally unprecedented disruption to the conditions of their work, teachers took on the novel and distinctive role of pandemic navigators. This role required them to engage foursquare with both the affordances and the challenges of devising new interactions and relationships with their students, with parents and caregivers, with fellow teachers, with school leadership teams, with learning materials, with educational technologies, with teaching and assessment practices and with professional development imperatives. The success stories that these teachers enacted under these extraordinary circumstances differed considerably, ranging from necessarily adjusting existing arrangements to exploring genuinely innovative approaches to their work. Regardless of those differences, the study participants' experiences of COVID-19 analysed in this chapter certainly reflected teachers' widespread capacity to apprehend and negotiate complex and fast-paced changes and continuities in their students' and their own environments and lives. Accordingly, teachers as pandemic navigators simultaneously demonstrate specific instances of motivation and resilience, and encapsulate broader dimensions of teachers' work and identities that both frame and constrain who they are as educators and as persons.

References

Aiello, P., Pace, E. M., Sharma, U., Rangarajan, R., Sokal, L., May, F., Gonzalez Gil, F., Loreman, T., Malak, S., Martín, E., McIlroy, A., & Schwab, S. (2023). Identifying teachers' strengths to face COVID-19: Narratives from across the globe. *Cambridge Journal of Education, 53*(3), 357–374. https://doi.org/10.1080/0305764X.2022.2159013

Alves, R., Lopes, T., & Precioso, J. (2020). Teachers' well-being in times of Covid-19 pandemic: Factors that explain professional well-being. *International Journal of Educational Research and Innovation, 15*, 203–217.

Bascia, N. (2023). *Teachers' work during the pandemic (critical perspectives on teaching and teachers' work)*. Routledge.

Beames, J. R., Christensen, H., & Werner-Seidler, A. (2021). School teachers: The forgotten frontline workers of Covid-19. *Australasian Psychiatry, 29*(4), 420–422. https://doi.org/10.1177/10398562211006145

Billett, P., Turner, K., & Li, X. (2023). Australian teacher stress, well-being, self-efficacy, and safety during the COVID-19 pandemic. *Psychology in the Schools*, *60*(5), 1394–1414. https://doi.org/10.1002/pits.22713

Dempsey, T., & Mestry, R. (2023). Teachers' perceptions and experiences of navigating continuing professional development during the COVID-19 pandemic. *Education Sciences*, *13*(9), 933. https://doi.org/10.3390/educsci13090933

Fray, L., Jaremus, F., Gore, J., Miller, A., & Harris, J. (2023). Under pressure and overlooked: The impact of COVID-19 on teachers in NSW public schools. *The Australian Educational Researcher*, *50*(3), 701–727. https://doi.org/10.1007/s13384-022-00518-3

Hindun, I., Husamah, H., Nurwidodo, N., Fatmawati, D., & Fauzi, A. (2021). E-learning in COVID-19 pandemic: Does it challenge teachers' work cognition and metacognitive awareness? *International Journal of Instruction*, *14*(3), 547–566. https://doi.org/10.29333/iji.2021.14332a

Ismail, S. J., Tunis, M. C., Zhao, L., & Quach, C. (2021). Navigating inequities: A roadmap out of the pandemic. *BMJ Global Health*, *6*(1). https://gh.bmj.com/content/6/1/e004087

Lepp, L., Aaviku, T., Leijen, A., Pedaste, M., & Saks, K. (2021). Teaching during COVID-19: The decisions made in teaching. *Education Sciences*, *11*(2), 47. https://doi.org/10.3390/educsci11020047

Lim, P. L. (in press). *Navigating the pandemic: Talking sense and sensibility about COVID-19*. World Scientific.

Marshall, D. T., Shannon, D. M., & Love, S. M. (2020). How teachers experienced the COVID-19 transition to remote instruction. *Phi Delta Kappan*, *102*(3), 46–50. https://doi.org/10.1177/0031721720970702

Mecham, E., Newell, E. J., Reina, L. J., & Stewart, C. (2021). Navigating pandemic schooling for novice teachers. *Educational Research: Theory and Practice*, *32*(1), 90–96. https://files.eric.ed.gov/fulltext/EJ1288160.pdf

Nerlino, E. (2022). Navigating "the chaos": Teacher considerations while adapting curriculum and instruction during the COVID-19 pandemic. *Qualitative Research Journal*, *22*(4), 433–447. https://doi.org/10.1108/QRJ-02-2022-0026

Netolicky, D. M. (2020). School leadership during a pandemic: Navigating tensions. *Journal of Professional Capital and Community*, *5*(3/4), 391–395. https://doi.org/10.1108/JPCC-05-2020-0017

Newberry, M., & Hinchcliff, E. (2024). Navigating teacher–student relationships during and beyond the pandemic. *Educational Research*, *66*(2), 188–204. https://doi.org/10.1080/00131881.2024.2332221

Nosike, C. J., & Nosike, U. C. (2024). Navigating the challenges and seizing the opportunities amidst the COVID-19 pandemic: A comprehensive review. *Nigerian Journal of African Studies*, *6*(1). https://www.nigerianjournalsonline.com/index.php/NJAS/article/view/4440/4304

Ozamiz-Etxebarria, N., Berasategi Santxo, N., Idoiaga Mondragon, N., & Dosil Santamaría, M. (2021). The psychological state of teachers during the COVID-19 crisis: The challenge of returning to face-to-face teaching. *Frontiers in Psychology*, *11*, 620718. https://doi.org/10.3389/fpsyg.2020.620718

Psacharopoulos, G., Patrinos, H., Collis, V., & Vegas, E. (2020). *The COVID-19 cost of school closures*. Brookings Institution. https://coilink.org/20.500.12592/qdm653

Robinson, L. E., Valido, A., Drescher, A., Woolweaver, A. B., Espelage, D. L., LoMurray, S., Long, A. C. J., Wright, A. A., & Dailey, M. M. (2023). Teachers, stress, and the COVID-19 pandemic: A qualitative analysis. *School Mental Health*, *15*(1), 78–89. https://doi.org/10.1007/s12310-022-09533-2

Trust, T., & Whalen, J. (2020). Should teachers be trained in emergency remote teaching? Lessons learned from the COVID-19 pandemic. *Journal of Technology and Teacher Education*, *28*(2), 189–199. https://doi.org/10.70725/307718pkpjuu

Van Bergen, P., & Daniel, E. (2023). "I miss seeing the kids!": Australian teachers' changing roles, preferences, and positive and negative experiences of remote teaching during the COVID-19 pandemic. *The Australian Educational Researcher, 50*, 1457–1476. https://doi.org/10.1007/s13384-022-00565-w

West, J. J., & Bautista, A. (2022). Global perspectives on teacher professional development: Navigating the pandemic. *International Journal for Research in Education, 46*(2), Article 1. https://scholarworks.uaeu.ac.ae/ijre/vol46/iss2/1

Recommended Further Reading

King, R. B., Yin, H., & Allen, K.-A. (2023). Re-imagining teaching, learning, and well-being amidst the COVID-pandemic: Challenges, opportunities, and recommendations. *Educational and Developmental Psychologist, 40*(1), 1–4. https://doi.org/10.1080/20590776.2023.2148827

Kush, J. M., Badilo-Goicoechea, E., Musci, R. J., & Stuart, E. A. (2022). Teachers' mental health during the COVID-19 pandemic. *Educational Researcher, 51*(9), 593–597. https://doi.org/10.3102/0013189X221134281

Niemi, H. M., & Kousa, P. (2020). A case study of students' and teachers' perceptions in a Finnish high school during the COVID pandemic. *International Journal of Technology in Education and Science, 4*(4), 353–369. https://doi.org/10.46328/ijtes.v4i4.167

Pokhrel, S., & Chhetri, R. (2021). A literature review on impact of COVID-19 on teaching and learning. *Higher Education for the Future, 8*(1), 133–141. https://doi.org/10.1177/2347631120983481

Rahayu, R. P., & Wirza, Y. (2020). Teachers' perception of online learning during pandemic Covid-19. *Jurnal Penelitian Pendidikan, 20*(3), 392–406. https://doi.org/10.17509/jpp.v20i3.29226

6 Teachers as Policy Refractors

Introduction

Have you seen the English sub-titled 2023 Spanish film *El maestro que prometió el mar* (The Teacher who Promised the Sea)? Or perhaps you've even read the 2013 book in Spanish upon which it was based, *Desenterrant el silenci: Antoni Benaiges, el mestre que va prometre el mar*? (by Francesc Escribano with Sergi Bernal Ferrando and Francisco Ferrándiz Martin).

In the film, you'll be taken to and fro between present-day Spain and events of 1936 when Antoni Benaiges was teaching in a small village in *Bañuelos de Bureba* (Burgos). His commitment to a seemingly unorthodox pedagogy of student-centred learning finds favour with his young students and eventually their parents. However, as a most committed refractor of not only educational, but also economic and social, policies of his time, Antoni pays the ultimate price when the initially symbolic violence of the education system turns to actual physical violence perpetrated upon him from wider sociopolitical forces.

Such education policies as Antoni refracted were mediated through a plethora of institutional and individual identities, prefigurative pedagogical practices, professional beliefs, values and cultures. This was never work for the faint hearted. Intellectually, there were gossamer networks of like-minded teachers and social theorists throughout the world providing contextual traces of success and failures (e.g., Dewey, 1916; Durkheim, 1956; Freire, 1970; Vygotsky, 1978).

In exploring policy refraction through an Australian lens in this chapter, we are eschewing physical violence while exploring the experiences of nine teachers from the larger participant cohort. To begin this exploration, the concept of refraction and its enactment in policy spheres is defined through necessarily selective literature. Secondly, the results of analysis of 42 semi-structured interview transcripts are presented in accordance with this chapter's focus question: How do the processes of policy refraction mediate systemic narratives of education change impact teachers' professional lives? Implications emerging from these findings are distilled in the following section that is succeeded by concluding comments pertinent to teachers as professionals and the profession of teaching.

DOI: 10.4324/9781003564850-6

Selected Literature

In a recent publication from this project, a conceptual framework was presented depicting teacher resilience as being contingent upon commitment, agency, relationships, self-awareness and context (Peel et al., 2023, p. 4). In this chapter's review of selected literature, while the other four elements of resilience are encountered, context is prioritised (i.e., the contexts in which policy refraction may be understood). Policy documents are defined as "ideological texts that have been constructed within a particular context" (Codd, 1988, pp. 243–244), with policy response defined as "any course of action (or inaction) relating to the selection of goals, the definition of values or the allocation of resources" (Codd, 1988, p. 235). Therefore, context counts in identifying the ideologies constructing policies. Accordingly, it could be argued that in this project policy refraction is a teacher's response to ideologically framed policies that conflict with, contradict or even seek to reverse their own professional values, beliefs and practices as educators.

If policy formulation, dissemination and subordination are an ideological project constructed in and through socioeconomic, cultural and historical contexts, then its interpretation causes problems of refraction as messages are relayed imperfectly. It has been argued that "refraction refers to the process by which global standards are re-directed by rearranging them in their historical and cultural contexts" (Goodson & dos Santos Rosa, 2018, p. 299). Yet this reasoning goes only so far. Global educational standards and their governance such as those espoused by UNESCO's Office of Economic and Cultural Development (OECD) are themselves aggregated ideological texts of varying educational jurisdictions jostling for power in a "complex and competitive landscape of ideas, actors, and interests" (Martini et al., 2024, p. 2). For instance, the OECD's Program for International Student Assessment (PISA) global standards-based testing programme for 15-year-olds in reading, mathematics and an innovation domain (in 2022, that was creative thinking) is now integral to national assessment programmes across the world.

Based upon a systematic review of PISA results and their influence on policy development, Volante and Klinger (2021) found education policy inertia in Italy, policy avoidance in France and policy refraction in Finland. Policy refraction was characterised by "challenges that threaten its position as an equalitarian society" (Volante & Klinger, 2021, p. 51). Specifically, their analysis of the Finnish results identified socioeconomic segregation, truncated school choice options and socioeconomic status differentials evident in study pathways across comprehensive and selective schools. Policy reform initiatives in recent years are acknowledged but critiqued for their focus solely on pedagogy and curriculum rather than on the "difficult structural reforms needed to address increasing social stratification concerns in their education system" (Volante & Klinger, 2021, p. 51).

Systemically, education is in "a state of evidentiary symbolism" in which selective outcomes "are presented or promoted in order to rationalize specific policies or policy directions" (Volante & Klinger, 2021, pp. 52–53). Awareness of the political prisms of governments and those who would influence governments is essential because evidence itself may be politicised. "Whether it comes from PISA, other international large-scale assessments such as those administered by the International Association for the Evaluation of Educational Achievement (IEA), national administrative data, and/or empirical studies" (Volante & Klinger, 2021, p. 52), evidence may be magnified, obscured, discounted or even mutated.

So too with the evidentiary symbolism of teachers as professionals in school-based education systems and institutions, all of which exist courtesy of governments and those who would influence governments. Theoretically, a structural-functionalist analysis of professions and professionalism addresses "conflicts and tensions that arise within and between the bureaucracy in ways that make for complementarity and maintain an overriding tendency to social cohesion"; but equally and conversely "professionalism has too often merely benefited private interests at the expense of public good" (Kanes, 2011, pp. 5–6). Subsequent consequences, while not always intended, can range from professional trauma at its most severe to professional tensions and ethical dilemmas at the very least.

Policy refraction provides a resilience to teacher professionalism. As a conceptual tool, it can broker the fragilities of tensions and trauma in teaching that are more than a "metaphorical abstraction" (Stray, 2017). Refraction works both internally in "personal contexts" and externally among "local and professional cultures" (Goodson, 2014, p. 35).

> This *refraction* results in global trends being mediated by wider national histories, traditions and dominant ideologies and politics, and national policies being translated through institutional cultures and practice and redirected through actions arising based on individuals' and groups' own beliefs, values and trajectories.
> (Rudd & Goodson, 2016, p. 101; *italics in the original*)

In Chapter 1, we defined "profession and professionalism" as "Teachers' ethical and partly autonomous enactment and dissemination of knowledge, and their interactions with other educational stakeholders", which consist of people and their practices, as well as artefacts/objects, technologies, ideas and intentions of texts (e.g., curriculum, policies), organisations and institutions (Fenwick & Edwards, 2013). Together with global policy flows, national and jurisdictional professional standards are mediated by teachers embroiled in cultures of measurement and accountability that challenge the status of their professional knowledge (Biesta, 2017). The analytic accounts that follow illustrate the micro levels of policy refraction in local and social environments of schools, as expressed verbally by individual teachers (Stray, 2017).

Data Analysis

As noted in Chapter 1 and evident throughout the chapters in this book, the analytic heuristic developed for interview transcripts from our 42 participant teachers was not linear but recursive and conditional as four nodes (analytic categories) were constructed inductively with five dimensions of understanding. The focus dimension in this chapter is one of those five; namely, teachers' understanding of their profession and professionalism as seen through their ethical and partly autonomous enactment and dissemination of knowledge, and their interactions with other stakeholders (see Table 6.1).

In this section, you will encounter *in vivo* expressions of teachers' mediation of their profession and professionalism; between their individual ideologies with their contextualised teaching practices and those of globally impregnated national and institutional policies determining what they and others count as teaching (Goodson & dos Santos Rosa, 2018; Rudd & Goodson, 2016). Table 1.1 in Chapter 1 provides demographic information about the participants, as well as their assigned pseudonyms.

While Table 6.1 presents the analytic matrix upon which findings are reported, its elements are not meant to be read in isolation from one another. Rather, taken together these nodes illustrate the ways in which teachers as professionals demonstrate their professionalism. Before presenting evidence of each node, a case of one teacher has been constructed to illustrate the ways in which all four nodes interact.

Audrey: A Case of Complexities, Challenges, Contradictions and Comforts

The recent global health pandemic provided a useful lens for Audrey to articulate challenges she'd encountered that tested her commitment to the teaching profession. It is possible to imagine Audrey's classroom in which unnamed behaviour management policies were challenging her belief that she was there to teach what was expected of her as a professional:

> It's to help the kids; [they] should be in the green zone for learning, the red zone when they're really angry, and the blue zone when they're sad. The green zone is optimal for learning. We've got to incorporate that into our day as well as a bounce back program, which

Table 6.1 Data Analysis Matrix for Teachers as Policy Refractors

	Profession and professionalism
Complexities	Audrey; Stella; Harriet; Marnie
Challenges	Audrey; Emily; Doug; Alexa; Kylie
Contradictions	Audrey; Doug; George; Alexa
Comforts	Audrey; Sally; Keira

is for health. There's all these little things that keep getting added into your day and you wonder, "When can I actually do the maths that you want me to do?"

Here the ethics of Audrey's dilemma are starkly articulated. One can see the influence of those classroom behaviour management, health and wellbeing policies that were not of Audrey's choosing. They posed challenges for her. The challenges were not because of their intent (coloured zones for deployment of students when certain behaviours are exhibited) or content (as in the "bounce back" programme). Rather, the challenges and thus her ethical dilemma arose because Audrey views them as "all these little things" that were seemingly being "added into" her day while "the maths" was still waiting to be taught. It was "the maths that you want me to do". While the "you" is never explicitly identified, it is reasonable to presume that "you" is a euphemism for the collective of school-based colleagues, systemic institutions, curriculum frameworks and assessment regimes, as well as jurisdictional teaching standards of the particular state/territory in which she was teaching.

During her interview, Audrey fleshes out this "you" through critical reflections on one complex, challenging issue:

> COVID actually saved me, because in Term One I didn't think I'd make it through the year. I'd been hit three times; I'd been threatened with scissors.
> …. I was crying at the end of every day [in] Term One. I spoke to leadership; they know what the battles were; they were more than supportive. I just said, "I'm losing faith in my own teaching; why can't a 15-year train[ed] teacher cope with this class? What's wrong here?"
> …. The previous teachers of this child have had to have stress leave or have only worked half of the year and left. I wasn't special; I wasn't any different to anyone else.

Now Audrey believes that "this stuff isn't taught at university to these people who are starting off". Yet, even if it had been, "this stuff" is beyond even an experienced teacher.

Audrey elaborates further on the policy-driven issue impacting a particular student, other students and herself:

> You've got a high-needs students in a mainstream school because of the government's belief in inclusion …. You're trying to teach a mainstream classroom with a child who needs to be in a specialised classroom and they're not coping. He was jumping out the window, he was running away, he was hurting me, he was hurting the school officer, and I had no control over the room or him and he was scaring the class.

From her perspective, can you picture Audrey's dilemma? What followed was potentially disastrous because "Then COVID came and he had to go home"; but "It's saved me".

Physically and emotionally, the shutdown of face-to-face schooling and transition to online teaching and learning impacted Audrey in ways she could not have foreseen, but which she knows were needed:

> COVID meant I got a break, and he got a break, and it gave us a chance to get some specialist services to him and he's a different [child] now.
>
> .... We could start managed attendance in return from COVID and he gradually learned that school was a safe place, and he could trust me and his [specialist services] school officer.
>
> He only attends two days a week now for full-time and three days for part-time. I could make it through the day now.

In this recount, the parents'/caregivers' voices are silent. However, the outcomes were such that the student's legal guardians during that pandemic period and afterward would have been consulted in accordance with established procedures at the school level. There is an old saying in English, "It's an ill wind that blows nobody any good", meaning that sometimes even bad situations can have good outcomes. Audrey takes comfort from the fact that, for this student, he was now in a safe place at school with a teacher and specialist school officer whom he could also trust.

Audrey believes that, at the school level, in her classroom, an inclusion policy of locating this student with special learning needs was detrimental to him, other students and herself. She could not avoid that policy. She could not ignore it. Nor could she refract it on her own. Other professional colleagues such as the school leadership team and specialist services were just as hamstrung as Audrey. The contradictions she encountered, the complexities she lived and the challenges she overcame provided some comfort for her that this student was safe to learn and that she was safe to teach.

Let us now examine further evidence from each of these nodes in turn, beginning with complexities, then journeying through challenges, contradictions and comforts as per Table 6.1.

Complexities

A hallmark of being a professional is accepting accountability and expecting autonomy to enact that accountability. Mediating legal, socioeconomic and cultural norms highlights the complexity of enacting professionalism in teaching. Complexities are demonstrated through transactional interactions, interpersonal relationships and ethical dilemmas.

For instance, Stella has "never been a big fan of national testing", yet acknowledges that "you need something" to know if students are learning. However, national testing "only provides one very small part of a picture" of a student. This is difficult for Stella because "I've worked with so many teachers like me, who are very professional. You would trust their judgement in so many areas, regardless of what a national test said". Here Stella is mediating results of national testing outcomes of students' abilities against her own knowledge of her students' capabilities. The latter she trusts. Stella also trusts her colleagues. There are "so many teachers like me"—because they are professionals who know their students "in so many areas", not just those covered in national testing regimes.

However, Stella is the first to acknowledge that "we're not infallible; we are human". Accordingly, she thinks "there's got to be a balance of both. ... We do need both". In other words, teachers as professionals can accommodate other measures of their students' learning as well as their own knowledge of their capabilities that encompass so much more than that measured on comparative testing external to the classroom and a particular school. Such testing could be seen as teachers' transactional interactions with wider policy imperatives, while their professionalism values interpersonal relationships as well.

In this profession, though, the world around teachers is "constantly changing from year to year" (Harriet). Just as internationally and nationally policy changes have brought wide-scale testing regimes, "your kids are constantly changing from year to year" (Harriet). Parents, caregivers and whole communities are changing too. Harriet believes that, as a professional, you have to be "very critical of yourself and what you do and your performance and how things work so that you can continually change and get better" because "you just can't afford to keep things the same all the time because it's just not going to work. You have to be willing to learn from situations or reflect on things and change" (Harriet).

Marnie warns against complacency in the face of complexity as the years go by:

> You don't know what you don't know and, the further along you get, you realise there's a whole lot that you don't know, and there's a whole lot you should be doing, and you get very wise at choosing to prioritise things.

The ability to prioritise, and the insight to know when to prioritise, are considered markers of wisdom Marnie has gained over time. Like Harriet and Stella, trusting one's judgement to know what you do not know while being willing to reflect critically on performance of self and others facilitates Marnie's mediation of ethical dilemmas encountered along the way.

Challenges

Emily confirms the need for balance in mediating challenges in teaching. She argues that, "if you are really good in life in balancing everything, and, you know, your social life, your personal life, your spiritual life..., I think you can preserve your sanity" and not be overwhelmed by complexities. She still believes that "teaching is very enjoyable profession; really it's very rewarding", despite the complexities encountered along the way. That is not to ignore the challenges of such complexities as those noted above bring to teachers and teaching.

As Audrey's case above demonstrates, while teaching is an "interesting" profession that has "some pretty high highs", it also has "some pretty low lows", according to Doug. Prior to teaching for the last decade at the time of the interview, Doug had worked in a "high stress", "pretty high demand" job. He reflected that, in contrast to his previous work:

> ... the one thing I think about teaching that's different than a lot of professions in other areas is that you're constantly surrounded at certain times of the year by people who are all in the same state of mind. It's almost like everybody drags each other down at times.

This outsider–insider insight is further elaborated and clarified:

> Usually, when it's reporting writing or exam time, there's a lot of stress and a lot of snappiness and that sort of thing. At the same time, when the good things ... happen, everybody celebrates those together. There is a sense of family.

However, Doug warns that:

> It's one of those jobs to me that's very, very unstable in terms of emotion because it's almost like a rollercoaster that there's good times, but, within one phone call or one mistake, it goes into complete bad times as well.

The challenge of the emotional rollercoaster that can come from one phone call is noted by Alexa as emanating also from parents. While considering herself an experienced teacher who can distinguish between a student's content-related distress versus emotional distress, Alexa believes that demands from parents question teachers' professional credentials and professionalism. In her experience:

> Parents are bullies. They bully teachers all the time. That's probably the next biggest issue for teaching, is the demands of parents. I mean, would they ring up some other professional and have a go at them? No. They do it to teachers all the time....Get a grip, parents.

Now it would be methodologically presumptuous to claim that all parents fit Alexa's descriptor; however, it was evidently a significant challenge encountered that impacted on her self-perception as a professional. Likewise, Kylie believes that challenges could be overcome if teachers are respected with no assumptions made about their practices: "It's just time for giving teachers time to reflect, giving teachers time to collaborate, giving teachers time to plan, respecting, and not making assumptions on teachers' practice".

Contradictions

Teachers' professionalism is most at risk when assumptions about their practice are contradictory. Contradictions highlight the transitions, tensions and politics of changes that teachers identify as impacting their conduct, competence and skills. Audrey believes that:

> They want us to teach it a certain way, and they want us to have this many assessments, and they want us to have these many documents, and they want us to tick this many boxes, and they want it all written a certain way.

Doug concludes that "teaching is just very much a data collection process". He is perplexed as to "why there is so much data collection around student learning". Echoing the tenets of professionalism espoused by Audrey, Doug sees teaching being reduced to:

> A lot of literally just ticking boxes that seems to be done here. I don't understand why we need to do so much of that given that we're teachers; we know how to help students progress in their learning. We don't need to be recording it every single time in a numerical form.

If teachers are professionals and know how to help students progress in their learning, then Doug cannot see the value of these data because, after the data have been collected, collated, aggregated and disseminated far and wide, then eventually returned to the school, "there's not really a correlation between the data that's being provided to schools and student learning progressing".

It's not that teachers do not see the potential of data to inform so as to improve their practices and students' learning. "I think you need to have data. You need to have something to base your programming on"; however, "Its purpose is to ultimately increase student learning, not to tick a box and sit in some dusty filing cabinet somewhere" (Doug). George concurs: "We should have up-to-date data, at our fingertips at any given moment, about every aspect of that individual child".

George notes wistfully that "if only some of that concept was applied to the people who worked in the school":

> ... you know, tick the box, you are what you are .... We all bring incredibly different skills and strengths to the job, and I think it works

best when that's understood and recognised [that] one person is going be brilliant at doing the paperwork for programming; people like me are not. Yet I have the same expectation upon me. ... I can deal with students and parents ..., but it doesn't necessarily get a tick in the box.

Individuals such as George who take on the intellectual and cultural challenges of teaching may ironically be positioned in ways that deterritorialise them from the profession. The contradictory conundrum thus emerging is that teachers too "should be able to play to our strengths and we should be appreciated, all, for our strengths" (George).

In a similar vein, Alexa takes issue with contradictions inherent in her mandatory membership of the state-based institute of teaching and registration with the same institute that enforces registration requirements, teaching standards, and associated rules and regulations:

The XXX Institute of Teaching, which we all have to belong to, which all it does is publicise the fact of when things go wrong. In their online—because it's an online newsletter now—but it's all about things that have gone wrong. It's not ever talking up the positives. That's supposed to be our professional body, which all it is is a registration. But it's always focusing on this person did this wrong or had a relationship with a student. It's never talking about the good stuff. That doesn't help. ... If your own professional body can't do that, what's society going to do?

The contradiction here is that teachers themselves are subjected to the "tick a box" of formal and informal credential creep, with professional standards being policed by agencies at local, systemic and national levels, and with regulation of knowledge production and its dissemination. For Alexa, the politics of this for a profession in which practitioners have access to and responsibility for vulnerable young people during their formative years are questionable.

Comforts

When teachers mediate their positioning as units of production, and as cost centres to deliver on the latest social, economic and political imperatives of education policies, the sense-making comforts of this profession emerge. There is something about teaching, because "you don't do teaching for the money; you don't do teaching for [the] status; you don't do teaching for lifestyle. You do teaching because you want to teach" (Sally).

It is a profession in which its practitioners "are in that absolute[ly] privileged position, that we are making an imprint on a young person's life for the rest of their life" (Sally). While data and comparative rankings of assessment outcomes may be important, students take their teachers with them into their futures. Sally recalls fondly:

> When you've been teaching for as long as I have, you will go out and you will have an adult come up to you and say, "I know you; you taught me in Year Eight, and remember that time –", and sometimes you remember it, sometimes you don't [...] or the number of times you get a thank you note sent to you from a child you taught 10 years ago. ... I always have a new group I'm focusing on, but they've gone away, and they've taken you with them.

Within her first eight years of teaching, Keira found herself with a group of 25 children deemed to be gifted and talented:

> That was challenging; I was the dumbest in the room. I had Grade Threes who were, oh, brilliant. ...That growth mindset, feeling like you know nothing, it's a real freedom when it comes to teaching. I think that class made me as a professional because I was willing to take a chance. I was willing to acknowledge that, "Hey, I don't know everything. That this Grade Three child can actually know more, ask more complicated questions than me" was, I believe, a blessing in my career. I'm still in touch with a lot of those kids, so I feel that that was really important in my career.

These teachers are tethered to their profession by choice. In turn, the profession requires that the work of teaching is tracked, measured and ranked through processes not necessarily recognised by their students with whom they learn and teach. It is also parents and others in institutionalised schooling who may not recognise or respect the markers of being a professional.

Implications

The implications of these findings for the teaching profession and the professionalism of teachers are threefold. Firstly, in their interactions with other educational stakeholders, these teachers were only ever partly autonomous professionals. Secondly, the ethical dilemmas they encountered exacted a multifaceted toll—a toll that was manifested emotionally, intellectually, and in some cases physically. Thirdly, and more portentously, the very fabric of teaching as a profession is at risk at this time in history as globally and locally educational institutions, curriculum frameworks and pedagogical practices are under siege.

Nevertheless, our interviewees have provided hope that not all teachers succumb to despondency and despair. There is still joy to be found in the refraction of policies at the local level that is demonstrated through:

- Pursuing knowledge, not presuming knowledge
- Respecting self, students and others
- Accepting difference as strength, not weakness.

Teachers' work will continue to evolve, mutate and respond to the political imperatives of local, state and national policies. Teachers in this study have read the global through the local. They were cognisant of the implications of "small-scale niche innovations and large-scale technological transitions" (Törnberg, 2021, p. 83).

The implications of this for initial and continuing teacher education are significant (Day, 2019). Within Australia alone, the profession is regulated through the inexorable power of bodies such as the Australian Institute for Teaching and School Leadership (AITSL), the Victorian Institute of Teaching, the Queensland College of Teachers, the NSW (New South Wales) Education Standards Authority, the Teacher Quality Institute (Australian Capital Territory), the Teacher Registration Board of the Northern Territory, the Teachers Registration Board of South Australia, the Teachers Registration Board of Tasmania and the Teacher Registration Board of Western Australia. Education departments of state/territory governments as well as systemic and non-systemic schools of varying persuasions interpret national and international policy-driven curriculum frameworks and pedagogical practices, some of which have been mentioned earlier in this chapter.

In this context, the very notion of professionalism is under scrutiny. Its old adages may no longer sustain such structures for the regulatory and social organisation of teaching. The implication for teachers, no matter where or what or whom we may teach, is clear: policy refraction offers amelioration of the forces of deprofessionalisation.

Conclusion

As Stray (2017) concluded in her doctoral dissertation on the idiosyncratic cultural responses to global educational reform movements, there is a "need for listening ears" (p. 200). Who listened to Antoni? Who listened to the children who wanted to learn with him? Neither the village priest nor the mayor listened, although the latter eventually capitulated as a parent only to recant when faced with the dire implications of policy refraction at individual, familial and village levels. A district inspector listened initially when faced with incontrovertible, classroom-based evidence viewed by himself that the children were being educated. They were learning.

The student-centred learning movement of that time in the 1930s was truly international (Kumar Shah, 2020). Those of us who came of age as teachers in the 1960s–1970s were on the cusp of change as previous conceptions of professionalism shifted towards purportedly more democratic and inclusive professional actions (Biesta, 2017). For the teachers in Australia of the 2020s, professionalism may well be a mirage, shapeshifting between distortions of students and their parents as clients, what counts as accountability and the sociocultural status of teachers' professional knowledge. Policy refraction provided a way in to the teaching profession's elusiveness in dealing with the tensions and dilemmas of being a teacher at this time in history. In professionalism's very elusiveness lies its potential for multidimensional, complex yet connective relationships capable of transforming people's lives.

References

Biesta, G. (2017) Education, measurement and the professions: Reclaiming a space for democratic professionality in education. *Educational Philosophy and Theory*, 49(4), 315–330. https://doi.org/10.1080/00131857.2015.1048665

Codd, J. (1988). The construction and deconstruction of educational policy documents. *Journal of Education Policy*, 3(3), 235–247. https://doi.org/10.1080/0268093880030303

Day, C. (2019). Policy, teacher education and the quality of teachers and teaching. *Teachers and Teaching*, 25(5), 501–506. https://doi.org/10.1080/13540602.2019.1651100

Dewey, J. (1916). *Democracy and education: An introduction to the philosophy of education*. New York: Macmillan.

Durkheim, E. (1956). *Education and Sociology*. New York, NY: Free Press.

Fenwick, T., & Edwards, R. (2013). Performative ontologies: Sociomaterial approaches to researching adult education and lifelong learning. *European Journal for Research on the Education and Learning of Adults*, 3(1), 49–63. https://doi.org/10.3384/rela.2000-7426.rela0104

Freire, P. (1970). *Pedagogy of the oppressed*. New York: Continuum Books.

Goodson, I. (2014). Context, curriculum and professional knowledge. *History of Education: Journal of the History of Education Society*. 46(3), 768–776. https://doi.org/10.1080/0046760X.2014.943813

Goodson, I., & dos Santos Rosa, M. (2018). The journey of school knowledge in high school and the concept of refraction. *Pro-Posições*, 29(1), 296–320. http://dx.doi.org/10.1590/1980-6248-2016-0052

Kanes, C. (Ed.). (2011). Challenging professionalism. In C. Kanes (Ed.), *Elaborating professionalism: Studies in practice and theory* (1st ed.) (Vol. 5, pp. 1–15). Springer. https://doi.org/10.1007/978-90-481-2605-7

Kumar Shah, R. (2020). Concepts of learner-centred teaching. *International Journal of Education*, 8(3), 45–60. https://doi.org/10.34293/education.v8i3.2926

Martini, M., Moscovitz, H., Fernández Ugalde, R., Hansen, M., Hughson, T., Marfán, J., & Tozan, O. (2024, April 19). In search of a global community: A multivocal critique of UNESCO's education commons discourse. *Journal of Education Policy*, 1–17. https://doi.org/10.1080/02680939.2024.2339914

Peel, K. L., Kelly, N., Danaher, P. A., Harreveld, R. E. & Mulligan, D. L. (2023). Analysing teachers' figurative language to shed new light on teacher resilience. *Teaching and Teacher Education*, 130, 104175. https://doi.org/10.1016/j.tate.2023.104175

Rudd, T., & Goodson, I. (2016). Restructuring, reform and refraction: Complexities of response to imposed social change. *Educational Practice and Theory*, 38(2), 5–21.

Stray, I. E. (2017). Teachers' ways in times of fluidity: Idiosyncratic cultural responses to global educational reform movements. Unpublished doctoral dissertation. Faculty of Humanities and Education, University of Agder. Kristiansand, Norway.

Törnberg, A. (2021). Prefigurative politics and social change: A typology drawing on transition studies. *Distinktion: Journal of Social Theory*, 22(1), 83–107.

Volante, L., & Klinger, D. A. (2021) PISA and education reform in Europe: Cases of policy inertia, avoidance, and refraction. *European Education*, 53(1), 45–56. https://doi.org/10.1080/10564934.2021.1987839

Vygotsky, L. (1978). *Mind in society: The development of higher psychological processes*. Cambridge, MA: Harvard University Press.

Recommended Further Reading

Edling, S., & Frelin, A. (2016). Sensing as an ethical dimension of teacher professionality. *Journal of Moral Education*, *45*(1), 46–58. https://doi.org/10.1080/03057240.2015.1127801

European Commission. (2020). *Equity in school education in Europe: Structures, policies and student performance*. Eurydice report. Publications Office of the European Union. https://eacea.ec.europa.eu/national-policies/eurydice/content/equity-school-education-europe_en

Evans, L. (2008). Professionalism, professionality and the development of education professionals. *British Journal of Educational Studies*, *56*(1), 20–38. https://doi.org/10.1111/j.1467-8527.2007.00392.x

Goodson, I., Moore, S., & Hargreaves, A. (2006). Teacher nostalgia and the sustainability of reform: The generation and degeneration of teachers' missions, memory, and meaning. *Educational Administration Quarterly*, *42*(1), 42–61. https://doi.org/10.1177/0013161X05278180

McLeod, J., & Wright, K. (2008). *Social values and schooling: Curriculum, counselling and the education of the adolescent, 1930–1970s*. Paper presented at the annual conference of the Australian Association for Research in Education, Queensland University Technology, Brisbane, December.

Rancière, J. (1991). *The ignorant schoolmaster: Five lessons in intellectual emancipation*. Translated, with an introduction, by Kristin Ross. Stanford University Press.

Rudd, T., & Goodson, I. (Eds.). (2017). *Negotiating neoliberalism: Developing alternative educational visions*. Sense.

Slezáková, K., Kissová, L., & Felcmanová, L. (2022). When policy clashes with practice: The case of teaching assistants in the Czech Republic. *Journal of Pedagogy*, *13*(2), 77–103. https://doi.org/10.2478/jped-2022-0009

Taylor, S. (1997). Critical policy analysis: Exploring contexts, texts and consequences. *Discourse: Studies in the Cultural Politics of Education*, *18*(1), 23–35. https://doi.org/10.1080/0159630970180102

7 Teachers as Relationship Brokers

Introduction

Relationship brokering can be defined as a process involving individuals—in this case, teachers—strengthening their collaborative communication in order to achieve successful interpersonal and professional outcomes. They may do this through a number of avenues that include the following (teacher specific) strategies:

- Enabling positive and effective policy and curriculum outputs such as tailoring learning episodes to meet diverse needs within a student cohort
- Helping others such as students to traverse the educative process
- Guiding decision-making for best results such as supporting parents
- Mentoring others such as practicum students or less experienced peers
- Evaluating school processes for effectiveness and relevance such as navigating student behaviour programmes
- Negotiating own work/life balance and caring for Self

The successful brokerage of relationships with a myriad of other stakeholders is a key aspect of a teacher's life. These stakeholders include students, parents, colleagues, organisational management, policymakers and members of the wider school community. It is also pertinent to acknowledge the role of relationship with Self as this is the basis upon which all other interactions are conducted.

Efficient and positive relationship brokering is an expectation put upon teachers who are generally not formally trained in the various processes involved with the psychological nuances of working with such a broad range and dynamic set of people and circumstances. Paradoxically, it is a pivotal role around which the teacher builds authenticity and professionalism.

As a further professional complication, often teachers are called upon to enact "bridgework" (Johnson et al., 2022). This is the process whereby teachers are required to act as mediation interventionists and to provide a neutral third party in order to broker damaged relationships successfully such as those that may occur between student and colleague, teacher and management, student

DOI: 10.4324/9781003564850-7

and parent, student and student, etc. This form of mediation requires delicacy, tact and an inhouse knowledge of contextual nuance.

Selected Literature

Teachers play a vital role in the operational functioning of an educative environment. Anderson et al. (2024) stated that: "Teachers can be seen as 'boundary workers' who broker a sense of (un)welcome and (un)belonging" (p. 3487). Relationships matter, and this sense of belonging is an important element of teaching and interacting within a school and a community. Belonging and inclusion were highlighted by Maslow (1943) in his seminal work on the hierarchy of human needs. He hypothesised that human behaviour is driven by certain requirements. In order to ascend the hierarchy successfully, the rudimentary physiological needs (air, food, water), safety needs (security) and social needs (love, belonging) must be fulfilled. Teachers as "boundary workers" play a pivotal role in brokering relationships of acceptance and belonging (students, peers, curriculum)—and, in some cases, safety—within an educative environment, thereby servicing the essential early rungs upward in the hierarchy of needs.

The philosophical assumptions held by teachers form the basis of their praxis and their understanding of workplace considerations around the concepts of ethics, skill acquisition and personal representation. Perceptions based on axiological, epistemological and ontological beliefs provide the professional framework upon which teachers build their interactions when addressing interpersonal relationships. Somekh and Lewin (2011) defined axiology as referring to "... philosophical questions relating to the nature of values" (p. 320).

As well as demonstrating and explicitly clarifying their own professional values, teachers are expected to impart a sense of an ethical Self to their students. The relationships that educators broker with students reflect axiological insights and enable students to examine, identify and clarify their own values in light of their own experiential worlds. Successful axiological role modelling allows students to encounter integrity and respect safely, and affords them opportunities to utilise this further in their interactions outside the classroom/school environment, thereby enhancing their own relationship brokering.

Epistemology concerns the nature of knowledge and the manner in which it is acquired (Merriam, 2009, p. 8). In order to engage students in effective learning, teachers need to broker relationships in a manner that imparts learning in ways that foster students' ways of knowing. Epistemic teaching (Mor-Hagani & Barzilai, 2022) focuses on knowledge building, which implies a dynamic relationship between learner and teacher that encourages academic risk-taking and trust.

Ontology, as defined by O'Leary (2010), broadly refers to "the study of what exists, and how things that exist are understood and categorized" (p. 5). This is translated by teachers into adjustments in the acquisition and amount of knowledge relative to the student cohort and their ability to ingest and comprehend knowledge formally at any given time. Tkachenko et al. (2024) posited that ontologically responsible teachers ensure the customisation of the educative process to suit the audience.

The use of ontologies is advisable, in particular, for:

- Personalization of learning aspects, such as learning processes (organization, management, control, etc.)
- Personalization of the learning process itself (providing educational content)
- Overcoming the heterogeneity and difficulty of processing large amounts of data (including information taken from the Internet) (p. 90)

In order to achieve these targets, teachers need relationships whereby they are familiar with students' academic and personal characters so that students accept/consider the information given to them by the teacher. This brokering of trust is foundational to teachers' successful professional goals.

Theoretically, the notion of boundary work noted above provides insights into how teachers in this study brokered relationships among individuals, social groups, education systems and cultures of the teaching profession and beyond to wider contexts of educational practice. In their initial review of boundary literature from sociocultural and psychosocial perspectives from the 1970s to the early 2020s, Akkerman and Bakker (2011) recognised boundaries as "dialogical phenomena" (p. 132). It is here—on, in and through in the boundary—that learning potentialities emerge as boundary objects that bridge dialogical inter/actions in their various forms. Boundary objects are inclusive, but not mutually exclusive of physical entities or cognitive processes (Groot & Abma, 2021; Star & Griesemer, 1989; Trompette & Vinck, 2009). These concepts of boundary, boundary objects and boundary crossing "refer to on-going, two-sided actions and interactions between contexts" (Akkerman & Bakker, 2011, p. 136) in which sociocultural and psychosocial differences are valued as resources for learning through and with people's diverse differences.

In this chapter, relationships are the boundary objects of interest. Teachers broker relationships when working within the boundaries between their personal and professional worlds. Brokers have a capability to be outsiders within, to "hear" multiple voices from multiple directions. to work with difference: "… a person situated at the boundary of two practices is typically considered as a broker, a significant yet challenging position from which connection between contexts can be made" (Kluijtmans et al., 2017, p. 647).

In a qualitative study with teachers in higher education institutions, Oonk et al. (2020) identified an educational broker as a "boundary crosser or bridge builder" (p. 713). Brokers manage, participate in and integrate various practices simultaneously, connecting knowledge and understandings between different social practices, both within schools as well as in their interface with parents and other community stakeholders. As brokers, teachers are "connecting, exchanging, switching, adapting and aligning" (Oonk et al., 2020, p. 713) relationships. The following section now explores teachers as relationship brokers through analysis of interview transcripts undertaken as part of the study reported in this book.

Data Analysis

As noted in Chapter 1, our data analytic strategy for engaging with the nearly 300,000 words of interview transcripts related to the Australian research project on which this book focuses included the elicitation of four "nodes":

- Complexities (CY): Engaging with multifaceted events and issues
- Challenges (CE): Encounters with difficult and potentially stressful events and issues
- Contradictions (CN): Events and issues with at least two competing influences and pressures
- Comforts (CT): Sources of encouragement, motivation and pleasure

Five "dimensions" were then applied to each of these nodes. These included psychosocial; profession and professionalism; changes and continuities, naming, framing and shaming; and teaching by design. This chapter focuses on the dimension referencing the "psychosocial dimension". In Chapter 1, we defined this dimension as "The interdependence of personal thoughts and behaviours with the contextual and relational influences of being a teacher".

Table 1.1 in Chapter 1 presented applicable demographic information about the participants, who are represented by their respective assigned pseudonyms and whose lived emotional experiences are investigated in this exploration. Building on the data analysis matrix presented in Table 1.2 in Chapter 1, Table 7.1 illustrates the approach taken to data analysis in this chapter, referencing teachers as relationship brokers. The data are illuminated in the psychosocial dimension. Data are further categorised within the four nodes—i.e., complexities, challenges, contradictions and comforts. These nodes are broken down into relevant categories such as relationship brokering with students, graduate teachers, pre-service teachers, Self, teaching colleagues, parents and school management.

Table 7.1 Data Analysis Matrix for Teachers as Relationship Brokers

	Psychosocial
Complexities	Harriet; Sylvia; Sally
Challenges	Sally; Doug; Rosalie; Shirley
Contradictions	Sylvia; Ella
Comforts	Marnie; Harriet

Complexities

Brokering relationships is complex as teachers' personal thoughts and behaviours are juxtaposed with those of the contextual and relational aspects of being a teacher. These complexities are now explored through Harriet's relationship with her students, Sylvia's and Sally's relationships with parents; and Sally's relationship with her graduate teacher.

Harriet connects with her students by letting them "see me as a teacher" and "also as a person":

> Yes, I think being able to have built those relationships with your students and have your students feel like they know you and they can trust you, I think it impacts on everything, not just academically.

By aligning with students personally, being able to switch between the academia of teaching and enjoying one another as people, Harriet trusts not only that learning will occur, but also that students' behaviour will be more manageable:

> If the students have respect for you and if they enjoy you as well as a person, then they're more likely to engage in your lessons and hopefully pick up on all your teaching, but as well with the behaviour management, I find that that really goes a long way as well.

Unfortunately, the complexities of relationships with parents are compounded in these digitised days. Sylvia thinks that "the digital age and all of the parents that are on Facebook, et cetera, and they have these communities that talk about what goes on at school, and with kids, and with students and teachers, that's a nightmare". Sally concurs. She also identifies the complexities of brokering relationships with parents as contributing to burnout:

> I think the fact that parents feel like they've got access to us all the time makes a big difference. I'm very good at doing those types of things, but it still is that three o'clock in the morning wake up .... There comes a point you have to leave it here. You can't just keep taking it home and doing more and more and more. There comes a point when you have to just leave it because the burnout is just huge.

Teaching is not a walk-in/walk-out, clock-on/clock-off job. Sally's experience is that parents seem to think it acceptable to contact teachers at any time. One consequence of this is not being able to "switch off" at night, waking up at three o'clock in the morning. This omnipresent psychosocial vulnerability is one that Sally is sharing with a graduate teacher whom she is mentoring. This graduate teacher is "absolutely fabulous":

> I think what probably built our relationship initially was that she actually did her fourth placement with me, so that's where I got to meet her. She got to see me working before she did anything as well, and then I got to see her and mentor [her] through her final placement.

Sally's relationship with her then-pre-service teacher was productive. They really connected. Sally admired her because "she was just so great with the students and really connected with them and knew how to hold her ground but still be compassionate". Later, this now-graduate teacher obtained a position at the same school. These days, Sally continues to mentor her and finds "her academic understanding is at really quite a decent level for a brand-new graduate as well":

> Like I said, it's just that youth and that enthusiasm and that passion you get with your graduates. It's just so easy to work with, for those that are genuinely built to be teachers, which isn't all of them. She's a good one.

Sally's philosophy of teaching aligns with that of the graduate teacher. From the complexities of relationships with parents and the resilience required there, to the mentoring relationship with "a good one", Sally switches, adapts and aligns her personal thoughts with those of the contextual and relational aspects of being a teacher and a mentor, and at the beck and call of parents.

Challenges

Sally was at a "pretty tumultuous time" in her life when professional challenges and a personal relationship breakdown were occurring at the same time. Coping with life in these complex contexts showed her that she "actually needed to spend more time for myself as well and focus a lot less on my job and spend a lot more time focusing on myself" (Sally). However, the challenge of focusing on Self remains as relationships with others are equally and contemporaneously challenging.

Doug and Rosalie highlight a range of challenges when teaching. Doug had another professional life before teaching and he is "a huge believer" that "teaching would be such a much more reputable and stronger profession" if his colleagues had experienced life prior to being "allowed into a classroom":

> I mean, I know it helped me immensely coming in as a 35-year-old with the life experience I had prior to that. I could never imagine coming into

a classroom as a 21-year-old or 22-year-old with no experience at all and expect to develop those relationships.

Doug already knew how to connect with other professionals in the workplace, and he believes that enabled him to cope with the challenges of classroom teaching more than if he had no life experience outside schools and schooling. He was better equipped to broker relationship with students and colleagues because of his past experiences.

For Rosalie, teaching is "a social justice job" that requires "a huge mixture of skills". Like Doug, she too finds teaching "requires a higher degree of skill than any other job I've ever done":

> It definitely requires more skill than being a lawyer or being a political advisor ... in terms of emotional intelligence, people management, relationship building, intellectual ability, abstract thinking, being able to pull things apart, being able to recognise different situations and think on the spot.
>
> It's so many skills and then, on top of that, you're working with this group that is going through a very difficult time of their life and the behaviours [that accompany that]. You're also working within a system. You've got all that system stuff going on and bureaucracy and stuff that you don't necessarily agree with. There's a lot to manage.

There is indeed a lot to manage. In fact, there is a lot of high-level skills and knowledge needed to teach. Furthermore, if teachers are also committed to providing equal rights and opportunities for all young people within systems with which they may not agree, then it is no wonder that a teacher such as Rosalie finds it challenging.

Challenging relationships with school management were encountered by Shirley to the point that she "finally ended up seeing the psychologist". In recounting a fraught relationship with her school principal, Shirley's psychologist is reported to have consoled her:

> I know you don't feel it at the moment, but one day, and not in that distant future, you actually will get back to where you were, you will be enjoying it again and you will have a working relationship, even with that principal who betrayed you. You will be back to your old self.

With the psychologist, Shirley exchanged her perspective on her relationship with that principal. That one relationship in one context (Shirley and her principal) was connected with another relationship in another context

(Shirley and her psychologist) so as to work through challenges in the first relationship.

Contradictions

Brokering relationships with school management can also be quite contradictory. Sylvia is a teacher of Japanese who has a new principal. Her brokerage strategy is described as "duck and weave":

> It's really inappropriate to say, but I don't want to be in his space; I don't want to have anything to do with him, I don't want him to know me, and yet he wrote the most fabulous card to me to thank me for the Japan trip and what the wonderful feedback he got was. ... Now I don't know if that's my colleagues, from the kids, from the parents, but that was in my pigeonhole the first day back, I think that strategy works. I'd rather he doesn't know diddly-squat about me.

Initially, at first glance, this teacher's perspective may seem contradictory in a context where second language teaching can have a perilous existence if student numbers are at risk of not justifying staffing and physical resourcing expenditures. Sylvia elaborates further:

> I'm not going to talk to him directly, he can get his information from other ways, but he doesn't need to know me. For the deputy [principal], I can avoid that .... Again, I will try not to be in this space.

Why is this so? Sylvia reflects critically: "It is a fear of the unknown. I don't know them yet, so I don't trust them. That's interesting because I trust everybody equal [to me] ... but I don't trust them". She identifies "trust" as fundamental to relationships and is fearful that, without yet knowing the principal and deputy principal, she cannot yet trust them. Sylvia then delves more deeply into her psychosocial assumptions about this trust/fear binary:

> That's a gender thing too as well and it's because they're younger and it's because they're both from another school, they've come together, and we've got a new structure at school. We haven't had a deputy before, but the new principal is a man, when a female did it for 15 years, and he needs a deputy. It's a whole lot of assumptions that I've made.

Sylvia's introspection has elicited gender, age and professional backgrounds as other contributory variables in her avoidance of a relationship with her new principal and deputy principal. By now, she is naming and framing the contradictions she is experiencing:

> They don't need to be bombarded by the minutiae that is my life, but I categorically want them to leave me [alone], and I categorically want

them to be involved and across everything that I'm doing, and I don't want to be responsible.

At this stage, Sylvia just does not want to be responsible for brokering a relationship with the new principal and his new deputy principal whom she sees as his (i.e. the principal's), but not yet as her, deputy principal.

Let us stay with Sylvia a little longer:

> Do I think these two men are operating at a level where they can question and challenge what I'm thinking? No, I don't think they understand my area well enough. Therefore, I'm not sure that they're doing their job properly because I'm not sure that they can question at a high enough level and support me appropriately …

The interview did not elicit any resolutions. However, Sylvia does provide an insight that may suggest the core of her concern and the hindrance it is posing to brokering any meaningful relationships (as at the time of interview):

> I think being in that era where you actually have relationships with people, you have discussions, you don't post things online, you can say completely inappropriate things because it's not recorded. That all helps. I think that's the way you manage your change. I think young people, they're growing up in a different environment and they don't have those skills.

The young people to whom Sylvia refers incorporated the aforementioned new principal and deputy principal as well as the students whom she teaches.

Brokering relationships with students can be quite contradictory. On the one hand, school attendance and progression in learning as measured by assessment outcomes are important. Officially, this is one measure of teacher effectiveness as educators and a marker of positive learning relationships with students. On the other hand, the mental health and well-being of young people in schools are also important because officially that is also a marker of teacher effectiveness. In reality, though, the boundaries between such two-in-one contexts are blurred, as Ella demonstrates:

> He's a really nice kid but he's got a lot of stuff going on and missed heaps [of] school each term. Last term because a parent was sick and he didn't come to school, and the previous term because he broke up with his girlfriend. That was too much to come to school. But he was just such a nice kid, and we would communicate over email heaps, and I would just like every time he missed class, I would email him and be

like, "Hey, just checking up on you. You doing okay? We're really missing you in class." That sort of stuff and it just formed like a really nice relationship.

Ella prioritised her relationship with that young man so that she did not lose him as a learner. Yet the relationship was more than that:

That was [the] bigger picture than doing this assessment for me, like I would in my email address write, "Look, this is what we did today. If you're up to doing it, have a go; it's all online. If not, then you just do what you can and prioritise your mental health" because that was not good. I think it just strengthened the relationship between us and then meant that I then chased up all of the other people at school that can provide more mental health support and all that sort of stuff. He was sort of one that really stuck out over the last semester.

Ella connected with this student (via email and presumably face-to-face during school time). She was exchanging updates on classroom happenings, adapting where necessary, switching focus from academic outcomes of assessment to mental health, and aligning her relationship with her student's overall well-being. Her interactions with others on his behalf brought comfort that she was doing all she could in that context at that time.

Comforts

Relationships with colleagues further demonstrate the interdependence of personal thoughts and behaviours with the contextual and relational influences on being a teacher. Both Marnie and Harriet had experienced positive interactions with colleagues in diverse contexts.

Marnie is in a small school where, in contrast to a big school, "everybody knows what's going on, and everybody just steps in and does what needs doing". There is no siloing of responsibilities when it comes to the welfare of students: "You don't have to know that's your job, or that's your job":

An example: one of the boys that I have is on medication at morning tea, and everybody is responsible. If he turns up and you're the one there, you're the one that gives it to him. There just doesn't seem to be that "It's your job to do".

Marnie's colleagues in this small school look out for one another. They are also forgiving when mistakes are made such that "somebody else will help you and fix it with you".

Such collegiality is a source of encouragement, motivation and even pleasure for Harriet, although she does acknowledge that "it can be very rare for sometimes teachers to have … that collegiality". Carpooling with one of her teaching partners sets Harriet up as they will "talk about plans for the day". Then once at school:

> I guess a good day is [when] I have a chance to debrief with my colleagues in the morning and you have that chance to not just talk about the plans for the workday but just have that social aspect.

Administrators (i.e., management) at Harriet's school are "very supportive". By Year 6, her 31 students (at the time of the interview) are used to the routine of "how the school works". This harmony contributes to her motivation for and pleasure in teaching.

Implications

Relationship brokerage was found to occur in institutional, interpersonal and intrapersonal contexts as teachers engaged with the complexities, challenges, contradictions and comforts of teaching. There are both practical and theoretical implications of these findings, although the aphorism attributed to Lewin (1945) that "There is nothing so practical as a good theory" signals the significance of both.

Practically, there are implications for professional development in both initial and continuing teacher education. For school teachers supervising pre-service teachers and also for university academics involved in the development of initial teacher education programmes in Australia, Standard 7 of the Professional Engagement domain of practice is the most pertinent here. At any of the four stages of development (graduate, proficient, highly accomplished and lead), teachers must "engage professionally with colleagues, parent/carers and the community" (Australian Institute for Teaching and School Leadership, 2011/2018). Demographic information shared earlier in this book shows the majority of teachers who participated in these interviews to be in any one of these stages.

Domain: Professional Engagement
Standard 7: Engage professionally with colleagues, parents/carers and the community
Focus area 7.1 Meet professional ethics and responsibilities
Focus area 7.2 Comply with legislative, administrative and organisational requirements
Focus area 7.3 Engage with the parents/carers
Focus area: Engage with professional teaching networks and broader communities.

(AITSL, 2011/2018, p. 14 of 15)

Therefore, teachers in all stages would also benefit from professional development activities mapped against these focus areas of Standard 7 of the Professional Engagement domain.

For individual teachers and teams in the study by Oonk et al. (2020) reported earlier in this chapter, there was even a card game developed from their findings called "Wanted Brokers!" which supported "awareness raising on brokering tasks and competencies, and peer exchange on related competence performance" (p. 714). Now, at the time of writing this chapter, that card game has not been experienced by either author of this chapter or by the other authors in this book. However, it is intriguing enough to be on our respective professional development agenda going forward because we too need to examine our practices for the extent to which we improve our capabilities in school–university–society relationships brokerage.

To return to the theoretical perspectives on teachers as relationship brokers, framing relationships as boundary objects enriches understandings of boundaries and of teaching as boundary work, with boundary crossing as contributing to teacher resilience. The findings reported in this chapter conceptualise mechanisms that point to the learning potentiality of boundary crossing in general and to the use of relationships as boundary objects in particular. The earlier work of Bakker et al. (2019) with vocational curriculum found four learning mechanisms at play in the brokerage of border crossing activities: namely, "identification, coordination, perspective making and taking (or mutual reflection), and transformation" (p. 349). Further research is needed to test this proposition in the cauldron of scholarly debate around what constitutes boundary objects and the sociocultural and the psychosocial positioning of relationships in teachers' boundary work.

Conclusion

This chapter has explored the personal thoughts, assumptions, perceptions and representations of Self and others of eight of the 42 Australian teachers who participated in the larger study with which this book engages. It has delved into their contextualised boundary work in which they broker relationships with welcoming, and sometimes unwelcoming, people, processes and policies. Their descriptions and imageries in this chapter show both subtlety and explicitness in the conduct of this boundary work (Anderson et al., 2024). Brokering relationships is integral to teachers' professionalism and should be built-in to initial and continuing teacher education, not bolted-on. It is of equal importance with curriculum development and implementation, pedagogical expertise, and managing assessment and reporting requirements. As relationship brokers, teachers navigate different epistemic practices, experiencing in the process convoluted complexities, enormous challenges, perplexing contradictions, and personal and professional comforts that valorise their educational boundary work.

References

Akkerman, S., & Bakker, A. (2011). Boundary crossing and boundary objects. *Review of Educational Research*, *81*(2), 132–169. https://doi.org/10.3102/0034654311404435

Anderson, V., Ortiz-Ayala, A., & Mostolizadeh, S. (2024). Schools and teachers as brokers of belonging for refugee-background young people. *International Journal of Inclusive Education*, *28*(14), 3487–3501. https://doi.org/10.1080/13603116.2023.2210591

Australian Institute for Teaching and School Leadership. (2011/2018). *Australian professional standards for teachers*. Australian Institute for Teaching and School Leadership.

Bakker, A., Akkerman, S., Guile, D., & Unwin, L. (2019). The learning potential of boundary crossing in the vocational curriculum. In D. Guile & L. Unwin (Eds.), *The Wiley handbook of vocational education and training* (1st ed.) (pp. 349–372). John Wiley & Sons.

Groot, B., & Abma, T. (2021). Boundary objects: Engaging and bridging needs of people in participatory research by arts-based methods. *International Journal of Environmental Research and Public Health*, *18*, 7903. https://doi.org/10.3390/ijerph18157903

Johnson, T. D., Aparna, J., & Kreiner, G. E. (2022). Bridgework: A model of brokering relationships across social boundaries in organizations. *Organization Science*, *34*(4). https://doi.org/10.1287/orsc.2022.1631

Kluijtmans, M., de Haan, E., Akkerman, S., & van Tartwijk, J. (2017). Professional identity in clinician-scientists: Brokers between care and science. *Medical Education*, *512*, 645–655. https://doi.org/10.1111/medu.13241

Lewin, K. (1945). The research center for group dynamics at Massachusetts Institute of Technology. *Sociometry*, *8*(2), 126–136. https://doi.org/10.2307/2785233

Maslow, A. H. (1943). A theory of human motivation. *Psychological Review*, *50*(4), 370–396.

Merriam, S. B. (2009). *Qualitative research: A guide to design and implementation*. Jossey-Bass Publishers.

Mor-Hagani, S., & Barzilai, S. (2022). The multifaceted nature of teachers' epistemic growth: Exploring teachers' perspectives on growth in epistemic performance. *Teaching and Teacher Education*, *115*. https://doi.org/10.1016/j.tate.2022.103714

O'Leary, Z. (2010). *The essential guide to doing your research project*. Sage Publications.

Oonk, C., Gulikers, J. T. M., den Brok, P. J., Wesselink, R., Beers, P.-J., & Mulder, M. (2020). Teachers as brokers: Adding a university–society perspective to higher education teacher competence profiles. *Higher Education*, *80*(4), 701–718. https://doi.org/10.1007/s10734-020-00510-9

Somekh, B., & Lewin, C. (Eds.). (2011). *Theory and methods in social research* (2nd ed.). Sage Publications.

Star, S. L., & Griesemer, J. (1989). Institutional ecology, 'translations' and boundary objects: Amateurs and professionals in Berkeley's Museum of Vertebrate Zoology. *Social Studies of Science*, *19*(3), 387–420. https://doi.org/10.1177/030631289019003001

Tkachenko, K., Tkachenko, O., Tkachenko, O., Mazur, N., & Mashkina, I. (2024). Ontological approach in modern educational processes. *CEUR Workshop Proceedings*, 88–97. https://ceur-ws.org/Vol-3654/paper8.pdf

Trompette, P., & Vinck, D. (2009). Revising the notion of boundary object (N. Draper, Trans.). *Revue d'Anthropologie des Connaissances*, 3–1. https://doi.org/10.3917/rac.006.0003

Recommended Further Reading

Akkerman, S. F., Bakker, A., & Penuel, W. R. (2021). Relevance of educational research: An ontological conceptualization. *Educational Researcher, 50*(6), 416–424. https://doi.org/10.3102/0013189X211028239

Haye, A., & González, R. (2021). Dialogic borders: Interculturality from Vološinov and Bakhtin. *Theory & Psychology, 31*(5), 746–762. https://doi.org/10.1177/0959354320968635

Holquist, M. (Ed.). (1981). *The dialogic imagination: Four essays by M. M. Bakhtin* [Translation of *Vorosy literatury i estetiki* by Caryl Emerson and Michael Holquist]. University of Texas, USA: University of Texas Press Slavic series; no. 1.

Sequevin, P., Pattyn, V., Jungblut, J., & Blum, S. (2024). There, across the border – Political scientists and their boundary-crossing work. *Policy Sciences, 57*, 437–457. https://doi.org/10.1007/s11077-024-09530-z

8 Teachers as Self-Regulated Learners

Introduction

Teachers at all school levels play key roles as agents of self-regulated learning (SRL) in developing their own professional competencies and their students' capabilities as self-regulated learners (Karlen et al., 2023). Within these dual roles, teachers demonstrate their competencies by proactively controlling their cognition, motivation and behaviour in pursuit of their desired goals, while also knowing how to support students to think, feel and act as active participants in their own learning process (Peel, 2019). Researchers have consistently substantiated the importance of SRL for academic achievement (Adams et al., 2015; Dent & Koenka, 2016), social and emotional wellbeing (Boekaerts, 2011; Steinbach & Stoeger, 2016) and lifelong learning (Nguyen et al., 2024; Winne, 2017). It follows then that empowered teachers, who have an understanding of SRL, play a significant role in supporting students develop self-regulatory capabilities (Landberg & Partsch, 2023) and indeed in developing epistemic fluency; "different ways of thinking about creating knowledge" (Goodyear & Ellis, 2007, p. 65) to thrive within the profession.

In this chapter, we explore how the teachers talked about embracing different types of knowledge and ways of knowing to demonstrate their capacity to be flexible and adaptive in their professional contexts. The data were collected from participants in the Australian research project that explored the narratives of teachers to identify their sources of resilience. Frequent references are made in this data to the teachers' improvisations and adaptations in response to the changing teaching profession. When faced with challenges, contradictions and complexities they acted with epistemic fluency to knowledgeably generate new insights and to shape their environment (Markauskaite & Goodyear, 2017). Furthermore, the interviews prompted the teachers' self-awareness where they talked about their comforts as sources of motivation and encouragement. The teachers self-reflected on their professional experiences as self-regulated learners, providing proactive examples that also demonstrated how their SRL competencies influenced their students' success as lifelong learners.

DOI: 10.4324/9781003564850-8

Selected Literature

SRL refers to one's active and constructive processes in response to personal thoughts, feelings and actions that are directed towards meeting goals (Zimmerman, 2013). Over the past five decades, research has proliferated to explain the many theoretical perspectives and complexity of SRL (Boekaerts & Cascallar, 2006; Järvelä & Hadwin, 2024; Schunk & Usher, 2013; Zimmerman, 1986; Zimmerman & Schunk, 2011), and this has continued to generate a range of teaching practices that empower self-regulated learners (Alvi & Gillies, 2021; Peel, 2020a, 2020b; Perry & Rahim, 2011). We adopt the definition of SRL suggested by Pintrich (2000) as "an active, constructive process whereby learners set goals for their learning and then attempt to monitor, regulate and control their cognition, motivation, and behaviour, guided and constrained by their goals and the contextual features in the environment" (p. 453).

Characteristically, SRL is cast as processes that involve the three cyclical phases of forethought and planning, performance monitoring, and reaction and reflection (Zimmerman, 2011). The self-regulatory cycle is perpetuated by a belief that one has the ability to achieve the desired outcome, activate strategies and adapt situationally, as SRL is highly context dependent. Accordingly, the self-regulatory cycle relies on the interactional influences of personal, behavioural and environmental determinants (Bandura, 1986). In other words, this triadic reciprocation view of self-regulatory functioning acknowledges that individuals can impact their environment as much as the environment can have an impact on how they think and behave. Pintrich and Zusho (2002) emphasised: "Self-regulation is not just afforded or constrained by personal cognition and motivation, but also privileged, encouraged, or discouraged by the contextual factors" (p. 279). Figure 8.1 presents the triadic interplay among the thought processes and feelings, the observable behaviours and the environmental events in explaining the reasons why SRL is highly situationally specific and context dependent.

Fundamentally, metacognition and motivation are important dimensions of SRL to be developed by recognising what strategies are feasible to realise a goal in the sense of creating an expectation of success (Efklides, 2011). Green (2019) contended, "Metacognition is conducive to individual success and epistemic flourishing" (p. 124), whereas the motivational dimension relies on an individual's self-awareness to prime emotional competence through positive self-reflections (Wosnitza et al., 2018). Self-awareness is empowering as it is conducive to understanding oneself and knowing how to regulate and control motivation and effort when applying and monitoring strategies for given purposes (Peel, 2019). Bandura (1986) articulated the notion of agency to describe how being self-aware of thoughts influences motivation and subsequent behaviours, stating, "People use the instrument of thought to comprehend the environment, to alter their motivation, and to structure and regulate their actions" (p. 1). The agentic teacher holds the self-efficacy beliefs to perform a specific task for a successful outcome (Bandura, 1997).

Teachers as Self-Regulated Learners 113

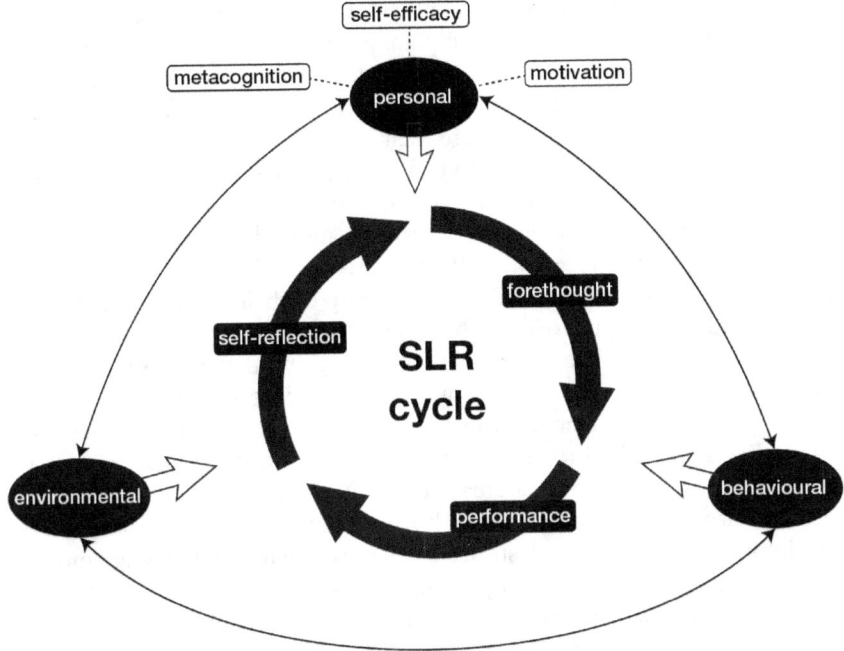

Figure 8.1 The triadic reciprocation view of self-regulatory functioning

Although not explicit in the literature, there are recognised similarities between SRL competencies, such as activating strategies to achieve a goal (Greene, 2018), and epistemic fluency, which involves one's ability to know and apply different ways of thinking, evaluate different perspectives and create new knowledge for solving real-world problems (Markauskaite & Goodyear, 2017). Manning and Payne's (1993) earlier portrayal of teachers as self-regulated learners characterised them as reflective practitioners and decision-makers, whose professional introspection enables them to monitor their professional situations and learn from their experiences. Kremer-Hayon and Tillema (1999) deemed that teachers' increased self-regulatory capacity would lead to greater autonomy, reflective practices and internalisation of knowledge. Subsequently, there was a call for more research to understand the strategies of teachers, as situationally adaptive learners who need to develop epistemic fluency, to thrive within the profession. In response, Barr and Askell-Williams (2019) researched teachers' reflexive examination of their knowledge and epistemic beliefs about SRL to confirm the value of teacher self-awareness for improving students' abilities to engage in SRL.

Considering the complex demands of teaching, it is proposed that how teachers draw on their epistemic fluency influences their self-regulatory functioning within diverse school contexts. In other words, teachers' knowledge and application of strategies to plan, perform and evaluate impacts their successful management of challenges, complexities and contradictions in their professional contexts. Sautelle et al. (2015) confirmed: "It is likely that teachers with self-regulatory skills manage their workload better and seek feedback on their teaching from students and colleagues, thus working to improve their teaching" (p. 56). Furthermore, it is well established in the literature that teachers can self-regulate their practice to activate students' SRL as a proactive process (Kramarski & Heaysman, 2021). Paris and Winograd (2001) asserted that teachers' self-awareness and understanding of their learning enable them to nurture the self-regulatory capabilities of their students.

Given the many different contexts of teaching and that SRL is contextually specific, teachers are required to improvise and adapt strategies in changing and novel situations. Teachers can find themselves in challenging positions, where they are required to respond to many factors outside their control, yet in many cases they also have a great deal of autonomy to guide the direction of their learning process. To portray how teachers professionally navigate the terrain of their work, they tell stories of their experiences expressing emotions such as amusement, frustration, admiration and satisfaction. It is through these narratives that we explore teachers as self-regulated learners and their strategies for success in the profession.

Data Analysis

From the five dimensions of teachers' work and identities discussed in Chapter 1, *Profession and professionalism* was selected as it incorporated the teachers' ethical and partly autonomous enactment and dissemination of knowledge, and their interactions with other educational stakeholders. The data analytic strategy implemented as outlined in Chapter 1 involved engagement with the interview transcripts related to the Australian research project with a specific focus on investigating the narratives of teachers as self-regulated learners. The approach taken to data analysis for this chapter of the book was inclusive of four nodes to investigate teachers as agents of SRL in developing their own professional competencies and their students' capabilities as self-regulated learners. The narratives are captured as *Complexities, Challenges, Contradictions* that were expressed as the teachers narrated them, through mixed emotions that included their identified sources of *Comforts*. As such, the data analysis followed the nodes that categorised the complexities the teachers faced when engaging with multifaceted events and issues; the challenges they encountered during difficult and potentially stressful times; the contradictions they experienced due to competing influences and pressures; and the sources of comforts that provided encouragement, motivation and pleasure.

Drawn from the interview data were teachers' narratives that related to their experiences in the profession, enacting and interacting as professionals, while adhering to ethical expectations. Nine participants' narratives that were

Table 8.1 Data Analysis Matrix for Teachers as Self-regulated Learners

	Profession and professionalism
Complexities	Paul; Cindy; Marnie
Challenges	Jalena; Maurie; Kelly
Contradictions	Doug; Helen; Norman
Comforts	Paul; Cindy; Marnie; Jalena; Maurie; Kelly; Doug; Helen; Norman

considered useful for understanding teachers as self-regulated learners were selected. The narratives were categorised by the nodes, as encounters of complexities, challenges, contradictions; and through discovering the sources of comforts that are embedded into each teacher story. Conveyed in Table 8.1, and specific to this chapter, are the nine participants who are represented by their respective assigned pseudonyms (Table 1.1 in Chapter 1 presents the demographic information about the project's participants).

Complexities and Comforts

Paul, a secondary school teacher, depicts a vicious cycle of emotions by reflecting on a chain of events that could be detrimental to his future teacher-student interactions. Reinforced by a negative feedback loop, his feelings of being stressed and underappreciated are articulated as motivational and emotional influences that act as barriers for effective SRL:

> I think about the impact of being stressed, coming in [to the classroom] feeling like you're stressed, and you're underappreciated, and the impact that has on the relationships that you make with the students. It's the vicious cycle. You go, "Oh, I'm not making a difference. No one's listening to me. They [the students] don't care," and then they pick up on that and they just respond negatively.

By associating negative feelings with the potential consequences, Paul reflects on how his interpretations could impact subsequent interactions with the students, and how such apprehensive self-talk could damage his future relationships. Of significance here is that it is not the emotion that feeds the vicious emotional cycle but the interpretation of the emotion (Rolston & Lloyd-Richardson, 2017). Being self-aware enables Paul to generate new insights, which in turn empowers him to be adaptive within his professional context:

> I've been thinking about the kinds of spirals that we get into that make the next day harder to get up from. I guess when I recognised that that was what was happening, I ended up seeking the help of the board [school leadership team] and just trying something different to actually change things up a bit.

Paul's use of self-regulatory strategies, such as self-evaluating and seeking social assistance to diffuse negative emotions, demonstrates his ability to effectively respond. He applies these coping strategies to manage the stressful situation and related emotions. An understanding of strategies for emotional regulation and how to apply them to complex situations assists teachers as self-regulated learners to adapt to the demands of their work and allows a greater understanding of what led to the emotional experience. Paul strategically demonstrates how he pays attention to possible triggers of strong emotions and strategically plans how he could meet expectations by creating a list to assist with time management:

> I think the biggest stress is just that feeling of not having enough time to do a good job. I've got like 15 tabs on my computer. I've looked them up and I need them to do the work; so they're basically my to-do list; and the to-do list is huge. It's always growing and never seems to get smaller. I know exhaustion creeps in more towards the end of the term and I am looking forward to a new term, and the fact that I've got the break helps me reset my emotional state. Of course, we all like holidays.

Paul recognises the emotional drain of working in the teaching profession and refers to school holidays as an emotional reset switch. At the end of a school term, Paul anticipates and appreciates the holidays as a source of comfort. Accordingly, this self-consequating strategy, of acknowledging holidays as a self-reward, motivates his return to work in the new school term.

The complexity of the work of teachers is highlighted by Cindy, an experienced primary school teacher, who perceives that teachers are now being made more accountable for the teaching of students' basic self-regulatory social skills, such as manners and communication:

> The jobs or the hats we wear as teachers these days are so varied. It's a job where no two days are ever the same. It's always changing, always interesting and never dull. I've seen a big difference in the last 25 years— even the last 10 years or so. There's a lot of almost pseudo parenting that we have to do, where we're teaching skills that I wouldn't have taught years ago, because they [the students] already came to school with those skills: how you hold a conversation; how you talk politely with your, please and thank you; all the basic manners and etiquette and politeness.

Research justifies that, prior to children attending school, parents and caregivers are seen as being responsible for teaching the basic social rules (Landberg & Partsch, 2023). Once they begin school, although parents and caregivers are consistently associated with the development of their children's basic self-regulatory skills (Lengua et al., 2021), Cindy contends that responsibilities are changing. In response to these changes, she accepts, in accordance with the research, that schools are seen as the central context for fostering lifelong learning competencies (Landberg & Partsch, 2023):

> I think it's my role to encourage lifelong learning like teaching them [the students] how to learn, to be learners; all the holistic things and the pastoral care like how to be a good person; teaching them how to self-manage and regulate their emotions; and then how to socialise well with other people and to respect others.

Strong parallels have been made between the qualities of lifelong learning and SRL (Winne, 2017). The associated strategic actions can be taught irrespective of personality traits or dispositions for learning (Perry & VandeKamp, 2000). Furthermore, teachers' attitudes towards learning are exemplified to their students (Landberg & Partsch, 2023). As such, Cindy's attitude towards and modelling of lifelong learning is highly relevant to fostering her students' capabilities for SRL:

> I think to be a teacher is also to acknowledge that we are all lifelong learners because I learn something every day from my students, as well as me teaching them. They teach me a lot. If by the end of the day, I've got them wanting more; like when you come to the end of a chapter of a book, the writer normally makes you want to read to the next chapter. If some or most of my students feel that they want to come back the next day to learn more, or I've inspired them to learn more about a certain topic then I've activated that lifelong learning. They actually want to find out about things. I think that I would call that a very successful day.

From this motivational dimension, Cindy talks about lifelong learning as engagement in learning being an integral and valued part of her students' lives. The literature supports that teachers are powerful influencers who can empower students by triggering an interest in their learning and developing their sense of agency, where they are in control of their actions and feel an expectation of success (Peel, 2020b; White, 2017).

Cindy's own motivation, as a source of comfort that encourages her as a self-regulated learner, comes from the sense of purpose and satisfaction that rewards her work in the profession: "I think being a teacher gives you a real purpose to life where you feel that you are doing something; you are achieving something worthwhile".

Marnie, also an experienced primary school teacher, reflects on the complexities that she has encountered during her years of teaching. She expresses an overwhelming and perpetual seeking of knowledge when discussing the different ways of thinking about what is known in a profession that is recognised as a "continual learning experience" (Pugach, 2023, p. 4): "I think [teaching] has gotten harder. It's probably easier back when you're beginning because you don't really realise what you're doing wrong". At the same time, she acknowledges the continuing presence of teaching's complexity: "The thing is, it doesn't actually go away. You never actually finish the year and go, 'Yes, I got that right'".

When describing an effective teacher, Tomlinson (2010) stated, "... teachers never fall prey to the belief that they are good enough. The best teachers I have known are humbled by how much more they need to learn" (p. 24). Marnie embraces the value of self-reflection to initiate changes to her teaching as an ongoing everyday occurrence that informs her practice (Peel, 2021). Reflecting on experiences in the profession enables teachers to understand why they do and know what they do so that they can subsequently do what they do well (Seidman, 2012). Correspondingly, Marnie demonstrates her ability to see the complexities of teaching from the perspective of early career teachers as she connects with empathy to show understanding:

> I think teaching is one of those professions where you can take things very personally. It's a very hard profession to feel like you do it well, so to see someone with my years of experience say to a first-year, or a second-year teacher, "Yes, I'm like that too".

Barriers to humanistic collaboration among teachers in schools have been associated with the structural conditions that isolate teachers and the pressures placed on teachers that can be overwhelming and make them competitive rather than collaborative (Sage et al., 2012). In contrast to being impersonal and competitive, Marnie talks about how she develops an atmosphere with colleagues that encourages safety and a sense of belonging:

> Sometimes it's just enough to talk, and to listen to people for a bit, and have a bit of perspective. Sometimes it's just that confidence to go, "Yes, that's what I'm doing too" or "That's how I'm feeling too". It's actually comforting just to know that's what happens. I think it shows an understanding that we're human beings, and we have lives outside of teaching; that's helpful.

Furthermore, Marnie's humanistic approach is comforting and confidence building for other teachers, and for herself, and as such acts as a source of motivation that is fundamental for SRL (Peel, 2019; Zimmerman, 2011).

Challenges and Comforts

The focus on the humanistic experience and the challenges that impact teachers' professional functioning introduces Jalena's narrative as a secondary school teacher of Languages (that is, teaching a language other than English). The Australian Curriculum (Australian Curriculum Assessment and Reporting Authority [ACARA], 2024) supports the inclusion of Languages, stating,

"Learning a language(s) broadens students' horizons in relation to the personal, social, cultural and employment opportunities that an increasingly interconnected and interdependent world can offer" (n.p.). Languages is one of the eight learning areas that students learn, although the majority of students in Australia choose not to study a language other than English once it is no longer compulsory for the curriculum year level. Jalena concedes this is a reality at her school, but despite this she recognises the broader rationale for language learning from a humanistic perspective:

> Teaching a language, a lot of people don't see [that] as very important. They think of the subject [language as a learning area] as just a bit of a side-line. I don't see it that way at all. The good thing about learning a second language, I think, is that it's more about the person, the student, than it is about the content. What we do is a human job. It's not a mass production job. It's not about producing people for the workforce.

Furthermore, Jalena identifies herself and other teachers as being *helpers*, and this is reported in the literature to have challenging implications in relation to teacher self-care: "Teachers, as helpers, have a stressful profession" (Sage et al., 2012, p. 211). As such, there are risks, including that of burnout, in this helping profession that can be managed through a teacher's heightened self-awareness of the choices and their consequences that support their decision-making:

> I see my job is teaching students and helping them [students]. Helping train them; helping guide them to be better thinkers; to be better organised; to be more independent; to see that they can problem solve without someone holding their hand.

The competencies that Jolena acknowledges that are important for her students are also what teachers require to build their strong sense of self and knowledge of strategies for awareness, management and problem-solving as self-regulated learners in the profession.

As a source of comfort, Jalena shares how she is intrinsically motivated by a motto that has meaning for her as a teacher and inspires her professionally to thrive. A motto is a statement that creates a personal mission, affirms core values and provides a sense of purpose that empowers internally a self-regulated learner (Houston & Sokolow, 2017):

> I follow a particular blog ... a middle high school teacher in the States [United States of America]. He does short articles. It's just really common sense. His motto is the humanity of teaching, "Our job as teachers is to promote the long-term flourishing of young people." That's the bottom-line. You know, that's my motto now.

Maurie, a secondary school maths and science teacher, similarly is challenged by the demands placed on students' academic achievement that can divert the focus from the importance of the emotional, social and self-regulatory competencies:

> The focus changes the way that I feel, the shifting from the content focus to the learning environment focus, much towards individual students, the class dynamic, plus a bit of content. As someone who has an interest in the learning of the kids, it's not just the content itself, although I think that's important; a student grows not just academically, but as a person and should feel valuable as an individual. That value that's given to that student is independent of how well they're doing in school.

It is generally agreed in the literature that students' SRL competencies, such as behavioural regulation, persistence when facing frustration, control of emotions and ability to apply strategies to solve problems, encompass the strongest predictors of students' academic outcomes (Pintrich, 2000; Schraw, 2010; Zimmerman, 2000). Yet, Maurie emphasises the challenging dilemma of balancing teaching the content of his learning area and engaging students holistically in learning. He takes comfort in the knowledge that he is a role model to his adolescent students:

> A bit of ... almost leadership or mentoring or guidance or role modelling these roles, which perhaps aren't being filled elsewhere in society or are more fragmented in society— nowadays almost a supplement to the family itself. I want those things. I want to be that thing myself, and I want the family members that I care about to have those experiences as well.

As an early career secondary school teacher, Kelly talks about empowering students as self-regulated learners but is challenged by her lack of confidence to connect with her students:

> What I always come back to is about giving to kids, empowering them with the knowledge and skills to become independent, to open up opportunities later in life. For me, that's what it means to be a teacher. Then on my side, I would need to be as organised and as knowledgeable as possible to help make that happen. But I just lacked a lot of confidence in how I presented myself to the class.

Central to SRL is the experience of a sense of agency that is directly related to having the self-efficacy beliefs to perform a specific task for a successful outcome (Bandura, 1997). Kelly's lack of self-efficacy in her classroom was reflected in her teacher presence:

> I had everything really well organised to compensate, but I realised that it had to be my non-verbal language, my tone of voice, all of the physical

appearances, the presence in the classroom, that's what I really had to work on. The way I gave instructions, that was the key.

Bromley (2017) described teacher presence as "owning your classroom space" (n.p.) and advised that this could be "achieved by means of body language, eye contact and tone of voice" (n.p.).

Kelly's self-awareness enabled her to monitor what was and was not working in her instructional approach and to develop practices to grow her classroom presence. SRL involves experiencing an expectation of success by anticipating the possibility that there will be a successful outcome (Peel, 2019). The ways in which a teacher as a self-regulated learner adapts to the teaching context and learns new practices form cumulative cycles (Zimmerman, 2002) that contribute positively to future teaching experiences. When teachers understand and own their practices, they learn new skills that can be transferred to classroom (Spruce & Bol, 2015), as Kelly reflects:

> Teaching does give you a lot of skills with organisation and time schedules. I like to be really organised, have all of the technology working in the classroom, and have the children engage with the tasks that were designed. Having them also just enjoying it as well and going beyond what we were expecting them to learn for the day.

Kelly is comforted and motivated by her capacity to develop the self-regulatory skills of organisation and time management that she applies to her teaching for the students to experience a love of learning. Lumsden (1999) proposed, "Today's educators face a great opportunity and responsibility: To make learning something students will want to incline their hearts toward for their own personal reasons" (p. 108).

Contradictions and Comforts

The relationship between teacher motivation and students' academic outcomes is well researched (Lazarides & Schiefele, 2021). Furthermore, it is well established that teacher motivation is central to teachers' competence (Kunter & Holzberger, 2014). Doug, a secondary school teacher of ten years of experience in the profession, came to teaching as a career change. He talks about the enthusiastic teachers who demonstrated an enthusiastic approach to teaching, in contrast to teachers he speculates are employed for the purpose of gaining a financial income:

> You see right away the teachers that are passionate and making a difference and the teachers who are just seeing the school as a bank machine. My theory around that is we need every teacher to be as passionate. That's what I try to be for my students and for my school. Lead by example. The most frustrating thing for myself and other people in my

position [leadership role] that I've spoken with is that the biggest emotional killer in teaching right now is dealing with staff that are under-motivated and under-prepared.

Given the connection between teachers' motivation and their productive performance, it follows that fostering teacher motivation should be of a high priority for school leadership and educational policy decisions. In contradiction, Doug relates his experience:

I think the educational system actually rewards people who are under-motivated by not giving them more [work]. It's almost one of the only jobs in the world where being confident means you're going to get more and more and more work till you crumble. When there's somebody or a number of people who don't pull their weight; that weight then needs to shift onto somebody else. It's just a matter of time before that somebody else crumbles.

The consequential misappropriation of incentives, as described by Doug, is concerning as it tests the resilience of motivated teachers in relation to them being able to sustain their enthusiasm and effectiveness with an increased workload. Doug identifies the paradox of teacher competency being disregarded and perceived as a disadvantage: "In terms of emotion, to me the most emotionally draining aspect of teaching is being competent, and rather than getting rewarded and patted on the back for that, your job becomes harder". Not all teachers have the life experience or expertise to be able proactively to self-reflect and maintain their professional enthusiasm should they find themselves in the position that Doug has observed.

As a source of motivation, Doug is comforted by the appreciation he welcomes from his students for whom he has been a teacher role model:

Nothing makes me happier than seeing a kid who could be an engineer, or a rocket scientist come to me and tell me, "You know what, I'm inspired to be a teacher now," because those are the people that we need to be teachers, those who are able to have that passion in the classroom.

Helen teaches in a secondary school and speaks about her teacher–student interactions that are built on empathy and care about students' learning. Teacher empathy is founded on knowing students' personal and social situations, feeling care and concern and responding compassionately, while maintaining focus on their learning (Meyers et al., 2019): "Obviously, overall, the main emotion as a teacher is empathy for the students you teach. Enjoying being with them and having fun. Also, learning from them and being inspired by young students. It's probably the personal connection".

The powerful combination of empathy, teacher effort and students' successful learning goal progress provide for Helen the comfortable feeling of self-respect. The research confirmed that self-respect supports teachers as self-regulated learners by promoting their autonomy and pursuit of personal goals that reciprocate respect for self and others (Roland & Foxx, 2003). Helen reflects:

> I guess what we all strive for as a teacher is to feel that at the end of the lesson or the end of the week or at the end of the semester you can see the progress in the kids and when you do that then you will have a real self-respect. When your self-respect gets boosted, you feel really good about yourself. Your content with the effort that you've put in.

As opposed to a successful learning outcome resulting from teachers' dedication, Helen speaks about the frustration and disappointment she feels when the goals are not met and how she recognises inconsistencies in teaching success:

> On the other hand, when you don't see that [success] and there's not a single teacher who doesn't occasionally not see that, you get frustrated that you did put in all this effort. I guess it's a certain let down that you feel because you did everything that you could to help the students. You just never know how each day is going to go.

Norman is a secondary school teacher who questions whether teachers have a grasp of the strategies that are effective for managing their time, balancing work-life commitments and controlling their emotions to maintain healthy functioning:

> Teachers need to do a better job at managing their time, disconnecting from work, having good self-care and separating the emotion from the problem. You can have a problem, but it doesn't have to be anyone's fault, or it doesn't have to be personal. I think sometimes teachers do a lot of talking but don't do a lot of walking the talk. We say that to the kids all the time, "You got to be really good time managers", but we at times are not good time managing ourselves.

In contrast to teachers being role models as self-regulated learners for their students, teachers who are struggling to manage themselves are less likely to promote strategies of which they have not experienced as being effective. If teachers expect students to self-regulate their learning, then it is assumed that teachers will teach and demonstrate what that looks like in the learning context. Peeters et al. (2014) described self-regulated teachers as "(pro) active agents who trigger certain educational beliefs, construct appropriate instructional practices accordingly and proactively control the teaching environment and conditions" (p. 1965).

Sharing a source of comfort, Norman describes himself as being fortunate to be at his school where he interacts with many students. He is inspired in his leadership position to develop strategies for supporting the motivation of other teachers:

> I've spent the past about five-years at this school and really loving it. I'm really lucky to have a wide variety of teaching as I get to know all the kids, which is great. Now I'm about to do acting head of department and thinking about what strategies I can develop as a leader to inspire other teachers.

Implications

For teachers to be effective in teaching SRL in their context they require a clear understanding of what SRL is and how it impacts lifelong learning. Geldhof and Little (2011) contended that SRL "represents a core aspect of human functioning that influences positive development across the lifespan" (p. 45). As such, teachers' knowledge about and ascribed value to teaching SRL would have a significant impact on student lifelong learning. It follows then that teachers' ethical and partly autonomous enactment and dissemination of knowledge includes developing good quality teacher knowledge about improving students' development as self-regulated learners. Furthermore, research has highlighted the importance of teachers having professional competences as self-regulated learners as well as being agents to promote their students' SRL (Karlen et al., 2023).

The extracts of data from the interview transcripts related to the Australian research project were drawn out to investigate the narratives of teachers as self-regulated learners. The teachers shared their success strategies to highlight that SRL is understood from two perspectives, where there is an expectation on teachers to demonstrate the dispositions of a self-regulated learner and a responsibility to enact their knowledge to effectively teach SRL competencies to their students. Furthermore, in accordance with the basic triadic reciprocation view of self-regulatory functioning (Bandura, 1986), it is emphasised teachers can impact their teaching context as much as the professional context can have an impact on how they think and behave. There is no doubt that a teacher's awareness of themselves as a self-regulated learner can be enhanced by understanding the success strategies that are situationally adaptive for improving students' abilities to engage in SRL. The following four success strategies are elaborated from the teacher participants' narratives.

Firstly, the competencies that teachers acknowledge as important for students are also what they require to build their strength of self and knowledge of strategies for awareness, management and problem-solving as self-regulated learners in the profession. By recognising what strategies are feasible to realise a goal, teachers are metacognitively thinking and monitoring their strategic decisions and actions (Karlen et al., 2023). Furthermore, knowing how to apply strategies for emotional regulation when faced with complex situations assists teachers as self-regulated learners to adapt to the demands of their work and allows for a greater understanding of what led to the emotional experience. Therefore, the teacher serves dual roles, as a self-regulated learner, while also knowing how to support students as self-regulated learners (Karlen et al., 2023).

Secondly, teachers' improvisations and adaptations in response to the changing teaching profession provide opportunities for continual learning. Teachers need to be perpetually seeking new knowledge and be epistemically open to different ways of thinking. By reflecting on their experiences in the profession, teachers gain deeper understandings of what it is to be a self-regulated learner. As such, teacher reflection triggers new ways of thinking about and exploring knowledge of practices that enable an internal sense of agency. Teachers are empowered by being personally aware of and in control of their actions rather than being overwhelmed by the challenges and complexities that are inherent to the teaching profession. However, teachers also need to be self-aware that promotion of agency is situationally influenced and is collectively developed from what teachers bring to their practice and from what is afforded from the wider school community (Biesta et al., 2015).

Thirdly, a teacher's attitude towards and modelling of lifelong learning are highly relevant to fostering students' capabilities for SRL. Lifelong learning involves applying skills, promoting personal fulfilment, being flexible and adaptable and exercising respect; all recognised as a highly desirable attribute of learners (Watson, 2003). Among other influences, capacities for developing the habits of lifelong learners are a "result of the role models provided by individual teachers—both as learners themselves and as illuminators of specific attitudes regarding the importance of learning in our lives" (Pendergast et al., 2005, p. 8). Furthermore, lifelong learning, from a humanistic perspective, is seen as an internal and natural process that considers students' needs, motivation and emotions (Sage et al., 2012). Subsequently, a humanistic approach diverts the demands that are placed on students' academic achievement towards promoting their emotional, social and self-regulatory competencies. Teachers' humanistic dispositions are individual, such as being empathetic, and relational, through modelling, as well as contextual by creating a teaching context that encourages safety and a sense of belonging for all. Unfortunately, schools are reported as being a neglected context for fostering lifelong learning (Landberg & Partsch, 2023), which is perturbing considering the associated SRL skills are a necessary component for nurturing teachers and students as self-regulated learners.

Fourthly, fostering teachers' motivation should be of a high priority for school leadership and educational policy decisions as it is fundamental for SRL (Peel, 2019) and is a key component of teachers' professional competencies in promoting students' SRL (Jud et al., 2023). Self-regulated learners require the motivation to engage in the learning and the perceived confidence that they have the capabilities to perform the strategies. As such, both will and skill are central for the agentic teacher and is directly related to them having the self-efficacy beliefs to perform a specific task for a successful outcome (Bandura, 1997). Self-efficacy, or lack of, influences the ways in which teachers adapt to the complexities they face in their teaching context and determines what they learn as new practices that will contribute positively or negatively to their teaching experiences in the future. This highlights the significance of the motivational dimension of SRL that calls on teachers' positive self-awareness and self-reflections to prime their emotional competence (Wosnitza et al., 2018). Research contended self-efficacy as one of the strongest predictors of teachers' SRL promotion (Dignath-van Ewijk, 2016).

Finally, the teacher participants, through their narratives, expressed the outcomes from their strategies for success by acknowledging the sources of encouragement, motivation and pleasure that nourished them as a teacher. They spoke of the sense of purpose and satisfaction gained from a rewarding profession and the appreciation derived from being an influential role model that empowers internally a self-regulated learner. Highlighted also was the motivational power of humanistic collaboration and being empathetic to emotionally understand. These actions were perceived as being confidence building for themselves, and for other teachers, and provided a source for self-respect. The teachers referred to learned and applied strategic actions that were both goal directed and insightfully spontaneous for supporting them and their students as self-regulated learners.

Conclusion

This chapter presented the narratives of nine teachers who self-reflected on their professional experiences as self-regulated learners. Four success strategies were shaped by an analysis of the narratives through the teachers' experiences of complexities, challenges, contradictions and comforts. The competencies that teachers acknowledge as important for students are also what are required by teachers as self-regulated learners. Furthermore, teachers' improvisations and adaptations in response to the changing teaching profession provide opportunities for their continual learning to build their strengths as self-regulated learners. Accordingly, as self-regulated learners, teachers' attitudes towards and modelling of lifelong learning is highly relevant to fostering students' capabilities for SRL. Essentially, fostering teachers' motivation should be of a high priority for school leadership and educational policy decisions as it is fundamental for SRL. Teachers with a capacity to be self-aware and self-regulate as learners can steer themselves towards being positive, confident and capable to thrive within the profession.

References

Adams, C. M., Forsyth, P. B., Dollarhide, E., Miskell, R., & Ware, J. (2015). Self-regulatory climate: A social resource for student regulation and achievement. *Teachers College Record*, *117*(2), 1–28.

Alvi, E., & Gillies, R. M. (2021). Self-regulated learning (SRL) perspectives and strategies of Australian primary school students: A qualitative exploration at different year levels. *Educational Review*, *75*(4), 680–702. https://doi.org/10.1080/00131911.2021.1948390

Australian Curriculum Assessment and Reporting Authority [ACARA]. (2024). *Teacher resources. Understand this learning area/Languages.* https://www.australiancurriculum.edu.au/curriculum-information/understand-this-learning-area/languages

Bandura, A. (1986). *Social foundations of thought and action: A social cognitive theory.* Prentice-Hall.

Bandura, A. (1997). *Self-efficacy: The exercise of control.* Freeman.

Barr, S., & Askell-Williams, H. (2019). Changes in teachers' epistemic cognition about self-regulated learning as they engaged in a researcher-facilitated professional learning community. *Asia-Pacific Journal of Teacher Education*, *48*(2), 187–212. https://doi.org/10.1080/1359866X.2019.1599098

Biesta, G., Priestley, M., & Robinson, S. (2015). The role of beliefs in teacher agency. *Teachers and Teaching*, *21*(6), 624–640. https://doi.org/10.1080/13540602.2015.1044325

Boekaerts, M. (2011). Emotions, emotion regulation, and self-regulation of learning. In B. Zimmerman & D. H. Schunk (Eds.), *Handbook of self-regulation of learning and performance* (pp. 408–425). Routledge.

Boekaerts, M., & Cascallar, E. (2006). How far have we moved toward the integration of theory and practice in self-regulation? *Educational Psychology Review*, *18*(3), 199–210. https://doi.org/10.1007/s10648-006-9013-4

Bromley, M. (2017). Developing your presence in the classroom. *Secondary Education*, *2017*(21). https://doi.org/10.12968/sece.2017.21.12

Dent, A. L., & Koenka, A. C. (2016). The relation between self-regulated learning and academic achievement across childhood and adolescence: A meta-analysis. *Educational Psychology Review*, *28*, 425–474. https://doi.org/10.1007/s10648-015-9320-8

Dignath-van Ewijk, C. (2016). Which components of teacher competence determine whether teachers enhance self-regulated learning? Predicting teachers' self-reported promotion of self-regulated learning by means of teacher beliefs, knowledge, and self-efficacy. *Frontline Learning Research*, *4*(5), 83–105. https://doi.org/10.14786/flr.v4i5.247

Efklides, A. (2011). Interactions of metacognition with motivation and affect in self-regulated learning: The MASRL model. *Educational Psychologist*, *46*(1), 6–25. https://doi.org/10.1080/00461520.2011.538645

Geldhof, G. J., & Little, T. D. (2011). Influences of children's and adolescents' action-control processes on school achievement, peer relationships, and coping with challenging life events. *New Directions for Child & Adolescent Development*, *133*, 45–59. https://doi.org/10.1002/cd.303

Goodyear, P., & Ellis, R. (2007). The development of epistemic fluency: Learning to think for a living. In A. Brew & J. Sachs (Eds.), *Transforming a university: The scholarship of teaching and learning in practice* (pp. 57–68). Sydney University Press.

Green, J. L. (2019). Metacognition as an epistemic virtue. *Southwest Philosophy Review*, *35*(1), 117–129. https://doi.org/10.5840/swphilreview201935112

Greene, J. A. (2018). *Self-regulation in education.* Routledge.

Houston, P. D., & Sokolow, S. L. (2017). *The empowering leader: 12 core values to supercharge your leadership skills.* Rowman & Littlefield.

Järvelä, S., & Hadwin, A. (2024). Triggers for self-regulated learning: A conceptual framework for advancing multimodal research about SRL. *Learning and Individual Differences, 115*, 102526. https://doi.org/10.1016/j.lindif.2024.102526

Jud, J., Hirt, C. N., Rosenthal, A., & Karlen, Y. (2023). Teachers' motivation: Exploring the success expectancies, values and costs of the promotion of self-regulated learning. *Teaching and Teacher Education, 127*, 104093. https://doi.org/10.1016/j.tate.2023.104093

Karlen, Y., Hirt, C. N., Jud, J., Rosenthal, A., & Eberli, T. D. (2023). Teachers as learners and agents of self-regulated learning: The importance of different teachers competence aspects for promoting metacognition. *Teaching and Teacher Education, 125*, 104055. https://doi.org/10.1016/j.tate.2023.104055

Kramarski, B., & Heaysman, O. (2021). A conceptual framework and a professional development model for supporting teachers' "triple SRL–SRT processes" and promoting students' academic outcomes. *Educational Psychologist, 56*(4), 298–311. https://doi.org/10.1080/00461520.2021.1985502

Kremer-Hayon, L., & Tillema, H. H. (1999). Self-regulated learning in the context of teacher education. *Teaching and Teacher Education, 15*(5), 507–522. https://doi.org/10.1016/S0742-051X(99)00008-6

Kunter, M., & Holzberger, D. (2014). Loving teaching: Research on teachers' intrinsic orientations. In P. W. Richardson, S. A. Karabenick, & H. M. G. Watts (Eds.), *Teacher motivation* (pp. 105–121). Routledge. https://doi.org/10.4324/9780203119273

Landberg, M., & Partsch, M. V. (2023). Perceptions on and attitudes towards lifelong learning in the educational system. *Social Sciences & Humanities Open, 8*(1), 100534. https://doi.org/10.1016/j.ssaho.2023.100534

Lazarides, R., & Schiefele, U. (2021). Teacher motivation: Implications for instruction and learning. Introduction to the special issue. *Learning and Instruction, 76*, 101543. https://doi.org/10.1016/j.learninstruc.2021.101543

Lengua, L. J., Ruberry, E. J., McEntire, C., Klein, M., & Jones, B. (2021). Preliminary evaluation of an innovative, brief parenting program designed to promote self-regulation in parents and children. *Mindfulness, 12*(2), 438–449. https://doi.org/10.1007/s12671-018-1016-y

Lumsden, L. (1999). *Student motivation: Cultivating a love of learning*. ERIC Clearinghouse on Educational Management.

Manning, B. H., & Payne, B. D. (1993). A Vygotskian-based theory of teacher cognition: Toward the acquisition of mental reflection and self-regulation. *Teaching and Teacher Education, 9*(4), 361–371.

Markauskaite, L., & Goodyear, P. (2017). *Epistemic fluency and professional education: Innovation, knowledgeable action and actionable knowledge* (Vol. 14). Springer.

Meyers, S., Rowell, K., Wells, M., & Smith, B. C. (2019). Teacher empathy: A model of empathy for teaching for student success. *College Teaching, 67*(3), 160–168. https://doi.org/10.1080/87567555.2019.1579699

Nguyen, A., Lämsä, J., Dwiarie, A., & Järvelä, S. (2024). Lifelong learner needs for human-centered self-regulated learning analytics. *Information and Learning Sciences, 125*(1/2), 68–108. https://doi.org/10.1108/ILS-07-2023-0091

Paris, S. G., & Winograd, P. (2001). The role of self-regulated learning in contextual teaching: Principles and practices for teacher preparation. *Office of Educational Research and Improvement*. http://files.eric.ed.gov/fulltext/ED479905.pdf

Peel, K. L. (2019). The fundamentals for self-regulated learning: A framework to guide analysis and reflection. *Educational Practice and Theory, 41*(1), 23–49. https://doi.org/10.7459/ept/41.1.03

Peel, K. L. (2020a). Classroom behavior management in middle level education: A self-regulatory approach to empower teachers and adolescent learners. In D. Virtue

(Ed.), *International handbook of middle level education theory, research, and policy* (pp. 179–193). Routledge.

Peel, K. L. (2020b). Everyday teaching practices for self-regulated learning. *Issues in Educational Research, 30*(1), 260–282. http://www.iier.org.au/iier30/peel.pdf

Peel, K. L. (2021). Professional dialogue in researcher-teacher collaborations: Exploring practices for effective student learning. *Journal of Education for Teaching, 47*(2), 201–219. https://doi.org/10.1080/02607476.2020.1855061

Peeters, J., De Backer, F., Reina, V. R., Kindekens, A., Buffel, T., & Lombaerts, K. (2014). The role of teachers' self-regulatory capacities in the implementation of self-regulated learning practices. *Procedia - Social and Behavioral Sciences, 116*, 1963–1970. https://doi.org/10.1016/j.sbspro.2014.01.504

Pendergast, D., Flanagan, R., Land, R., Bahr, N., Mitchell, J., Weir, K., Noblett, G., Cain, M., Misich, T., & Carrington, V. (2005). *Developing lifelong learners in the middle years of schooling.* The University of Queensland. http://mceetya.edu.au/verve/_resources/lifelonglearn_midyears.pdf

Perry, N. E., & Rahim, A. (2011). Studying self-regulated learning in classrooms. In B. J. Zimmerman & D. H. Schunk (Eds.), *Handbook of self-regulation of learning and performance* (pp. 122–136). Routledge.

Perry, N. E., & VandeKamp, K. J. O. (2000). Creating classroom contexts that support young children's development of self-regulated learning. *International Journal of Educational Research, 33*(7–8), 821–843. https://doi.org/10.1016/S0883-0355(00)00052-5

Pintrich, P. R. (2000). The role of goal orientation in self-regulated learning. In J. Boekaerts, P. R. Pintrich, & M. Zeidner (Eds.), *Handbook of self-regulation* (pp. 452–502). Elsevier Academic Press.

Pintrich, P. R., & Zusho, A. (2002). The development of academic self-regulation: The role of cognitive and motivational factors. In A. Wigfield & J. Eccles (Eds.), *Development of achievement motivation* (pp. 249–284). Academic Press.

Pugach, M. C. (2023). *Because teaching matters: An introduction to the profession.* John Wiley & Sons.

Roland, C. E., & Foxx, R. M. (2003). Self-respect: A neglected concept. *Philosophical Psychology, 16*(2), 247–288. https://doi.org/10.1080/09515080307764

Rolston, A., & Lloyd-Richardson, E. (2017). What is emotion regulation and how do we do it. *Cornell Research Program on Self-Injury and Recovery, 1*, 1–5.

Sage, S. M., Smith-Adcock, S., & Dixon, A. L. (2012). Why humanistic teacher education still matters. *Action in Teacher Education, 34*(3), 204–220. https://doi.org/10.1080/01626620.2012.694021

Sautelle, E., Bowles, T., Hattie, J., & Arifin, D. N. (2015). Personality, resilience, self-regulation and cognitive ability relevant to teacher selection. *Australian Journal of Teacher Education, 40*(4), 54–71. https://doi.org/10.14221/ajte.2015v40n4.4

Schraw, G. (2010). No school left behind. *Educational Psychologist, 45*(2), 71–75. https://doi.org/10.1080/00461521003720189

Schunk, D. H., & Usher, E. L. (2013). Barry J. Zimmerman's theory of self-regulatory learning. In H. Bembenutty, T. J. Cleary, & A. Kitsantas (Eds.), *Applications of self-regulated learning across diverse disciplines* (pp. 1–28). Information Age Publishing.

Seidman, I. (2012). *Interviewing as qualitative research: A guide for researchers in education and the social sciences* (4th ed.). Teachers College Press.

Spruce, R., & Bol, L. (2015). Teacher beliefs, knowledge, and practice of self-regulated learning. *Metacognition and Learning, 10*(2), 245–277. https://doi.org/10.1007/s11409-014-9124-0

Steinbach, J., & Stoeger, H. (2016). How primary school teachers' attitudes towards self-regulated learning (SRL) influence instructional behavior and training implementation in classrooms. *Teaching and Teacher Education, 60*, 256–269. https://doi.org/10.1016/j.tate.2016.08.017

Tomlinson, C. A. (2010). Notes from an accidental teacher. *Educational Leadership*, 68(4), 22–26.

Watson, L. (2003). Lifelong learning in Australia. In *Lifelong Learning Network, Division of Communication and Education*, University of Canberra. Department of Education, Science and Training.

White, M. C. (2017). Cognitive modeling and self-regulation of learning in instructional settings. *Teachers College Record*, 119(13), 1–26. https://www.tcrecord.org/Content.asp?ContentId=21924

Winne, P. H. (2017). The trajectory of scholarship about self-regulated learning. In T. Michalsky & C. Schecter (Eds.), *Yearbook of the National Society for the Study of Education: Volume 116. Self-regulated learning: Conceptualizations, contributions, and empirically based models for teaching and learning*. National Society for the Study of Education.

Wosnitza, M., Delzepich, R., Schwarze, J., O'Donnell, M., Faust, V., & Camilleri, V. (2018). Enhancing teacher resilience: From self-reflection to professional development. In M. Wosnitza, F. Peixoto, S. Beltman, & C. F. Mansfield (Eds.), *Resilience in education* (pp. 275–288). Springer. https://doi.org/10.1007/978-3-319-76690-4_16

Zimmerman, B. J. (1986). Development of self regulated learning: Which are the key subprocesses? *Contemporary Educational Psychology*, 11, 307–313. https://doi.org/10.1016/0361-476X(86)90027-5

Zimmerman, B. J. (2000). Attaining self-regulation: A social cognitive perspective. In M. Boekaerts, P. Pintrich, & M. Zeidner (Eds.), *Handbook of self-regulation* (pp. 13–39). Academic Press.

Zimmerman, B. J. (2002). Becoming a self-regulated learner: An overview. *Theory into Practice*, 41(2), 64–70. https://doi.org/10.1207/s15430421tip4102_2

Zimmerman, B. J. (2011). Motivational sources and outcomes of self-regulated learning and performance. In B. J. Zimmerman & D. H. Schunk (Eds.), *Handbook of self-regulation of learning and performance* (pp. 49–64). Routledge.

Zimmerman, B. J. (2013). From cognitive modeling to self-regulation: A social cognitive career path. *Educational Psychologist*, 48(3), 135–147. https://doi.org/10.1080/00461520.2013.794676

Zimmerman, B. J., & Schunk, D. H. (Eds.). (2011). *Handbook of self-regulation of learning and performance*. Routledge.

Recommended Further Reading

Dignath-van Ewijk, C., & van der Werf, G. (2012). What teachers think about self-regulated learning: Investigating teacher beliefs and teacher behavior of enhancing students' self-regulation. *Education Research International*, 2012, 1–10. https://doi.org/10.1155/2012/741713

Greene, J. A., Bernacki, M. L., & Hadwin, A. F. (2023). Self-regulation. In P. A. Schutz & K. R. Muis (Eds.), *Handbook of educational psychology* (pp. 314–334). Routledge.

McLennan, B., & Peel, K. (2011). Inspire to connect a learning desire. In L. Abawi, J. M. Conway, & R. Henderson (Eds.), *Creating connections in teaching and learning* (pp. 33–45). Information Age Publishing.

Randi, J. (2004). Teachers as Self-Regulated Learners. *Teachers College Record*, 106(9), 1825–1853. https://doi.org/10.1111/j.1467-9620.2004.00407.x

9 Teachers as Situated Ethicists

Introduction

A long-standing assertion is that one of the defining features of a profession is a code of ethics. For instance, Greenwood (1960) contended: "Succinctly put, all professions seem to possess: 1) systematic theory, 2) authority, 3) community sanction, 4) ethical codes, and 5) a culture" (p. 169). Three decades later, Strike (1990) listed among the characteristics held to define a profession the following: "… the possession of an esoteric knowledge base, a long and substantial amount of training required for entrance, the existence of a professional association that can speak authoritatively for the occupation, a code of ethics, significant professional autonomy, and a strong orientation toward service and client welfare" (p. 91).

This enduring emphasis on the centrality of ethical decision-making in professional practice, including that of teaching, reflects the complex and nuanced character of that practice: if it were straightforward, it would not require the careful thinking and weighing of alternative options in resolving multifaceted situations to which many of the study participants referred in highly diverse contexts. This form of ethical decision-making is the kind that keeps teachers awake at night, wondering if they have done "the right thing" in relation to their students, their colleagues and other stakeholders. Moreover, the associated ethical dilemmas have long-term and deleterious effects on individual teachers and on the profession at large, to the extent that "… teaching as an occupation is ethically charged and … teachers may be exposed to ethical dilemmas over time" and the well-being of "… present and future generations of teachers is a key element in alleviating teachers' attrition, reducing intentions of leaving the profession and keeping the teaching profession attractive …" (Heikkilä et al., 2023, p. 11).

While noting the considerable body of literature critiquing claims to separate professional status for certain occupations (see for example Adams, 2010; Light & Levine, 1998), our focus in this chapter is on elaborating the ramifications of this bald but provocative proposition: "Ethical conduct is both the most fundamental tenet of professionalism and the most challenging" (Krishnaveni & Anitha, 2007, p. 156). In particular, we seek to elicit what we can understand about Australian teachers' success strategies as gleaned from the participants' narratives of motivation and resilience specifically related to their accounts of ethical dilemmas and how they engaged with those dilemmas.

In doing so, we deploy the concept of situated ethics (Simons & Usher, 2000) as a lens for making sense of the participants' strategies elaborated below. This concept illuminates how the teachers analysed the multifaceted contexts in which their everyday practices were enacted in order to devise and implement locally intelligent actions that "made sense" in their respective contexts to work through complicated situations towards what they identified as just consequences. As the narratives presented in the chapter make clear, they were not always successful in their actions, yet they persisted in their efforts as situated ethicists to seek ethically appropriate outcomes for their students, their colleagues and themselves.

Selected Literature

The ethical dimension of teachers' work is explored in considerable and growing depth in the scholarly literature (Bárcena et al., 1993; Forster, 2019; Lyons, 1990). For example, Mangubhai (2007) described three ethical dilemmas that he contended were specific to Languages Other Than English (LOTE) teachers: "(1) the concern that everyone has a worth, (2) the concern that students should not hurt each other's feelings, and (3) the concern that students should learn to tolerate differences" (p. 178) (although we note that the participants in this study might see these dilemmas as having wider applicability to them). Similarly, Husu and Tirri (2001) distilled "... the ethical dilemmas in early childhood education [as] relational and [as] deal[ing] with competing interpretations of 'the best interest of the child'" (p. 361); that is, such dilemmas derive directly from the distinguishing features of the respective education level and sector. From a corresponding perspective, Sumsion (2000) applied "... an enduring ethical dilemma" with which many educators resonate—"... How to enact my commitment to professional practice grounded in an ethos of caring ... for my students, without being drawn into the abyss of endless and ultimately disempowering emotional labour that caring can entail ...?" (p. 167)—to the particular context of teacher education.

Intriguingly, Ehrich et al. (2011) identified "... several strategies that may help to minimise the impact of ethical dilemmas" (p. 173). These strategies included:

> ... the importance of sharing dilemmas with trusted others; having institutional structures in schools that lessen the emergence of harmful actions occurring; the necessity for individual teachers to articulate their own personal and professional ethics; acknowledging that dilemmas have multiple forces at play; the need to educate colleagues about specific issues; and the necessity of appropriate preparation and support for teachers. (p. 173)

We endorse all these proposed strategies, particularly if they contribute to reducing teachers' professional and personal isolation in engaging with the complex ethical dilemmas that they encounter in their work, a number of which are considered in this chapter.

Likewise, Chen et al. (2017) referred to the concept of "dilemmatic spaces", thereby locating such dilemmas "… in extended and dynamic spaces, in which the actions and interactions of the actors are taken into consideration", again emphasising the contextual specificities framing these ethical conundrums for teachers. Relatedly, Edling and Frelin (2016) highlighted the ethical implications of teaching being a microcosm of broader society with its attendant inequities and injustices that impact in diverse ways on teachers' work when they elaborated "… the notion of *sensing* within the *ethics of alterity* and the *ethics of dissensus*, both of which express a desire to contest the various forms of violence in society" (p. 46; *italics in the original*). A variation on this focus on sensing in teacher ethics was enunciated by Osawaru and Omatseye (2017) in their account of teachers' discipline of their students: "… ethical decision making requires more than a belief [in] the importance of [the] ethics of discipline[;] it also requires ethical sensitivity" (p. 66).

While acknowledging the ubiquity of teacher ethics and the complexity of teachers' ethical decision-making, Joseph (2016) used her study of the experiences of 36 beginning secondary school teachers in the United States to affirm the capacity of teachers to "… realise their potential as moral agents by preparing them to become moral educators" (p. 31). In doing so, Joseph linked that capacity with broader and deeper elaborations in teachers' personal and professional growth, whereby "… one's self-concept as a moral person is crucial to the development of a teacher as an ethical practitioner", and "Moral identity is important to an individual's overall identity …" (p. 35). Furthermore, "… moral identity can be understood not just as an end product of ethical knowledge but [also] as a dynamic construct of ethical knowledge and self-formation" (p. 35). Critically, "… a telling way to think about teachers constructing their moral identities is to imagine this process both ethically and politically as 'identity work' (Clarke, 2009, p. 186) …" (p. 35). Joseph's analysis certainly resonates strongly with the study participants' experiences reported in the next section of this chapter and also emphasises that teachers' ethical decision-making and their concomitant development of their moral identity are an ongoing work in progress that includes engaging proactively with the next ethical dilemma that they encounter.

Against this backdrop, we argue that the concept of situated ethics (Simons & Usher, 2000; see also Danaher & Danaher, 2008; McPherson et al., 2019) is particularly productive in analysing the study participants' experiences of ethical decision-making designed as success strategies for addressing the ethical dilemmas in their work. This is because situated ethics accentuates the contextualised and localised character of ethical practice, thereby focusing directly and explicitly on what happens in the "here and now" of ethical encounters. For Simons and Usher, "... ethical practices are mediated within different ... practices and these take on different significances in relation to those practices" (p. 1). Additionally, "A situated ethics is local and specific to particular practices. It cannot be universalized ..." (p. 2). Accordingly, "... we emphasize the inescapable necessity for making ethical decisions and the difficulty and complexity of such decision-making in situations where recourse cannot be had to indubitable foundations in incontrovertible principles" (p. 3). Moreover, "... making ethical decisions, in whatever situated context, is a process of creating, maintaining and justifying an ethical integrity that is more dependent on sensitivity to politics and people than it is on ethical principles and codes" (p. 11). Finally, Simons and Usher (2000) summarised the major common themes of the chapters of their edited book about situated ethics as follows:

- The challenge to universal principles and codes
- The importance of being sensitive to socio-political contexts
- The scope for being fair to disadvantaged groups; and taking account of the diversity and uniqueness of different ... practices (p. 11)

This focus on situated ethics as a conceptual framework for analysing the study participants' experiences is intended to highlight their contextual awareness and purposeful intelligence in evaluating each ethical dilemma that they encounter, rather than passively applying predetermined ethical guidelines. While such guidelines can often—but not always—be helpful in identifying options for decision-making by teachers in general and by the study participants in this particular example, the subtle complexities and nuances of the dilemmas require them to assess each situation on a case-by-case basis and to make their decisions accordingly. Considering teachers as situated ethicists accentuates the consistently high-level thinking in which they must engage and also underscores both the complexity and the politicisation of their professional status.

Data Analysis

Of the five dimensions of the analysed data that were identified in Chapter 1, this chapter contributes to demonstrating the enactment of the fourth dimension: "naming, framing and shaming". This was defined in Chapter 1 as "The social, cultural and political issues, tensions and changes that influence the public and sometimes politicised positioning of teachers' work and identities" (see also the coverage of this dimension in Chapter 4).

We posit in this chapter that there is a crucial correspondence between the naming, framing and shaming dimension of the data analysis related to this research project, on the one hand, and the proposition of teachers as situated ethicists engaged in intelligent and thoughtful professional action, on the other hand. This correspondence is linked also with the notion of constrained agency (Coe & Jordhus-Lier, 2010; Damman & Henkens, 2017; Gulati & Srivastava, 2014; Herndl & Licona, 2007; Lassalle & Shaw, 2021) as it applies to the work and identities of teachers (Porter, 2023) that was canvassed in Chapter 1, that is, the ethical decision-making by the study participants whose experiences are analysed in this chapter was rendered more complex and often more stressful because those decisions were made with limited professional autonomy, frequently involved multiple stakeholders and took place against the backdrop—and sometimes against the grain—of teachers being positioned in ways that diminished their professionalism. This was despite our argument at the start of the chapter that complicated and nuanced ethical situations are conventionally emphasised as a key defining feature of professionalism. From this perspective, we explore below how the participants' anomalous status required them to engage in contextually specific ethical decisions that in turn reflected the naming, framing and shaming dimension of their positioning.

As we noted additionally in Chapter 1, our data analytic strategy also elicited four "nodes", articulated in this way:

- Complexities (CY): Engaging with multifaceted events and issues
- Challenges (CE): Encounters with difficult and potentially stressful events and issues
- Contradictions (CN): Events and issues with at least two competing influences and pressures
- Comforts (CT): Sources of encouragement, motivation and pleasure

Building on Table 1.2 in Chapter 1, Table 9.1 illustrates the approach taken to data analysis in this chapter about teachers as situated ethicists, clustered around the naming, framing and shaming dimension, and organised around the four aforementioned nodes.

Complexities

For Ella, being a situated ethicist results from engaging with the complexities of her work as a teacher. She explicates some of these complexities in her response to the interviewer's question, "When the rules say one thing but you

Table 9.1 Data Analysis Matrix for Teachers as Situated Ethicists

	Naming, framing and shaming
Complexities	Ella; Jalena
Challenges	Rosalie; Chantelle
Contradictions	Sally; Stella
Comforts	Kylie; Doug

feel ethically that the rule is wrong, does that ... impact on other ... aspects of your teaching as well?":

> Yes, I think so. Not massively because the rules are all ultimately there. They've got the right idea behind them, but just time and place sometimes it doesn't feel like it's the best thing to do. Just doing the right thing—not the right thing, just doing things that might have a better outcome can often take a huge amount of time and effort, but they're usually worth it, but it's a ton of time and effort [so] that sometimes you can't do it all, I think. But yes, a school system is a very strong system that can get a bit bigger than itself, I think, sometimes.

Here Ella encapsulates neatly much of the messiness of ethical decision-making attendant on the complexities of teachers' work. This messiness includes the situation when teachers' beliefs and values prompt them to disagree with some aspect of their professional code of ethics as it is written down. In doing so, Ella exhibits considerable discursive dissonance (Harreveld, 2002) as she navigates working at the micro level of her classroom set against the meso level of her school and the macro level of the education system writ large. On the one hand, Ella acknowledges that "... the rules are all ultimately there" and that "They've got the right idea behind them ...". On the other hand, she refers to the situatedness of her decision-making in a particular "... time and place ..." in which "... sometimes it doesn't feel like it's the best thing to do". At this point in her narrative, Ella appears to recognise the fundamental contradiction between the overarching "rules" and the specific context of her work, then she seems to draw back from naming it as such, by diverting from articulating the corollary of "... doing the right thing ..." being associated with that context rather than with "the rules". Instead, she asserts that "... doing things that might have a better outcome can often take a huge amount of time and effort, but they're usually worth it ...". From this perspective, Ella implicitly affirms the moral value of the situated ethics of "doing things that might have a better outcome", even while confirming the personal toll of doing so: "... it's a ton of time and effort [so] that sometimes you can't do it all ...". This discursive dissonance accentuates Ella's diminished professional autonomy to make the ethical decisions that she considered appropriate to the situation, thereby reflecting her distinctive framing as a teacher with significantly constrained agency. Furthermore, while her ethical decision-making demonstrates a success strategy based on her personal motivation and resilience, she ends this part of her narrative by identifying the source of that constraint: "But yes, a school system is a very strong system that can get a bit bigger than itself, I think, sometimes".

Jalena highlights a different form of the complexities of teachers' ethical decision-making by evoking a stark contrast between education leaders such as heads of department who are "human[s]" and those who are "ladder climber[s]":

> ... we've had a big turnaround in our school in the last couple of years, and particularly this year has seen a massive improvement. One of the improvement areas for us has been a head of department who is not climbing a ladder. She's there to stay and she wants to do the right thing by people, doing the right thing by the job, and she has a passion for good teaching and a passion for languages, and it's like, "Oh, God, a human, not a ladder climber". Whereas I think previously, last year, when we've had heads of department who were obviously ladder climbers, and I think that they're very frustrating because they don't make sense, they are not looking for common sense, and again it feels like we're not taken seriously, and that's when I would have a strong emotional reaction ....: "Hang on, this is about my job and the decisions you're making about my job are based on you, not about the welfare of kids". That's when I feel the strongest, and I think most teachers do. That's a common source of conversation in the staffroom.

For Jalena, the essence of her situated ethics is "... the welfare of kids". While the specific form of that essence can differ from context to context, it is clearly recognised as the antithesis of an education leader making decisions "based on" her- or himself, rather than acknowledging the expertise of teacher colleagues. Decision-making that positions teachers as lacking knowledge and that undermines their professional autonomy in ways that are implicitly shaming is unethical towards students and teachers alike. By contrast, the current head of department "... has a passion for good teaching ...", with "good" in this context manifesting itself as "... want[ing] to do the right thing by people, [and] doing the right thing by the job ...".

Challenges

Rosalie encapsulates the challenges of engaging in situated ethics in teaching by comparing it with two other and very different jobs that she had undertaken prior to taking up her current teaching position. In one of those jobs: "... by the end of it, I was emotionally burnt out and destroyed and morally felt like I didn't know who I was any more". Fortunately for Rosalie, that role was succeeded by one in which:

> ... I felt like I was able to get my [moral] compass back because I was doing community work to help communities engage with government. I felt like I was back on my social justice [mission] and my [moral] compass was back.

By contrast, in her current teaching position, Rosalie shares: "... again I felt that [moral] compass getting squished. I struggled a lot with being involved in practices that didn't sit well with me".

This juxtaposition of three very diverse jobs enables Rosalie to identify the diminution of her professional autonomy in her present teaching role, and also to discern the direct impact of that diminution on her reduced sense of her ethical self. She exemplifies this situation as follows:

> Yes, but then they will say they're interested in teacher feedback. What they'll do then is they'll say, "We want to create a teacher's student feedback learning loop where we're going to randomly interview students from your classes. We don't want to be intrusive so we want you to design the model and design the questions that we're going to ask. We're going to get you to design everything". Then you'd have a group of teachers sitting there going, "We don't even want to do this".

Here Rosalie evokes a situation in which her colleagues and she experience what she constructs implicitly as an unethical positioning of her fellow teachers and her whereby their professional autonomy is undermined. What comes through starkly in Rosalie's narrative is a strong emotion of mutual mistrust, and the sense of teachers being burdened with the additional work whereby "We're going to get you to design everything". Moreover, this process is potentially deceptive, even a kind of entrapment, given that "... randomly interview[ing] students from your classes" could easily turn into a form of coercive control of teachers perceived as not aligning with the school's dominant discourse of its supposed purpose and ethos.

Chantelle draws on a different perspective on the challenges of enacting situated ethics that derives from her having a leadership position in her school. She begins this part of her narrative with a telling encapsulation of teaching's moral purpose juxtaposed with an unheeding system: "Everybody wants to know they're doing a good job if they're putting in the hard work, and that's very rarely given in my experience here". Chantelle also evokes what happens when some teachers are seen to deviate from "... doing a good job ...":

> Then, just as a leader in the school in a position of leadership, I've had to deal with a lot of staffing issues in terms of just managerial things ... when people aren't doing the right thing, I suppose, and that's been a big learning curve for me as well. Just learning how to deal with people who aren't doing the right thing but believe they're doing the right thing, and trying to coach them through that.

For Chantelle, situated ethics informs her approach to her school leadership role, which requires her to differentiate between teachers who are "... doing a good job ..." and teachers who "... aren't doing the right thing ...". Significantly, despite her leadership position, her agency in enacting it is constrained, as seen by her attempted success strategy of "... trying to coach them through that". From one perspective, the uncooperative teachers might be seen as experiencing naming, framing and even shaming by the school leadership team. From a different perspective, Chantelle's account emphasises the ethical challenges associated with interdependent professionals whose capacity to "... [do] a good job ..." and to "... [do] the right thing ..." is contextually constructed and situationally constrained.

Contradictions

Sally reveals two very different situations that highlight fundamental contradictions framing her ethical decision-making that in turn accentuated the diminished autonomy of her teacher ethics. In doing so, she demonstrates how both these situations constrained her success strategies as a situated ethicist.

The first situation occurred when Sally had a school leadership position and involved a beginning teacher. Sally's perspective on the new teacher's capacity differed significantly from the perspective of her school principal:

> I think the big thing that probably really snapped it in for me at the end is that I actually shouldn't be listening to my leaders all the time. If I think, if my ethical core tells me, "That's not right", I need to do what I believe, not what I'm told, because we had a brand new graduate up there, who couldn't teach for two and a half years after working with [the principal]. She's finally teaching again because I was her mentor, and my principal said, "You know what? I'm cutting you off; you can't help her any more. She's got to drown and get out". I did that because I was told to [do so] ... not the right thing. Obviously, not something I'm proud of.

Here Sally neatly distils the essence of situated ethics with the powerful utterance, "... if my ethical core tells me, 'That's not right', I need to do what I believe, not what I'm told ...". This is not a matter of wilfully disobeying a more senior colleague, but rather acting on a nuanced and empirically grounded judgement derived from extensive experience of mentoring the beginning teacher. Some years later, the reality that "I did that because I was told to [do so]" still sits badly with Sally: "... not the right thing. Obviously, not something I'm proud of". Despite her leadership position at the time, Sally was framed by the principal as needing to accede to the principal's authority rather than being afforded the professional autonomy whereby her empirically grounded judgement could be carefully considered. This stark contradiction between holding an official position and recognising the realpolitik of a school leadership team had a deleterious effect on Sally's motivation and resilience.

The second situation related to Sally's relationship with one of her students who had been diagnosed with Autism Spectrum Disorder and who has acknowledged to Sally that his behaviour in the classroom can be challenging.

Furthermore, the student's mother has requested to Sally about her son in this way: "I don't care if he learns, I don't care what he does; all I want is [for] him to have his final year at your school to be fun", a request that Sally has resisted. Here Sally elaborates her situated ethical dilemma in working with this student:

> With him, I'm always second guessing how I approach him as well, and it's like, "Do I just let him go? 'Stick your headphones on; don't worry about it. You just do whatever you feel like right now, and we'll go off and do some learning". Like I said, morally and ethically, that's not what I can do. I think I need to help him be his best, but, when you hit brick walls like that, it's incredibly challenging, so I never know what to do in those situations. Some days I just think I don't have the energy …. Most days I try to find [the energy], but it doesn't always work.

This disparity between Sally's professional autonomy in her teacher work and an explicit request from her student's mother has generated a situated ethical dilemma for Sally as a consequence of a contradictory framing of her as simultaneously being responsible for communicating and assessing a formally sanctioned curriculum, on the one hand, and being expected by her student's mother to accede to the mother's request about her son's schooling experience, on the other hand. From this perspective, Sally's attempted success strategy in seeking to facilitate the student's learning was undermined by the student's admittedly challenging behaviour and by a lack of cooperation from his mother.

Stella draws on her extensive experience teaching refugee students to analyse what she sees as a fundamental contradiction influencing her ethical decision-making:

> And this is not just me speaking. I think this would be everyone who works with them. You're just so frustrated that they have no voice quite literally. They don't have the English words to actually communicate politically what they believe. It's really hard to take. I think you do feel as a teacher in that environment, but also with kids too from difficult homes and things. You think, "Somebody has to actually stand up for this situation". They have no agency themselves.

Here Stella emphasises two powerful and interlocking contradictions that impact directly on her position as a situated ethicist. On the one hand, there is a significant contradiction between the students' often very diverse and rich prior and current experiences as adult learners and their lack of capacity "… to actually communicate politically what they believe", so that "… they have no voice quite literally", and "They have no agency themselves". On the other hand, there is an equally significant contradiction between Stella's professionally constrained role as a refugee teacher and what she perceives as her ethical responsibility to advocate on her students' behalf. Both these contradictions reflect various variations on naming, framing and shaming in relation to the refugees and, to a certain extent, with regard to the teachers of those refugees, which in turn generate heightened ethical dilemmas: "It's really hard to take".

Comforts

By contrast, the two remaining study participants whose experiences provide evidence for the argument being pursued in this chapter report different manifestations of what occurs in relation to situated ethics when there is commensurate alignment among multiple stakeholders, and when the effects of specific situations are perceived as being ethically sound and as just outcomes. In some ways, both these final teacher accounts constitute idealised ethical decision-making in the spirit of teaching idealists traversed in Chapter 10. Certainly, both accounts reflect the comforts of what occurs in the ethical dimension of contemporary teaching when teachers are named and framed appropriately, and when their work as situated ethicists is allied with their success stories, thereby enhancing their motivation and resilience.

In this regard, Kylie crystallises with commendable clarity the "moral purpose" of teaching that lies at the heart of the comforts of situated ethics:

> If you can get below those behaviours into those beliefs and really go below … underneath, enable that mechanism and take that moral purpose of that teacher of why we do what we do, build the expertise and tell them we'll support them with how and when to use those strategies, that is all the professional learning that will help teachers discern when and what to do as the expert and professional in the classroom.

Kylie's utterance here implicitly positions "… that moral purpose of that situation …" as being located in the specific contexts of the here and now of everyday teaching, and yet also and simultaneously as animating and sustaining teachers' autonomy in their ethical decision-making. This autonomy in consequence maximises their framing as incontestably "… the expert[s] and professional[s] in the classroom", which likewise facilitates their design and enactment of multiple success strategies in enhancing their students' effectiveness as ethical decision-makers in their turn.

Finally, Doug accentuates the affective dimension of teachers' enactment of situated ethics and of their ethical decision-making when he encapsulates the comforts for teachers who are affirmed that they are "doing the right thing":

> There's an immense sense of …. I think it's that balance that a lot of teachers talk about … all those questions that ever go into your mind about whether or not you're doing the right thing, that one email or one phone call like that takes all of that away. The emotions around that would be just happiness and relief almost that this kid has found their

way. Again, just satisfaction that, despite everything else that's going on, at the end of the day, what we do is for the kids and sometimes it does work.

We sense something of the range of emotions underlying Doug's narrative here, including the self-deprecating "… sometimes it does work". Indeed, despite all the undoubted complexities, challenges and contradictions of teachers' ethical decision-making in contexts of situated ethics, the comforts related to facilitating the circumstances in which "… sometimes it does work" are immense. It is at those times that teachers are confirmed as "… doing the right thing …", and they are also framed as autonomous and knowledgeable professionals with their students' best interests at heart. In these situations, teachers as situated ethicists are clearly planning and implementing success strategies for their students' and their own ethical selves.

Implications

Preservice initial teacher education and inservice professional development for teachers still need to engage explicity with the profound connundrums of being and becoming a professional. Generations of teachers have graduated from such courses and inservice programmes that have been mapped against codes of conduct, competency frameworks and professional standards. Likewise, previous research has already identified what works at school and system levels to minimise the deleterious impacts of ethical dilemmas on teachers personally and in their professional practices (Ehrich et al., 2011). However, positioning teachers as situated ethicists provides implications for policy and practice yet to be identified in the literature.

Firstly, teachers have clear notions of right and wrong. The concept of "rightness" is individually interpreted and contextually justified by situated ethicists Ella, Jalena, Chantelle, Sally and Doug (see also Heikkilä et al., 2023). The narratives demonstrated constant comparison between right and—largely by its absence—wrong. The distinction between the two was a key determinant in morally justified ethical decision-making. This finding of the data analysis in this chapter underscores the productive power of teachers' narratives that courses thematically throughout this book.

Secondly, a sense of morality permeates the ethics of teaching. In some situations recounted by the participants, teachers-as-ethicists were shamed through the moralities of others such as parents, school leaders and teaching colleagues, while simultaneously sensing the enormity of their own morality in framing and naming thoughts and deeds (Ella, Chantelle, Sally, Rosalie, Chhantelle, Sally, Kylie, Doug). Sense is important to these teachers, including a sense of self that gives resilience to naming a sense of morality that frames their teaching (Simons & Usher, 2000).

Thirdly, discourses of deviancy are anomalous yet important for teacher motivation and resilience. Teachers' anomalous status was characterised by the discursive dissonances of ethical dilemmas that tested their moral fortitude and from which they did not resile (Edling & Frelin, 2016; Osawaru & Omatseye, 2017). Their anomalous status was both self-named and framed as well as named, framed and shamed by others (Jalena, Chantelle, Stella). In other words, participants positioned themselves in some situations as different from the norm, including expected patterns of behaviours and views for a teacher, so as to claim emotional resilience.

Strategic choices were made by these eight situated ethicists:

- Ethical decision-making was nuanced, predicated upon balancing sometimes competing and contradictory interests. The interviews provided safe spaces for these nuances to be articulated.
- Ethical decision-making was a personal project as much as a professional one. Teachers had to live with themselves morally, and it was that which often tipped the balance one way or another when responding to ethical dilemmas.
- Teachers do actually consult with others, even though in the end they may not agree with them, and act accordingly.

These strategic choices were made in diversely dilemmatic spaces (Chen et al., 2017) that had rules and right ideas sometimes inimical to the amount of time, contingencies of place and sheer effort required to negotiate them.

In distilling these implications from the preceding data analysis, we need to acknowledge the inherent messiness of these kinds of situations faced by the participants whose voices are presented in this chapter and by teachers more broadly, that is, the implications articulated here are highly contextualised—the essence of situated ethics—and they require considerable work and ongoing attention. Much of the unease and ambivalence reported in the data analysis reflect the point that this is "hard labour" and not amenable to "easy fixes" or "magic bullets" by teachers.

Conclusion

In conclusion, this chapter has used a thematic analysis of transcripts from interviews with eight Australian teachers working in primary and secondary schools across various states and systems. Consistent with other chapters throughout this book, we have deployed an analytic matrix to compare and contrast their identification of and reactions to social, cultural and political issues, tensions and changes in their day-to-day work. Findings illustrate their resilience when faced with challenges and contradictions from the ladder climbers, the system, the parents/guardians, fellow teachers and competing interests among themselves and others. Such resilience was bolstered by the warmth of encouragement, motivation and pleasure experienced in some situations.

Ethical dilemmas are not new in any profession. Professions such as teaching operate within powerful jurisdictional constraints and share a commonality of ethical care for students of all ages. Knowing the dimensions of ethical care and its moral lodestar is a multifaceted construct for teachers. Courage and resilience in the face of competing interests define the situated ethicists you have met in this chapter. Codifying such work has been undertaken, but like any profession it is through its enactments and self-critique that it will be known and judged.

References

Adams, T. L. (2010). Profession: A useful concept for sociological analysis? *Canadian Review of Sociology/Revue canadienne de sociologie, 47*(1), 49–70. https://doi.org/10.1111/j.1755-618X.2010.01222.x

Bárcena, F., Gil, F., & Jover, G. (1993). The ethical dimension of teaching: A review and a proposal. *Journal of Moral Education, 22*(3), 241–252. https://doi.org/10.1080/0305724930220305

Chen, X., Wei, G., & Jiang, S. (2017). The ethical dimension of teacher practical knowledge: A narrative inquiry into Chinese teachers' thinking and actions in dilemmatic spaces. *Journal of Curriculum Studies, 49*(4), 518–541. https://doi.org/10.1080/00220272.2016.1263895

Clarke, M. (2009). The ethico-politics of teacher identity. *Educational Philosophy and Theory, 41*(2), 185–200. https://doi.org/10.1111/j.1469-5812.2008.00420.x

Coe, N. M., & Jordhus-Lier, D. C. (2010). Constrained agency? Re-evaluating the geographies of labour. *Progress in Human Geography, 35*(2), 211–233. https://doi.org/10.1177/0309132510366746

Damman, M., & Henkens, K. (2017). Constrained agency in later working lives: Introduction to the special issue. *Work, Aging and Retirement, 3*(3), 225–230. https://doi.org/10.1093/workar/wax015

Danaher, M. J. M., & Danaher, P. A. (2008). Situated ethics in investigating non-government organisations and showgrounds: Issues in researching Japanese environmental politics and Australian Traveller education. *International Journal of Pedagogies and Learning, 4*(1), 58–70. https://doi.org/10.5172/ijpl.4.1.58

Edling, S., & Frelin, A. (2016). Sensing as an ethical dimension of teacher professionality. *Journal of Moral Education, 45*(1), 46–58. https://doi.org/10.1080/03057240.2015.1127801

Ehrich, L. C., Kimber, M., Millwater, J., & Cranston, N. (2011). Ethical dilemmas: A model to understand teacher practice. *Teachers and Teaching: Theory and Practice, 17*(2), 173–185. https://doi.org/10.1080/13540602.2011.539794

Forster, D. J. (2019). Teaching through ethical tensions: Between social justice, authority and professional codes. In R. Scott Webster & J. D. Whelen (Eds.), *Rethinking reflection and ethics for teachers* (pp. 33–50). Springer.

Greenwood, E. (1960). Attributes of a profession. *Journal of Visual Impairment & Blindness, 54*(5), 169–178. https://doi.org/10.1177/0145482X6005400504

Gulati, R., & Srivastava, S. B. (2014). Bringing agency back into network research: Constrained agency and network action. In D. J. Brass, G. Labianca, A. Mehra, D. S. Halgin, & S. P. Borgatti (Eds.), *Contemporary perspectives on organizational social networks (research in the sociology of organizations vol. 40)* (pp. 73–93). Emerald Group Publishing Limited.

Harreveld, R. E. (2002). *Brokering changes: A study of power and identity through discourses* [Doctoral dissertation]. Central Queensland University, Australia.

Heikkilä, M., Mauno, S., Herttalampi, M., Minkkinen, J., Muotka, J., & Feldt, T. (2023). Ethical dilemmas and well-being in teachers' work: A three-wave, two-year longitudinal study. *Teaching and Teacher Education, 125*, 104049. https://doi.org/10.1016/j.tate.2023.104049

Herndl, C. G., & Licona, A. C. (2007). Shifting agency: Agency, kairos, and the possibilities of social action. In M. Zachry & C. Thralls (Eds.), *Communicative practices in workplaces and the professions: Cultural perspectives on the regulation of discourse and organizations* (pp. 133–154). Routledge.

Husu, J., & Tirri, K. (2001). Teachers' ethical choices in sociomoral settings. *Journal of Moral Education*, 30(4), 361–375. https://doi.org/10.1080/03057240120094850

Joseph, P. B. (2016). Ethical reflection on becoming teachers. *Journal of Moral Education*, 45(1), 31–45. https://doi.org/10.1080/03057240.2016.1156521

Krishnaveni, R., & Anitha, J. (2007). Educators' professional characteristics. *Quality Assurance in Education*, 15(2), 149–161. https://doi.org/10.1108/09684880710748910

Lassalle, P., & Shaw, E. (2021). Trailing wives and constrained agency among women migrant entrepreneurs: An intersectional perspective. *Entrepreneurship Theory and Practice*, 45(6), 1296–1521. https://doi.org/10.1177/1042258721990331

Light, D., & Levine, S. (1998). The changing character of the medical profession: A theoretical overview. In R. Stewart (Ed.), *Management of healthcare*. Routledge.

Lyons, N. (1990). Dilemmas of knowing: Ethical and epistemological dimensions of teachers' work and development. *Harvard Educational Review*, 60(2), 159–181. https://doi.org/10.17763/haer.60.2.v71123u7768r47w6

Mangubhai, F. (2007). The moral and ethical dimensions of language teaching. *Australian Journal of Education*, 51(2), 178–189. https://doi.org/10.1177/000494410705100206

McPherson, A., Forster, D., & Buchanan, R. (2019). Situated cases of ethical tensions when working with children and young people in educational contexts. *Global Studies of Childhood*, 9(2), 103–108. https://doi.org/10.1177/2043610619845735

Osawaru, A. E., & Omatseye, B. O. (2017). An ethical dimension to discipline and teachers' use of power. *Sokoto Educational Review*, 17(1), 66–75. https://doi.org/10.35386/ser.v17i1.18

Porter, K. (2023). *As easy as ABC? A novel psychological approach to teacher agency: Exploring the influence of affect on behaviour and cognition* [Doctoral dissertation]. University of St Andrews, Scotland. https://research-repository.st-andrews.ac.uk/handle/10023/28376

Simons, H., & Usher, R. (2000). Introduction: Ethics in the practice of research. In H. Simons & R. Usher (Eds.), *Situated ethics in educational research* (pp. 1–11). Routledge/Falmer.

Strike, K. A. (1990). Is teaching a profession: How would we know? In R. L. Schwab (Ed.), *Research-based teacher evaluation* (pp. 91–117). Springer.

Sumsion, J. (2000). Caring and empowerment: A teacher educator's reflection on an ethical dilemma. *Teaching in Higher Education: Critical Perspectives*, 5(2), 167–179. https://doi.org/10.1080/135625100114821

"Teaching Through Ethical Tensions: Between Social Justice, Authority and Professional Codes": https://link.springer.com/chapter/10.1007/978-981-32-9401-1_3?utm_source=chatgpt.com

Recommended Further Reading

Bergviken Rensfeldt, A., Hillman, T., Lantz-Andersson, A., Lundin, M., & Peterson, L. (2019). A "situated ethics" for researching teacher professionals' emerging Facebook group discussions. In Å. Mäkitalo, T. E. Nicewonger, & M. Elam (Eds.), *Designs for experimentation and inquiry: Approaching learning and knowing in digital transformation*. Routledge.

Ebrahim, H. B. (2010). Situated ethics: Possibilities for young children as research participants in the South African context. *Early Child Development and Care*, 180(3), 289–298. https://doi.org/10.1080/03004430701822958

Henriksen, A.-K., & Schliehe, A. (2020). Ethnography of young people in confinement: On subjectivity, positionality and situated ethics in closed space. *Qualitative Research*, *20*(6), 837–853. https://doi.org/10.1177/1468794120904873

Palaiologou, J., & Brown, A. (2023). Ethical considerations and dilemmas for the researcher and for families in home-based research: A case for situated ethics. *Research Ethics*, *19*(4), 519–535. https://doi.org/10.1177/17470161231181860

Vivat, B. (2002). Situated ethics and feminist ethnography in a West of Scotland hospice. In L. Bondi, H. Avis, R. Bankey, A. Bingley, J. Davidson, R. Duffy, V. I. Einagel, A.-M., Green, L. Johnston, S. Lilley, C. Listerborn, M. Marshy, S. McEwan, N. O'Connor, G. Rose, B. Vivat, & N. Wood (Eds.), *Subjectivities, knowledges, and feminist geographies: The subjects and ethics of social research* (pp. 236–251). Rowan & Littlefield Publishers.

10 Teachers as Teaching Idealists

Introduction

What do we, as researchers, propose when we address the concept of a teaching idealist? Historically, the notions around idealism began with Plato (427–347 BC), who posited a theory of two "worlds"—the observable, external world, and the logical, internal world or the "world of ideas" (Salucci, 2022, n.p.). In more contemporary philosophy, the word "idea" has been reframed to refer to a "mental representation" (Salucci, 2022, n.p.) that reflects an individual's experiential understanding and construction of their reality. In the case of this research, teachers were asked to examine their individual professional philosophies and the manner in which their values/beliefs were reflected professionally. There was a significant focus on broader educational long-term goals. Simultaneously, the participants emphasised the short-term, relationship-enhancing principles and opinions that they enacted within the confines of the classroom as well as in their wider communication with stakeholders outside the classroom.

When examining the concept of a teaching idealist, it is difficult not to get caught up in rhetoric driven by the question: "What makes a good teacher?" This type of enquiry and the qualities listed by the responder are highly subjective and contextualised, and require personal judgement. It is dependent upon who is asked and the conditions around which the respondent provides an answer. Opinions such as these are fluid in nature in that an individual's response may be determined by the interaction that they may have had with that teacher at that particular time and within particular circumstances/parameters. Furthermore, attitudes held by others are similarly dynamic and may change at any time.

This chapter is not about exploring the notion of "good" or the sentiments of others regarding "good" teaching. Rather it focuses on teachers as they reflect upon their own particular situation and their values around fundamental questions like "What does teaching mean to you?" and "What constitutes the ideal of teaching for you?". Educational ideals, and the philosophies related to them, are at the heart of teaching relationships and methodological best praxis. They impact on all major areas of the educative process such as:

DOI: 10.4324/9781003564850-10

organisational goal setting; methodology in the classroom; the rights and responsibilities of teachers, students and other stakeholders; and the experiential effectiveness of learning.

The significance of exploring the proposition of teachers as teaching idealists is twofold. Firstly, it is inherently instructive to understand how the selected participants' narratives distil their sense of the essence of their work in its ideal form, pared back from, yet also situated in and framed by, their everyday practice. Secondly, that sense of the idealised foundation of their work helps to animate their diverse strategies for success. In other words, their efforts to facilitate their students' learning in highly varied contexts are motivated by seeking to fulfil their conceptions of the pure form of teaching that they might well not attain with every student in every interaction, but towards which they feel that they must continue to strive.

Selected Literature

The starting point for this selected literature review about teaching ideals and idealists is the second response by Hansen (2013) to his provocative question: "Do ideals and idealism have a role to play in teaching?" (p. 55). The response was as follows:

> Teachers must have ideals, and their ideals must reach beyond societal expectations. According to this argument, teachers are not bureaucratic functionaries whose only charge is to pass on to the young whatever knowledge and skills the powers-that-be have sanctioned. Teachers do play an important role in socializing students into expected custom and practice. But as teachers, rather than as mere socializers, they also help equip students to think for themselves, to conceive their own ideals and hopes, and to prepare themselves for the task of making tomorrow's world into something other than a tired copy of today's. (p. 56)

These sentiments certainly resonate with many of the prompted and unprompted statements by the participants in this study, who in varied ways expressed their commitment to supporting their students in attaining more than the prescribed curriculum and assessment outcomes, now and in the future. While importantly acknowledging the "Perils" as well as "The Promise...of Ideals" (p. 56), Hansen (2013) helpfully synthesised the broader relevance of teaching idealists with which this chapter is concerned, and which is exemplified in the next section:

> Ideals point to territory beyond the familiar, the known, the previously attainable. They embody possibilities the human spirit generates. Even though they may be out of reach, ideals can provide a source of guidance and courage. A teacher whose ideal it is for all students to learn, and enjoy learning, may not need a tap on her shoulder to remind her of

how challenging, or perhaps impossible, the ideal is to realize. Nonetheless, the teacher relies upon the ideal to strengthen and to broaden her pedagogical efforts. The ideal helps the teacher identify short-term goals and aims. It provides a wellspring, or source of inspiration, for choosing specific instructional activities and curricular materials—those that will help her, in her view, move closer toward realizing the ideal of universal student learning in her classroom. (p. 56)

From this perspective, teachers' ideals can be seen as being much more than private concerns or individual matters. Instead, they help to animate teachers' personal identities and to motivate their everyday practice. Moreover, they are crucial to generating teachers' conviction of professionalism and their sense of vocation. In this regard, teachers' ideals serve to justify their assertion that teaching matters, and that what they do with their students encapsulates profound significance beyond the confines of the "here and now".

At this juncture, and building on a point made in the preceding section, it is important to differentiate between this chapter's emphasis on teaching as an ideal form and a related but separate literature about "ideal teachers". Certainly, scholarship abounds about the latter, including attributes and dispositions gleaned from education policies, media representations and individual experiences of teachers and students alike (Moreno, 2022). By contrast, the focus here is more closely aligned with the evocation of types of teaching practices in their essential and ideal forms. One illustration of such forms was the "… three professional ideal types" (p. 173) distilled by Carmi and Tamir (2022) as being exemplified in "… the current landscape of teacher preparation" (p. 173): "… teachers as intellectuals, master craftspeople, and artists" (p. 173). By way of example, each of these "… professional ideal types" suggests particular behaviours and goals, yet they can all be discerned as exhibiting much more than such behaviours and goals, and as evoking higher-level actions and aspirations that communicate something profound about being human in and through educational relationships.

In addition to teaching being conceptualised as a number of "… professional ideal types" (Carmi & Tamir, 2022, p. 173), for many teachers teaching in its idealised form constitutes a vocation, while acknowledging that term's historical association with religious orders that set themselves apart from the contemporary world. Badley and Hughes (2022) illustrated the character of a teaching vocation by drawing a striking contrast between the terms of teachers' official contracts of employment, on the one hand, and the affective, spatial and temporal elements of the unofficial enactment of those contracts, on the other hand:

> The legal contract between a teacher and a school or board of trustees does not address the matter of working weeknights after dinner, the necessity of doing class preparation or grading papers on the weekends,

the worries about the success of a student who finds school challenging, or the deep questions about the teaching vocation itself. Interestingly, nor does that contract mention the joy teachers experience when their students graduate or when a student warmly greets them on the street months or years after leaving their classroom. (p. 2)

Against that backdrop, Badley and Hughes (2022) depicted "... the teaching vocation" as "... the calling to teach" (p. 3), and they recalled the derivation of the term "vocation" "...from *voce*, the Latin word for 'voice', in the sense of '...having heard a call or voice'" (p. 3). While it is important to recognise the multiplicity of reasons for teachers to take up teaching, many of the participants in this study certainly spoke about being motivated by something less tangible and potentially more mysterious that sat beside more pragmatic considerations such as salaries, employment security and being able to enjoy holidays with their school-age children. Given this chapter's alignment with the dimension of the study's data analysis identified as "Changes and continuities", as we elaborate below, it is timely also to note the longer-term backdrop to Badley and Hughes' account of teaching as a vocation: "Teachers' work has negatives and positives, and teachers at all levels struggle: some throughout their entire careers come to terms with the contrast between these aspects of teaching" (p. 5).

Furthermore, given this book's explicit focus on teachers' resilience, it is noteworthy that Sabino (2023) identified teaching vocation, as a powerful call to teach, explicitly as "... key to resilience in the teaching profession" (p. 1). It was noteworthy that Sabino made this identification in the context of Venezuelan primary school teachers engaging with the COVID-19 pandemic—certainly a dramatic period of unprecedented global change in education and more broadly, as well as exhibiting certain continuities, which are explored further in Chapter 5 of this book.

Finally, Delcheva-Dizdarevikj (2024) located her account of teaching as an ideal form in the specific context of contemporary Macedonian education. In particular, she drew on a range of philosophical treatises to assert baldly, "What all these works have in common is that they consider the teaching vocation to be more than a profession" (p. 90). Significantly, in presenting the case for this proposition, Delcheva-Dizdarevikj highlighted many of the affective elements of teachers' idealised work that are explored in diverse forms throughout this book: "I can only emphasize that we are on the right track—it just takes more energy, a greater dynamic and courage from all of us" (p. 93).

Data Analysis

As we noted above, this chapter contributes to illustrating the third dimension that emerged from our analysis of the interview transcripts completed for this study. This dimension, "changes and continuities", was defined in Chapter 1 as "Elements and experiences of teachers' work and lives that have been dynamic and/or constant" (see also Chapter 5).

Teachers as Teaching Idealists

As we also explained in Chapter 1, our data analytic strategy elicited as well four "nodes" that have helped to guide the presentation of the data analysis in the ten data chapters in this book, including this one:

- Complexities (CY): Engaging with multifaceted events and issues
- Challenges (CE): Encounters with difficult and potentially stressful events and issues
- Contradictions (CN): Events and issues with at least two competing influences and pressures
- Comforts (CT): Sources of encouragement, motivation and pleasure

Extending from Table 1.2 in Chapter 1, Table 10.1 encapsulates: the approach enacted to analyse data in this chapter about teachers as teaching idealists; an orientation towards the changes and continuities dimension; and a clustering around the four aforementioned nodes. More specifically, the argument pursued in this section of the chapter is that the selected participants mobilised particular aspects of their constructions of the ideal forms of teaching as distinctive success strategies to enhance their motivation and resilience against the backdrop of educational changes and continuities, and also with references to the complexities, challenges, contradictions and comforts of their work.

Complexities

Helen identifies a number of complexities arising from her teaching work, including the wide diversity of student backgrounds and behaviours, and the time required to develop enduring rapport and trust with students. At the same time, she finds continuing motivation and resilience in:

> ... see[ing] teaching as being a person who can try to be inspiring, who can have a light and optimistic approach so that young people feel that there is hopefulness in the world and in their day. I think it's about really helping young people to feel a sense of success, a taste of success. I would feel very bad if a young person, after being in one of my sessions, walked away saying, "Oh, I feel ... stupid", and feeling really negative about themselves. I'd feel that that would be a failure on my part.

Table 10.1 Data Analysis Matrix for Teachers as Teaching Idealists

	Changes and continuities
Complexities	Helen; Erin
Challenges	Jalena; Chantelle
Contradictions	Diana; Serene
Comforts	Paul; Perry

This strongly articulated sense of optimism, intended to counteract students "... feeling really negative about themselves", functions in parallel as a crucial ingredient in Helen's success strategy for engaging with the complexities of her work. Similarly, Helen's affective response to that work is echoed in her idealised evocation of how she hopes that her students will feel in turn about their work as well:

> I ... always ... try to pick out things and make note of it to young people—things that they're doing well so that they always feel that—so they do see themselves as learners, or see themselves as competent people. Yes, I think it's about joy and playfulness and creativity—inspiring those things in young people. I should think that every young person should feel that they are a valued person.

Importantly, Helen's idealised evocation is not presented as being divorced from the material reality of her students' and her working lives. Instead, it is juxtaposed with a pragmatic emphasis on the students' human rights that by implication apply to her colleagues and her as well:

> ... but that is what I think is really important. Helping young people to be in relationship, or helping young people to know how to find information for themselves and knowing that they have a right to information. Yes, helping young people feel that they have rights—human rights—and that life is worth living, and that they have something to contribute, that they are valuable.

Finally for Helen, her encapsulation of her idealised construction of teaching as empowering students and transforming their lives demonstrates, albeit implicitly, the parallel power of such a construction in helping to maximise the motivation and resilience of Helen and her fellow teachers:

> I think we should be nurturing and we should be inspiring. I think we should be gentle and kind, and offerers of hope, not too much negativity and, absolutely, helping young people access new worlds ..., or new abilities, new interests. Really nurturing interests that they already have, to help them follow their authentic path. Helping to build young people up. Help them deal with hard things like conflict, and deal with some of the hard learnings too, but not in a mean way—in a kind way.

Erin explicates a similarly hopeful, yet also distinctive, vision of teaching as an ideal form intended to support her navigation of the complexities of her work that at the same time implies an element of possible resistance, even subversion, of those complexities:

> I think that it's a teacher's job to work within the system and within the curriculum and the parameters that we've been given, but also using our own little discursive space to do maybe what's not part of the curriculum.

Erin's reference to "... our own little discursive space" evokes a place of safety and security for her students and her where they can co-construct learning that is potentially deeper, wider and more long-lasting than the formal outcomes of the standardised curriculum. Erin is clearly excited by what might eventuate from such an approach for her students and by extension for herself:

> I think that we should be looking at students' academic development, but also just trying to give them opportunities to find their way in life. They're young people: helping them to get to know themselves and what they like and what they don't like, giving them lots of opportunities to explore whatever there is in the world, to find their strengths and their weaknesses, to help them find what they might want to do in their lives, career-wise and everything else. Helping to cultivate them as human beings and not just as workers in the workforce of the future. Thinking a little more broadly than that; I think taking a more holistic view of children is pretty great.

Here Erin outlines an empirically grounded and experientially informed strategy for her students to succeed that is derived from an equivalent success strategy for her own practice that she has built up over time and in many different contexts. Importantly for the dimension of the data analysis being addressed in this chapter, these strategies have evolved and gained traction over time, yet they also exhibit continuities across place and time, in much the same way that teaching as an ideal form demonstrates such continuities.

Challenges

Jalena responds to the interviewer's question about "... any current issues or challenges or things that are worrying or bothering you in relation to your work" with an explicit reference to "... a lot of the changes in education that are around accountability ...":

> ... with accountability and, in a big organisation like EQ [Education Queensland] or [the] Queensland Education Department, of course that means more box-ticking and more forms and more paperwork .... [I]t is concerning because I think what we need more than anything is thinking time, and sometimes that's frustrating, not enough thinking time ...

Importantly, Jalena's depiction of ongoing changes in teachers' work, centred on increasing "accountability", as a significant challenge to that work is juxtaposed with an insightful self-reflection about changes in her development as a teacher over time:

> I wish I'd been more relaxed, especially as a beginning teacher .... I definitely take a much more—I come across as much more relaxed with kids

while at the same time keeping those boundaries. The boundaries are created in a relaxed way .... It's not about being ... taught about the rules. It's about—"We have a goal. This is how we're going to get there, and this is how we're all going to help [one another] along the way". Whereas, when I first started out, I think it was very much—it was just a lot of anxiety.

From this perspective, Jalena's success strategy for engaging with the challenges of her work includes trusting in her considerable and growing confidence and experience that allow her to put the undoubted challenges of teaching "in their place".

When asked about the changes that she has observed since she began teaching, Chantelle lists several such changes that she considers complex challenges for her students:

The issues that our students are dealing with are far more complex than what I feel like they used to be .... I think the issues that our kids are dealing with these days are very different to what I've experienced. Seeing that change over time and learning how to deal with that on the outside like cyberbullying and all that sort of a thing that definitely wasn't—I don't feel that old, but it's amazing how quickly all that changes.

Intriguingly, Chantelle provides an equivalent list of complex changes for her fellow teachers and herself with which to engage:

... in myself as an educator, and my experience, ... that's something else that's clearly changing over time as well. Overall, ... I feel like I'm being expected to do far more with my time now than I ever have. Even as my role in a position of leadership, I've been in it like five years, five or six years, and even that, the amount of time that we had to do the same tasks seems to be reducing every year. There's more deadlines and more things that we're getting asked to do.

Given these challenges developing over time for her students and herself, Chantelle's characterisation of the essence of teaching is noteworthy:

For me, what it means to be a teacher I've really recognised at this school is helping to prepare kids for our world .... We're trying to help them become responsible young citizens .... The other thing I always go on about is, if they have a passion, being able to voice that, and being able to have a good conversation with someone about something you're passionate about, but being educated, and asking the questions. Being able to have an opinion but back it up with something ...

Expressed in this vein, Chantelle's depiction of her students "... being educated" evokes authentic and knowledgeable citizens who are well equipped to contribute productively to their communities and the world. Given the challenging changes and continuities in which they live their lives, "... being educated" constitutes a set of success strategies for them that in turn derive from the success strategies of Chantelle and her fellow teachers in giving life to this characterisation of the ideal form of teaching, with the concomitant enhancement of motivation and resilience for both groups.

Contradictions

For Diana, many of the changes in the teaching profession that she has experienced relate to some of the contradictions evident in that profession:

> ... actually now I don't think anybody under five years' experience can be a good teacher. There's so many balls to juggle. There's so much to do—multitasking—so it really takes quite a long time to have this repertoire [of teaching strategies].

At the same time, a crucial continuity for Diana is her love for teaching, which she also envisages as the unchanging essence of her work, and as fuelling her continuing motivation and resilience in a sometimes difficult environment:

> I have not lost my enthusiasm. That has not changed, which is a blessing, otherwise I need to retire as soon as that goes. It hasn't really changed. All the angst and the anger and all of that, they're all the things around it, but the core aspect of teaching is relationship[s] with your learners, the joy you get out of being with those learners if they are nice and well-behaved ... hasn't changed.

Diana's differentiation here between the implicitly peripheral concerns—"All the angst and the anger and all of that ..."—and "... the core aspect of teaching" as the essential focus of her work aligns closely with her explication of what it means to her to be a teacher:

> To build the future .... To share my passion. Yes, to contribute to the future. That is specifically [with reference] to the future of my students, but also as a language teacher I think it implies cultural openness, hopefully, a love to travel .... There's a lot of power as well that comes with having the students for five years. You do a lot of exchanges of opinions, ... and you teach more than just your subject, obviously.

As an experienced teacher, Diana uses this enduring commitment "To build the future .... to contribute to the future" as an encapsulation of well-proven success strategies for navigating the more peripheral concerns in order to focus on, and to help to facilitate, this longer-term, and indeed lifelong, aspiration for her students and herself. Accordingly, this aspiration functions simultaneously as an idealised encapsulation of the essence of teaching and as a set of contextualised and practical techniques for bringing the ideal into the realm of the real.

In reflecting on the changes and continuities in her professional life, Serene highlights a fundamental contradiction at the heart of her self-identified development as a teacher:

> ... I've always been willing to work for myself. I've always been willing to look at what it is that I do, so I think the way I have changed and grown with education is I think ... because of my own interest, not because of the Education Department. I can see big picture stuff; I relate to kids really well. I know that there's something that I struggle with. I often read that it's a fine line between when you teach you're meant to be a teacher; you're not allowed to be [a] counsellor .... Sometimes I think I [cross over] that line. That's because of the experience I've had, and I know that I'm very careful with that, and sometimes when I do cross the line I make sure I contact parents and say, "I've had this conversation", or let the guidance counsellor know .... [I]t's come back to bite me, that I probably wouldn't have done that much in the past.

Serene's rationale for engaging in this consciously risk-taking behaviour, which constitutes a contradiction with the officially sanctioned conduct expected of teachers, relates to what she sees as a significant change in contemporary society:

> ... I think it's required more these days [to counsel students] ... because I think a lot of kids have a lot more problems ... [that are being] talked about. Maybe problems and issues and issues used to be pushed a bit under the carpet, and now they're coming out hard and fast. I don't know if we have enough staff to deal with all of that. Like health issues being more opened up and all the gender transitions issues .... Now that it's becoming more public, it's more in the face in schools. It's more visible. That's a big change too, and that has an impact also in how our education operates or fails to operate.

Against this backdrop, Serene also identifies a fundamental change in her response to the questions "... what does it mean to you to be a teacher? What do you feel is the essence of a teachers' work?":

> I remember during my interview to become a teacher, I [said], "I want to change everything; I want to change the system; I want to change that". Then that didn't happen .... What it means for me now to be a

teacher [is] to impact, have an impact and help kids grow and learn in as many kids that I can reach at the school as possible. That's my thing now, is to open up kids' eyes to show them that learning is fun and that it has a purpose and there's a big world out there.

From one perspective, this seeming narrowing of the scope of Serene's idealisation of teaching might be seen as a reduced and less ambitious vision. From a different perspective, simultaneously this reduced focus is a reflection of reality and potentially a more nuanced and carefully targeted assertion of the essence of teaching for Serene. At the same time, it affords Serene opportunities to demonstrate her desired impact in ways that engage productively with the changes and continuities in education and the broader society that she has identified, enacted in efforts to enhance her students' motivation and resilience that boost her own motivation and resilience as well.

Comforts

Turning our attention to the comforts that teachers derive from their work, Paul presents an extended and insightful account of his response to the questions, "… what does it mean to you to be a teacher? What do you think is the essence of teacher work?" He begins by recalling a lecture that he had attended with the provocative title "The meaning of life: Why should you care?": "… [The lecturer] said he was more interested in the question of finding meaning in life, and the fact that, if you have meaning in your life, you live longer, you live better, essentially".

In reflecting on the lecturer's argument, Paul uses the key concept of "meaning" as a springboard to articulate a powerful vision of the essence of teaching, including a sense of being an embodied teacher as well as meaning-making being co-constituted, dialogical and reciprocal:

> I think … [that] essentially it's actually the other way around. I find meaning in being a teacher, [although] there isn't necessarily anything really meaningful about teaching, though it's an important job. It's a job I feel I'm good at, that feels like I've got the skills to be able to do it, but, more importantly, I find meaning in being a teacher and a parent and a partner in a way that it makes me feel like a whole person, rather than just getting up to work and—There are days when I get up and go [sighs], "Not another feature", but it's fairly few. That's why I do it. I find meaning in doing that, meaning in doing, [being] of some influence instead of nudging some people potentially in the wrong direction. The majority is up to them. I do do what I can do, but they have to find their own meaning. Maybe if I can help them find their own meaning.

Clearly, the search for meaning is a profoundly human undertaking, and meaning is equally clearly a multifaceted and situated phenomenon. For Paul, meaning in his enactment of teaching has several distinctive features, centred on his relationships with his students and his capacity to exercise a positive influence on their current and future lives, and also incorporating the requisite knowledge, skills, energy and other attributes needed to carry out the work effectively. Although he does not address changes and continuities explicitly, we discern changes in the sense of Paul's meaning-making developing over time and in different contexts, as well as continuities in the underlying principles and values of that meaning-making. Moreover, given the articulateness of Paul's evocation of this meaning-making, we perceive several success strategies flowing from this highly honed understanding of the essence of his work, and furthermore that those strategies have a direct and positive impact on his students' and his own motivation and resilience.

Finally for the participants' voices traversed in this chapter, Perry uses the interview questions to reflect on a long-running and very diverse teaching career. While he had encountered a number of challenges in different schools during his career, he resists a hypothetical characterisation of the contemporary education system as being "broken". In doing so, he deploys a vivid car metaphor to highlight the diversity of current manifestations of that system:

> Maybe it gets you thinking about why, in a fleet of vehicles, … some are really running nicely, really running well, despite what they've been provided by the dealer, but others are running on three cylinders and some might suggest running on three wheels. There's a whole lot of things that's really hard to change.

Significantly, Perry derives comfort from the Australian education system whose strengths and complexities he knows so well, even when he evokes what is sometimes presented as an invidious comparison with the Finnish education system:

> It's a big system-wide thing [in Australia], but I think a good principal with regional support could probably do an awful lot. I don't think it's broken. I think it needs a lot more flexibility, and there's some things we're never going to have. We're never going to be like Finland, which doesn't have private schools. We are never going to be like that, because those decisions over there were made 50 years ago, and maybe they're running with the benefit of that.

Crucially for the argument in this chapter, Perry's self-construction of himself as a teaching idealist represents a judicious and purposeful balancing between this kind of clear-eyed realism, based on direct and extensive experience over time and in multiple places, on the one hand, and an enduring commitment to the ideal of what teaching could and should be and become, on the other hand. This self-construction includes sharing specific strategies that have assisted Perry to sustain his motivation and resilience as a teacher, including the self-care related to taking a break from teaching, and "... writing a little book for parents". After more than 25 years of teaching, Perry's closing reflection in his interview on his current teaching position simultaneously encapsulates his review of teaching as an ideal form and distils the ongoing hard work needed to move towards that ideal form: "It's taught me a lot of resilience, and it's taught me that I'm okay and I've still got something to offer".

Implications

The teaching idealists portrayed in this chapter employed a number of essential beliefs that they considered as their core business when interacting with students. Interestingly, they did not list detailed lesson planning or any form of paperwork as a fundamental principle when considering the essence of meaningful teaching. Most of their musings were interpersonal, student-centred and relationship-based. The notion of a teaching idealist is multifaceted and involves acknowledgements of factors such as: the importance of a healthy and diverse community; the significance of navigating academia so that it has relevance and currency; the need to attend to self-concept, both of the teacher and of the student; the value of recognising the tenets of student development, both mental and physical; the positive consequences of robust relationships and connections; and the power of professional integrity.

This chapter has uncovered a number of signposts for teaching idealists' resilience that include: adhering to social conscience; believing in the ideal of education and the societal value of effective teaching methodology; building and working on relationships (connections); finding and maintaining professional satisfaction and purpose; and sustaining passion. These elements are expanded below.

Adhering to Social Conscience

Teachers as community idealists see themselves as academic and cultural gatekeepers who seek to open minds to real-world issues. They are concerned with the well-being of others and with a healthy society. They bring real-world issues into the classroom to be discussed in a respectful and meaningful manner.

Believing in the Ideal of Education and the Societal Value of Effective Teaching Methodology

Teachers as philosophical idealists adopt a student-centred approach to teaching whereby each student comes to the learning environment as an individual in their own right, and as such has a unique set of values and needs.

These teachers believe in their educative approach as idealised teaching practice. They are accepting of (and embrace) student diversity.

Building and Working on Relationships (Connections)

Teachers as socially conscious idealists promote global citizenship. They understand the mental stages of development of their students and work within those parameters whilst providing for thought to expand their students' thinking beyond the classroom and the community. They model values such as ethics, critical thinking and social obligation.

Finding and Maintaining Professional Satisfaction and Purpose

Teachers as professional idealists recognise the promise of student potential and look for relevant methodology that will enhance their students' learning. They believe that challenging but attainable goals aid student success and mental growth. These goals keep the learning journey interesting for both students and teachers.

Sustaining Passion

Teachers as enthusiastic idealists demonstrate authentic excitement for their topic and work hard to inspire and encourage a love of learning in their students. These teachers sustain their passion through interaction with their students and a genuine regard for the learning process.

Conclusion

Teaching idealists are passionate about their chosen profession and are emotionally committed to their students' educative and personal progress. In the main, these teachers prioritise the holistic nature of teaching and concentrate on enabling their students to be well-rounded, interested/interesting and valuable members of society as well as confident academics. Teaching idealists believe that education can be transformative and that professionally they are uniquely positioned to influence the future positively. They consider the relationship with their students to be synchronistic in nature, and often cite the beneficial possibilities for both parties involved in the learning environment. They believe that the affirming relationships that they construct and maintain with their students provide them with a feeling of emotional well-being and fulfilment.

The teaching idealist is a holistic practitioner who works towards the betterment of educative practice for the student (and the teacher) that includes development of self-concept and self-awareness as well as academic success. The ripples felt from their enacted passionate educative philosophies in the classroom not only influence those they teach but also, through the student body, positively affect society as a whole.

References

Badley, K., & Hughes, M. C. (2022). The teaching vocation and the interior lives of teachers. In M. C. Hughes & K. Badley (Eds.), *Joyful resilience as educational practice: Transforming teaching challenges into opportunities* (pp. 1–10). Routledge.

Carmi, T., & Tamir, E. (2022). Three professional ideals: Where should teacher preparation go next? *European Journal of Teacher Education, 45*(2), 173–192. https://doi.org/10.1080/02619768.2020.1805732

Delcheva-Dizdarevikj, J. (2024). Being a teacher is more than a profession: Reflections on the teaching vocation in the XXI century. *Annals of the Faculty of Philosophy in Skopje, 77*(1), 77–94. https://doi.org/10.37510/godzbo2477077dd

Hansen, D. T. (2013). The place of ideals in teaching. In W. Hare & J. P. Portelli (Eds.), *Philosophy of education: Introductory readings* (4th ed.) (pp. 55–66). Brush Education Inc.

Moreno, V. M. (2022). The ideal teacher[:] Different images. *Human Arenas, 5,* 550–576. https://doi.org/10.1007/s42087-020-00148-0

Sabino, C. D. (2023). The vocation, key to resilience in the teaching profession. *HOLOS, 2,* 1–17. https://www2.ifrn.edu.br/ojs/index.php/HOLOS/article/view/15185/3639

Salucci, A. (2022). Idealism. In G. Tanzella-Nitti, I. Colagé, & A. Strumia (Eds.), *INTERS—Interdisciplinary encyclopedia of religion and science.* https://inters.org/idealism

Recommended Further Reading

Boulton, A., Grauer, K., & Irwin, R. L. (2016). Becoming teacher: A/r/tographical inquiry and visualising metaphor. *The International Journal of Art & Design Education, 36*(2), 200–214. https://doi.org/10.1111/jade.12080

Furlong, C. (2013). The teacher I wish to be: Exploring the influence of life histories on student teacher idealised identities. *European Journal of Teacher Education, 36*(1), 68–83. https://doi.org/10.1080/02619768.2012.678486

Hirst, P. H. (1971). What is teaching? *Journal of Curriculum Studies, 3*(1), 5–18. https://doi.org/10.1080/0022027710030102

Maaranen, K., Pitkäniemi, H., Stenberg, K., & Karlsson, L. (2016). An idealistic view of teaching: Teacher students' personal practical theories. *Journal of Education for Teaching: International Research and Pedagogy, 42*(1), 80–92. http://dx.doi.org/10.1080/02607476.2015.1135278

Ross, M. (2017). Conceptions of teaching: An illustrated review. *The Clinical Teacher, 14*(1), 8–14. https://doi.org/10.1111/tct.12622

11 Teachers as Technology Reframers

Introduction

Teachers in the 21st century have needed to respond to an increasing pace of technological change. As Shirley, one of the teachers in our study, shared, "... when I first started here, I think there was one desktop [computer] in a teacher's room, and to get it going we had to wait for, like, half an hour and whatever. It was different days". The last 50 years have seen technological change become ubiquitous in schools: the advent of the personal computer, local area networks, spreadsheets, presentation software, smartboards, the internet, tablets, artificial intelligence (AI) and many other changes. At the same time, it is important to recollect that educational technologies can include a stick that is utilised to draw symbols in a patch of dirt to explain a new idea to interested others, through to quill pens, slates and chalkboards, through to present day shared software on personal digital devices. One corollary of this recollection is that, to qualify as educational tools, technologies need to function as knowledge applications directed at facilitating learning and teaching. Another corollary is the requirement for the educational purpose and the technological orientation to be in sync if such learning and teaching are to be effective. Alternatively, there is a potential for them to be out of sync and hence to generate stress for students and teachers alike.

Accordingly, this chapter's focus on teachers as technology reframers is posited on the primacy of the pedagogical dimension of educational technologies if teachers are to be enabled to use such technologies effectively in their work. Often this occurs in the context of designing for learning, the focus of Chapter 2. From this perspective, reframing technologies is likely to begin with revisiting the purpose of the lesson or unit of study to reassert its pedagogical function. The next step is to evaluate particular technologies to establish whether and how they might facilitate the enactment of that function, and any opportunity costs in doing so. Assessing the pros and cons of applying a particular technology might entail considering contextual specificities such as the students' levels of understanding certain ideas mediated by one technology rather than another, as well as those same students' predicted classroom behaviours, including the safety of one another and of the technology.

DOI: 10.4324/9781003564850-11

Being a technology reframer can also involve moving between educational and technological discourses and appraising claims made in both those discursive realms, including understanding whose interests underly such claims.

In other words, teachers as technology reframers who seek to apply specific technologies as part of their intended success strategies need to incorporate such applications in an already highly complex and contextualised set of decisions being enacted in a dynamic and constantly shifting school and classroom ecology of networks and relationships. Consequently, their actions related to particular technologies in their work reflect the wider considerations and competing demands (Hughes, 2014) of their teaching practices. Our elaboration of teachers' technology reframing in this chapter exhibits a diversity of approaches and attitudes by the selected participants, ranging from enthusiastic take up and interest in technical innovation, to certain technologies enhancing disciplinary knowledge and driving positive social changes, to insistence on the primacy of the pedagogical over the technological, to pragmatic use of available technologies, to ambivalence and scepticism, and finally to refusal to adopt a technology celebrationist discourse in their teaching (Hodas, 1993).

Selected Literature

There are complex relationships between teachers and technology (Selwyn, 2021). Technology can reduce administrative and procedural work for teachers, yet at the same time it creates new forms of the same. It provides more options for pedagogical support in the classroom (e.g., through more interactivity and differentiation of activities), but it also creates new ways for lessons to go off the rails— Adriana, one of the teachers in our study, referred to technology not working as "the biggest frustration in a school". The connectedness of the internet and mobile devices has increased collegiality in the profession in many ways, with teachers supporting one another through email and countless online groups (Kelly et al., 2016), yet these same technologies can also serve to reduce the vibrancy of staffrooms, and to carry unhealthy and destructive communications in social media and unmoderated online forums (Arantes, 2023).

Indeed, there is a long tradition in the philosophy of technology to recognise this double-sided nature of technology. On the one hand, technologies are tools that can be put to various uses; it is up to the people using them to choose their practices given the affordances (or possibilities) of the technology (Norman, 2013). For this reason, Selwyn (2021) suggests that "our primary focus should be not on technological devices, tools and applications *per se*, but on the practices and activities that surround them" (p. 2; *italics in the original*). Such a view suggests that the technology itself is neutral or agnostic and that it is the people using it who make it useful or problematic.

Yet there is a flip side to this proposition. The technology in our world shapes our possibilities and changes us, even as humans likewise transform technology through applying and adapting it (Fleming & Sorenson, 2001). Our neural structures and our lifeworlds are transformed by the technologies that we use. A teacher who uses PowerPoint presentations in their teaching every day for a year has fundamentally changed as a person (and they are also changed further if they decide to vary that teaching approach in the future). In short, the technologies that we use lead us to see the world in different ways. Heidegger (1977/2009) summarises this position thus:

> ... we are delivered over to [technology] in the worst possible way when we regard it as something neutral; for this conception of it, to which today we particularly like to do homage, makes us utterly blind to the essence of technology. (p. 4)

Many people, including teachers, recognise the possibilities of technology to do good or evil in the world, yet this more subtle capacity of technology to change its user is often hidden.

Teachers' proficiency in integrating technological use for their teaching practices has been formalised in the TPACK model, an acronym that stands for Technological, Pedagogical and Content Knowledge (Koehler & Mishra, 2009). The model builds on Shulman's (1987) work in recognising that teachers need to integrate knowledge of how to teach (pedagogy) into knowledge of the curriculum content, and to integrate both with their general knowledge about the world. The contribution of Koehler and Mishra was to recognise that teachers also need to integrate their use of technologies into their teaching (though critics argue that this is simply a part of pedagogical knowledge). This echoes Selwyn's (2021) point above that it is the *integration* of technology into practices that matters most for teachers, and it also reinforces that effective educational technologies facilitate and potentially transform, rather than inhibit, teachers' pedagogical work.

In this regard, we see technology reframing by teachers as a conscious, agential, purposeful project for reasserting the pedagogical primacy of using such technologies in their work. This reframing project takes multiple forms, ranging from resisting technological capture (John, 2005), to teachers deploying their pedagogical reasoning to reframe their technological practice (Holmberg et al., 2018), to reimagining potential applications of particular technologies (Tellería, 2021), to potentially innovating technologies to facilitate transformed teaching and learning practice (Tarling & Ng'ambi, 2016). Moreover, we recognise this reframing project as a crucial contribution to teachers' success strategies more broadly: we posit a clear-eyed, evidence-based, experience-informed and highly contextualised approach to applying technologies in schools and classrooms as a pre-requisite of teachers' effective use of those technologies. Such an approach to technology use in learning might be called "designerly" in its response to context and openness to experimentation.

A particular aspect of teachers enacting success strategies in their role as technology reframers is what sometimes takes the form of a healthy scepticism about the pedagogical claims made on behalf of specific technologies. Theoretically, this "healthy scepticism" can be linked with a school of thought with contributors as varied as Debord (1967/1994) and Postman (2005) identifying how, within the present mode of production, the appearance of something (e.g., its exchange value) counts for more than the actual use of something (e.g., its use value). This plays out within schools, where the marketing potential of a technology to raise the status of a school ("Check out our BYOD policy and our amazing STEM program!") can often precede, and potentially conflict with, consideration of how these policies and technologies will affect learning (Buckingham et al., 2001; McGarr & Engen, 2022). This discursive dissonance (Harreveld, 2002) adds to the responsibility of teachers engaging in technology reframing by requiring them to navigate the sometimes competing educational and technological domains and to seek viable and sustainable bridges between those domains that can facilitate their students' learning and their own professional work.

Data Analysis

This chapter focuses on the fifth "dimension" elicited from our analysis of the interview transcripts completed for this study. This dimension, "teaching by design", was defined in Chapter 1 as "Curriculum, pedagogy and assessment as intentions, outcomes and effects, and opportunities for teachers to engage in adaptive, innovative and sometimes transformative educational practice" (see also Chapter 2).

As we elaborated in Chapter 1 as well, our analytical strategy also identified four "nodes" that have oriented the presentation of the data analysis in each of the ten data chapters in this book, including this one:

- Complexities (CY): Engaging with multifaceted events and issues
- Challenges (CE): Encounters with difficult and potentially stressful events and issues
- Contradictions (CN): Events and issues with at least two competing influences and pressures
- Comforts (CT): Sources of encouragement, motivation and pleasure

Building on Table 1.2 in Chapter 1, Table 11.1 illustrates the approach taken to data analysis in this chapter about teachers as technology reframers, organised around the teaching design dimension and clustered around the four aforementioned nodes.

Table 11.1 Data Analysis Matrix for Teachers as Technology Reframers

	Teaching by design
Complexities	Paul; Arthur
Challenges	Alexa; Adriana
Contradictions	Elspeth; Shirley
Comforts	Anthea; Serene

Complexities

In reflecting on the complexities of technologies in his colleagues' and his work, Paul exhibits considerable ambivalence and even scepticism about the degree to which such technologies have made a transformative difference to contemporary school teaching. On the one hand, he asserts that technology in schools "...hasn't changed as much as I hear my colleagues talk about it". His illustration to demonstrate his argument evokes the "death by PowerPoint" adage: "You can still be the person that gives out PowerPoints, da-da-da-da-da", suggesting that an expository teaching style simply changes one technology (chalkboard or whiteboard) for another (PowerPoint slides on a personal computer or laptop).

On the other hand, Paul presents a different viewpoint and what he sees as a more positive example that also highlights the complexities attending technological use in teaching:

> I've always been more interested in helping the students construct meaning rather than giving them meaning, and that hasn't really changed .... I've always been protected to some degree by being in science. That's how we do science, so it makes sense to teach that way, but that's not always how science is taught. It's never ... necessarily always been about [that]—it's been about memorising facts.

What is striking about Paul's argument here is the strength of his sometimes explicit privileging of the pedagogical discourse over the technological discourse pertaining to educational technologies. At the core of his mobilisation of the pedagogical discourse is his baldly asserted commitment to "... helping the students construct meaning rather than giving them meaning ...". In this regard, Paul's reframing of educational technologies is centred on his insistence that they enable him to continue "helping the students": "... that hasn't really changed". Intriguingly, his reference to having "... always been protected to some degree by being in science" elicits the hypothetical follow-up question: "protected from what?". One response seems to lie in Paul's implied critique of a focus on students "... memorising facts", which he concedes sometimes occurs in science teaching, which in turn deviates from his central proposition that science entails "... helping the students construct meaning ...". From this perspective, perhaps Paul feels it is important for science teachers to be "protected" from the ease with which contemporary technologies can be enlisted by, and become complicit with, expository and non-constructivist teaching approaches. More broadly, teachers' identity and practices can remain consistent in the face of technological change. Teachers who are grounded in their educational philosophy, who have a sense of their purpose and who have carefully considered their practices are able to use technologies to suit their own ends rather than feeling they must adapt slavishly to the technological trend *du jour*. In doing so, they resist the mobilisation of an automatically celebrationist discourse about such trends.

Arthur continues the theme of the complexities attending contemporary educational technologies by articulating a strong sense of ambivalence about the place of such technologies in current schooling:

> That's quite an unpopular line in a lot of schools, because technology forms this unholy alliance with marketing ...."Look how great our school is. All the kids have got computers. Look how great our school is. We've got this whiz bang network and superfast internet". Well, no, the kids aren't suffering, in Postman's terms, from a paucity of information. They're suffering from an overload of information.

Here Arthur echoes the pressures noted above on schools to market their uses of technologies (Buckingham et al., 2001; McGarr & Engen, 2022). He also recalls the discussion earlier in this chapter of technology potentially being about more appearance and spectacle (its exchange value) than about utility (its use value) (Debord, 1967/1994; Postman, 2005).

Like Paul, Arthur exhibits his technology reframing with a clearly and confidently explicated assertion of the pedagogical essence of his teaching work vis-à-vis the growing influence of educational technologies:

> What ... [students] actually need is an information-restricted environment where the information they're given is, one, of quality and, two, actually connected meaningfully to the rest of the information. That global idea of what curriculum can achieve is a bridge too far.

Despite the clarity of his articulation of this essence, Arthur is acutely aware of the complexities pertaining to turning it into an educational reality, including the fact that teachers receive a lot of top-down policies around how they ought to use technologies. There is a common refrain in the profession of teachers feeling that they should use a technology one way but being mandated to use it another way (Boonmoh et al., 2021; Yeung et al., 2012). From this perspective, a strategy for success for teachers is to understand the deeper motives for some of these superficially straightforward policies. As Arthur notes, schools and school systems are often driven by a spectacular imperative, a need to "appear" to be at the cutting edge of learning, even where resources might be better spent elsewhere to support actual learning more substantially.

Arthur continues this theme of the disparity between "appearance" and "reality", in doing so revealing a nuanced apprehension of the complexities at work regarding educational technologies:

> Certainly at our school, and I think in the sector generally, we really, really want to look like we're right on the money. Teachers are not cool.

> Learning is not cool. Again, this is a brutal thing to say .... We're the gatekeepers for something really important. At least, we used to be the gatekeepers for something important, but it wasn't cool. It was learning and reading and hard work and thinking.

Arthur's juxtaposition here of "... learning and reading and hard work and thinking" with technology as "making learning cool" is striking. Arthur is appreciating that learning requires rigorous thinking and dedication to a task, all of which is possible *with* technology; but the implication is that technology sometimes becomes a substitute *for* education: having the look and feel of learning, but without the rigour and dedication to give it substance. Moreover, Arthur's repeated reference to "... gatekeepers for something really important" constitutes a distinctive reframing of technology in which teachers enact a unique responsibility in translating valuable knowledge for their students to acquire and apply at present and in the future.

Challenges

In reflecting on some of the challenges associated with educational technologies, Alexa presents a timely reminder of the wider impact of such technologies on her students' everyday lives, which in turn have a profound effect on their learning experiences:

> I think one of the biggest challenges at the moment that we have students that have absolutely no resilience. Mental health issues are huge. I think social media has got a lot to answer for. Everyone just says that kids are digitally literate. I'm like, "No, they're not" .... They're just cruising the internet like everybody else. They're not coding. They're not actually using proper computing powers. Also, I think they all feel this need to be something that they're not and have all these friends on social media and all those things. That is creating a raft of problems for our young people today, and it's massive.

Alexa's juxtaposition of the misapprehension that young people are automatically "digitally literate" with the online ramifications of adolescent peer pressure emphasises the difficulty for individual teachers to reframe technologies positively in this kind of situation.

Adriana returns attention to the specific challenges facing teachers in using educational technologies, and in doing so she identifies particular strategies that are successful for her in the distinctive contexts of her work:

> There were seven different ways of connecting my computer to the system in the classroom that I am in. Sometimes it just doesn't work, and

nobody knows why. Fortunately, I always have my very old-fashioned flashcards with me. I have an uneasy relationship with technology. I think it's often overused, and I think a lot of people need to be able to do other things.

Here Adriana's self-professed "uneasy relationship with technology" can be seen as her agential reframing of the technologies available to her. Rather than being dependent on or intimidated by sometimes unreliable computing equipment, she finds that the pedagogical primacy guiding her teaching affords her a well-reasoned and eminently justifiable educational strategy.

The same pedagogical primacy is evident in this reflection by Adriana:

As a teacher, I use ... [technology]. I use the interactive whiteboard. I use YouTube clips, and all of those things. At the same time, I believe that there is enormous value in using an atlas, in using paper dictionaries. In fact, using an atlas has become part of the Australian curriculum for primary [school] kids.

In this comment, and despite the challenge of sometimes uncooperative computing equipment, Adriana attests to using a wide range of technologies appropriate to her teaching goals and her students' learning needs. At the same time, she resists a superficial binary between "sophisticated technology" and "basic teaching aids". This is at once a pragmatic response to inconsistent technology and a pedagogically grounded set of strategies directed at facilitating her students' and her own educational success.

Contradictions

Elspeth draws on her experience as a relieving teacher working in a number of schools in Queensland to illustrate a particular contradiction attending access to and availability of educational technologies in the same education system:

I can see some schools ... that are over resource[d], whereas, going to the other schools, they got absolutely nothing .... [T]hat's inequality or disadvantage .... Not only technology ... but books as well .... I was amazed to come here ... and they ... even used the interactive board .... [M]ore advanced than ... [her previous location] [Laughing] ... [where there was] The chalk and the board.

Elspeth is well aware of the educational effects of these kinds of material inequities and systemic contradictions, which she finds inexplicable given that the schools are located in the same Australian state and the same education system.

Shirley explicates a different but equally influential contradiction related to the impact of technologies on education:

> ... I probably have to mention technology because that has changed not just the teaching, but also everything we do as teachers. Accountability, professional development, teaching .... [W]hen I first started here, I think there was one desktop [computer] in a teacher's room, and to get it going we had to wait for like have an hour ... [or] whatever. It was different days .... Other than that, definitely the kids having the [mobile] phones. For the EALD [English as an Additional Language or Dialect] kids [it] is very positive because they can look up words really quickly, but everything else you have to be happy if you see any kids outside playing ball, because most of them are just with their phone somewhere. I find this to be a worry for the [students'] cognitive development and all this ... [but] there's not much you can do about it.

Here Shirley traces the impact of the now pervasive effects of technologies on seemingly "... everything we do as teachers", with networked systems functioning to monitor and evaluate teachers' "[a]ccountability, professional development, teaching". This sheer pervasiveness makes it increasingly difficult for teachers to retain their sense of pedagogical primacy. Similarly, Shirley highlights the stark contradiction between the positive outcomes of technologies for "... EALD kids" being able to "... look up words really quickly", on the one hand, and students more broadly being addicted to their mobile phones (as mentioned also by Alexa) and the corollary concerns about their disinclination to play outside and about their "... cognitive development", on the other hand.

Comforts

As a music teacher, Anthea expresses a discipline-specific comfort that reflects her successful reframing of educational technologies:

> ... [L]earning to read music ... has so many links to science, engineering ... because that's all that music is. It is just a set of instructions written in illegible code, but you just have to decode and follow the instructions. That's really the philosophical argument over what music actually is .... [I]t's something to experience, something human. I was actually reading an [article] last night and ... [the author is] talking about his musical choice is the computer because from that you can then interpret and create sounds that other musicians who have another instrument can then play and there's emotions that are attached to ... [enable students] to experience the world in [a] way they can then hang something on ...

In this reflection, Anthea shares an explicit and powerful analogy between music and technologies in relation to education. Both can be interpreted as "… just a set of instructions written in illegible code, but you just have to decode and follow the instructions". This technological reframing asserts the pedagogical primacy of the educational imperative over the technical aspect. Furthermore, Anthea communicates a profoundly felt truth about the positive effects of both music and technologies if that pedagogical primacy is enacted: they provide students with "… something to experience, something human", and also the opportunity "… to experience the world in [a] way they can then hang something on…".

Finally in this section of the chapter, Serene shares a highly developed sense of educational technologies as a comfort in her work. In doing so, she links such technologies with broader socioeconomic developments in society that influence the occupational pathways available to her students:

> Knowledge is huge. I love technology. I love going to workshops and innovation …. What else? Maybe a few more choices …. There's actually more opportunities now for boys and girls to do similar things. There's a lot of stuff that's changing things like girls do this, boys do this. Now with certificate courses … it's okay for guys to cook, it's okay for girls to become engineers, and that's a big change, that's a good change.

Here Serene reframes technology as being personally exciting and motivating, and more widely as driving positive developments in her students' lives outside and after school: "… that's a big change, that's a good change".

Implications

In the introduction, we posited technology reframing by teachers as a conscious, agential, purposeful project for reasserting the pedagogical primacy of using such technologies in their work. In the 21st century, teachers certainly have broad opportunities for using technologies in their teaching and the pace of technological development does not appear to be slowing down, with the widespread adoption of generative AI as a case in point. The teachers with whom we spoke had clearly reflected deeply upon the role of technologies in their teaching. They gave indications of an impressive capacity for framing and reframing technology in ways that suited their intentions. In this section, we draw attention to some of the implications for teachers and teacher educators about how the framing and reframing of technology can be part of teachers' success strategies.

As discussed in the selected literature, technology is rarely either all good or all bad, and the teachers in our study revealed an awareness of this multifaceted nature of technology. Arthur can see that technology is "cool", in the sense that it is useful for engaging students by giving them the latest shiny things. Yet he can also see that technology is "actually resulting in less wellbeing for students", a reference to the anxiety that typically accompanies social media use. In a similar way, Elspeth is concerned that some schools "are over resourced" while other schools get "absolutely nothing", an allusion to the problematic issues of unequal access to technology within our schools. In contrast to this issue of not enough access to technology, Shirley observes that "you have to be happy if you see any kids outside playing ball, because most of them are just with their phone somewhere", indicating a wistful longing for an era when children did not have technology surrounding them all the time. These are not paradoxes but rather are observations of the complicated relationships that teachers observe regarding students and technologies.

In this context, educational philosophies serve teachers as a guiding light that could be used in their decision-making around technology use. Paul presents a clear example of this when he asserts that he is "… more interested in helping the students construct meaning rather than giving them meaning". The implication is that this high-level commitment helps to guide him when he is designing for learning and discerning between different options that are available. Other teachers may have different educational philosophies (e.g., as discussed in Chapter 2, another teacher we spoke to prioritised the development of interpersonal relationships as a goal of their teaching), which would imply different ways of framing technology use.

Relatedly, teachers benefit from having the critical faculties to see through the "spin" that comes with much of the technology that teachers encounter. "EdTech" is a large industry claimed to be worth hundreds of billions of dollars per year, and that draws the attention of large corporations (Hogan, 2025). Teachers who have the critical faculties for making sense of the technological opportunities that they are presented with have a better chance of maintaining coherency in their use of technology in their teaching. Arthur gives an example of his ability to see that "technology forms this unholy alliance with marketing", and he is confident in his ability to see that what he believes students really need is at times at odds with this marketing. Having this insight allows him to ignore the opportunities for using technology that do not serve his overarching goals.

Teachers who have an underpinning educational philosophy as well as critical faculties can appreciate that older technologies may often be equal to, or in some cases superior to, newer technologies. Ariana discusses the value of having flashcards that she can rely upon when technology is broken, but she also notes that "I use the interactive whiteboard. I use YouTube clips, and all of those things. At the same time, I believe that there is enormous value in using an atlas, in using paper dictionaries". Teachers in the 21st century would ideally have it both ways: a literacy for using new technologies where appropriate alongside fluency with using pre-digital technologies in their teaching.

Teachers are professionals who design for learning (see Chapter 2) using a deep understanding of the learning context: *this* group of students in *this* environment. They make decisions about goals for their teaching and the learning activities that can achieve those goals. As the construct of TPACK (Koehler & Mishra, 2009) makes explicit, it is teachers' integration of technology into this decision-making that matters most for the successful framing and reframing of technology.

Conclusion

The pace of technological change in the 21st century is such that students' expectations and norms around technology and its uses can change from year to year. It would be unwise for any teacher to hold a fixed perspective on technology under these conditions. More broadly, these changing expectations and norms are symptomatic of the wider social tensions and cultural imperatives that impinge on teachers' work, whereby it is difficult to insulate individual classrooms and schools against the incursions of the outside world.

Rather than seeking to carry out such insulation, the study participants whose experiences have been presented in this chapter have mobilised educational values and pedagogical principles as their preferred compass bearings and navigational lodestars in engaging with the various technologies canvassed in the chapters. In doing so, the selected teachers have exhibited several different types of strategies to progress that engagement, ranging from enthusiastic take up to ambivalence and scepticism to declining to adopt an unthinking celebration of technologies in contemporary education. These strategies have included deploying alternative teaching techniques and "back up" plans in case of certain technologies proving uncooperative, as well as experimenting with different approaches to see "what works" with a particular group of students in a specific subject or context.

These various initiatives have reflected the teachers' reframing of technologies as intentional exercises directed at enhancing the effectiveness of students' learning outcomes as well as their own work practices. From this perspective, teachers as technology reframers can be seen as professional educators enacting diverse approaches to teaching by design in order to maximise their students' and their educational success.

References

Arantes, J. (2023). It's too late—the post has gone viral already: A novel methodological stance to explore K–12 teachers' lived experiences of adult cyber abuse. *Qualitative Research Journal*. Advance online publication. https://doi.org/10.1108/QRJ-01-2023-0014

Boonmoh, A., Jumpakate, T., & Karpklon, S. (2021). Teachers' perceptions and experience in using technology for the classroom. *Computer-Assisted Language Learning Electronic Journal*, 22(1), 1–24. https://callej.org/index.php/journal/article/view/320/251

Buckingham, D., Scanlon, M., & Sefton-Green, J. (2001). Selling the digital dream: Marketing educational technology to teachers and parents. In A. Loveless & V. Ellis (Eds.), *ICT, pedagogy and the curriculum: Subject to change* (pp. 20–40). Routledge.

Debord, G. (1967/1994). *The society of the spectacle* (D. Nicholson-Smith, Trans.). Black and Red. (Original work published 1967.)

Fleming, L., & Sorenson, O. (2001). Technology as a complex adaptive system: Evidence from patent data. *Research Policy*, *30*(7), 1019–1039. https://doi.org/10.1016/S0048-7333(00)00135-9

Harreveld, R. E. (2002). *Brokering changes: A study of power and identity through discourses* [Doctoral dissertation]. Central Queensland University, Australia.

Heidegger, M. (1977/2009). *The question concerning technology and other essays* (W. Lovitt, Trans.). Garland Publishing, Inc.

Hodas, S. (1993). Technology refusal. *Education Policy Analysis Archies*, *1*, 10. https://doi.org/10.14507/epaa.v1n10.1993

Hogan, A. (2025). *Commercialising public schooling: Practices of profit-making*. Routledge.

Holmberg, J., Fransson, G., & Fors, U. (2018). Teachers' pedagogical reasoning and reframing of practice in digital contexts. *International Journal of Information and Learning Technology*, *35*(2), 130–142. https://doi.org/10.1108/IJILT-09-2017-0084

Hughes, S. J. (2014). *Teachers as placemakers: How primary school teachers design, manage and maintain learning spaces as part of their daily workflow* [Doctoral dissertation]. University of Southern Queensland, Australia.

John, P. (2005). The sacred and the profane: Subject non-culture, pedagogical practice and teachers' perceptions of the classroom uses of ICT. *Educational Review*, *57*(4), 471–490. https://doi.org/10.1080/00131910500279577

Kelly, N., Clarà, M., Kehrwald, B., & Danaher, P. A. (2016). *Online learning networks for pre-service and early career teachers*. Palgrave Macmillan/Palgrave Pivot.

Koehler, M., & Mishra, P. (2009). What is technological pedagogical content knowledge (TPACK)? *Contemporary Issues in Technology and Teacher Education*, *9*(1), 60–70. https://citejournal.org/volume-9/issue-1-09/general/what-is-technological-pedagogicalcontent-knowledge/

McGarr, O., & Engen, B. K. (2022). By-passing teachers in the marketing of digital technologies: The synergy of educational technology discourse and new public management practices. *Learning, Media and Technology*, *47*(4), 440–455. https://doi.org/10.1080/17439884.2021.2010092

Norman, D. (2013). *The design of everyday things* (revised and expanded ed.). Basic Books.

Postman, N. (2005). *Amusing ourselves to death: Public discourse in the age of show business*. Penguin.

Selwyn, N. (2021). *Education and technology: Key issues and debates*. Bloomsbury Publishing.

Shulman, L. (1987). Knowledge and teaching: Foundations of the new reform. *Harvard Educational Review*, *57*(1), 1–23. https://people.ucsc.edu/~ktellez/shulman.pdf

Tarling, I., & Ng'ambi, D. (2016). Teachers pedagogical change framework: A diagnostic tool for changing teachers' uses of emerging technologies. *British Journal of Educational Technology*, *47*(3), 554–572. https://doi.org/10.1111/bjet.12454

Tellería, R. C. (2021). *By teachers for teachers: A toolkit to reimagine the futures of the teacher–technology symbiosis* [Masters dissertation]. Ontario College of Art & Design University, Canada. https://openresearch.ocadu.ca/id/eprint/3403/1/Chavez-Telleria_Rocio_2021_MDes_SFI_MRP.pdf

Yeung, A. S., Taylor, P. G., Hui, C., Lam-Chiang, A. C., & Low, E.-L. (2012). Mandatory use of technology in teaching: Who cares and so what? *British Journal of Educational Technology*, *43*(6), 859–870. https://doi.org/10.1111/j.1467-8535.2011.01253.x

Recommended Further Reading

Diao, J.-F., & Yang, J. (2021). Multiple-role perspectives on assessing teaching ability: Reframing TVET teachers' competency in the information age. *Journal of Educational Technology Development and Exchange, 14*(1), 57–77. https://doi.org/10.18785/jetde.1401.04

Garcia, A., & Nichols, T. P. (2021). Digital platforms aren't mere tools—they're complex environments. *Phi Delta Kappan, 102*(6), 14–19. https://doi.org/10.1177/0031721721998148

Goodyear, P., & Dimitriadis, Y. (2013). *In media res*: Reframing design for learning. *Research in Learning Technology, 21*(S1), 19909. https://doi.org/10.3402/rlt.v21i0.19909

Kitchenham, A. (2006). Teachers and technology: A transformative journey. *Journal of Transformative Education, 4*(3), 202–2025. https://doi.org/10.1177/1541344606290947

Whitesel, C. (1998). Reframing our classrooms, reframing ourselves: Perspectives from a virtual paladin. *The Technology Source*. http://www.technologysource.org/article/reframing_our_classrooms_reframing_ourselves/

12 Celebrating Teachers
Lessons for Teachers and Teaching Nationally and Globally

Introduction

Palmer (1998) wrote about having the *courage to teach* in relation to the demands educators face. He provided perspectives on the teaching profession to help inspire and reenergise a sense of connection and empathy with and among teachers. In this book, we have taken the experiences of practising teachers in Australia with a similar aim, demonstrating how responsiveness to change enables them to thrive, not just survive, in engaging with the inherent complexities, challenges, contradictions and comforts of their everyday work. This occurs in the context of a dynamic and demanding education system (Lemon & Turner, 2024), brought about by rapid changes in regulatory policy and accountability measures. Teachers have reported significant concerns about their well-being and the current status of the profession (Amitai & Van Houtte, 2022; Brun et al., 2022; Peel et al., 2024). Yet, rather than despair, we follow many of the teachers who spoke to us in adopting a perspective of "learned optimism" (Seligman, 1990), finding motivation in this exercise of distributed, collective reflection and resilience.

Teachers are at the centre of our education systems and in their daily tasks they are affected by real-time pressures to ensure coverage of the curriculum, to manage the collection of performance data, to safeguard the expectations of the students and their parents/carers, and to meet the national demands of testing for accountability. Supporting and valuing those in the teaching profession are essential for teachers to function effectively in classrooms, and their practices are at the centre of that functioning.

This book is about the strategies that Australian teachers use to succeed, where success may have different meanings for different teachers. As we have seen in the preceding chapters, Australian teachers are faced with many competing challenges, culminating in shocking statistics related to high rates of burnout and attrition. Our aim in this chapter, as in the book, is to celebrate teachers as professionals who manage to sustain motivation despite the many challenges of the profession. The book has adopted a strengths-based approach, looking to understand the resources that teachers have available and the creative ways that they make use of them. The teachers whose stories have been shared in this book are committed professionals who use a range of strategies to stay motivated, recover from adversity and continue achieving impressive outcomes with students and colleagues, working with situations as they encounter them. Here we bring together insights from the preceding chapters, identifying the types of success strategies used by teachers and discussing the relationships among those types.

This chapter suggests that Australian teachers' success strategies fall into four different categories: value-driven strategies, agentic strategies, adaptable strategies and relational strategies. These categories are expanded upon, with examples of each category provided. All four categories can be found within the literature, where scholars of teaching and teacher education have long advocated teacher agency (Cong-Lem, 2021; Molla & Nolan, 2020), collegiality (Shah, 2012) and adaptability (Loughland, 2019), as well as the importance of intrinsic motivation (Vansteenkiste et al., 2004) and educational philosophies (Biesta, 2015). Our contribution in this chapter is twofold. Firstly, we contextualise each of these kinds of strategies in the specific teaching practices described in the preceding chapters. Secondly, we identify relationships between these kinds of strategies and the scholarly literature.

The study that forms the basis for this chapter (and the book) is detailed in Chapter 1, drawing on a thematic analysis of interviews with 42 Australian teachers. Interviews were examined using a matrix of five dimensions (psychosocial; professional and professionalism; changes and continuities; naming, framing and shaming; and teaching by design) and four nodes (complexities, challenges, contradictions and comforts), with success strategies being identified as a part of the analysis. We have aimed to make use of teachers' self-reported narratives, "to understand how teachers make sense of their situations and how that enables them to thrive", as Marc Clarà writes in the Foreword to this book.

A summary of the strategies and the relationships between them is shown in Figure 12.1, providing a map for the rest of this chapter. Teachers' values are deeply held beliefs that matter to teachers, and teachers have strategies for establishing and maintaining this core. These are shown in Figure 12.1 as strategies that work from the inside to the outside and can be read through the lens of internal motivation (Peel et al., 2024). A complement are the three categories that involve more of an entanglement between the internal and external worlds. It is from these internal values that agency can flow, practices that involve taking actions that are in harmony with teachers' beliefs. Strategies of adaptability enable teachers to respond to the reality of situations as they are presented, the most extrinsic kind of strategy. Finally, strategies of relationality describe strategies that support the practice of teaching as a profession centred upon social relationships, particularly with students and with other teachers, among others. We recognise that this emergent framework resonates with much of the psychological literature on intrinsic/internal motivation, providing further empirical evidence of the basic human psychological needs for relatedness, competence and autonomy (Ryan

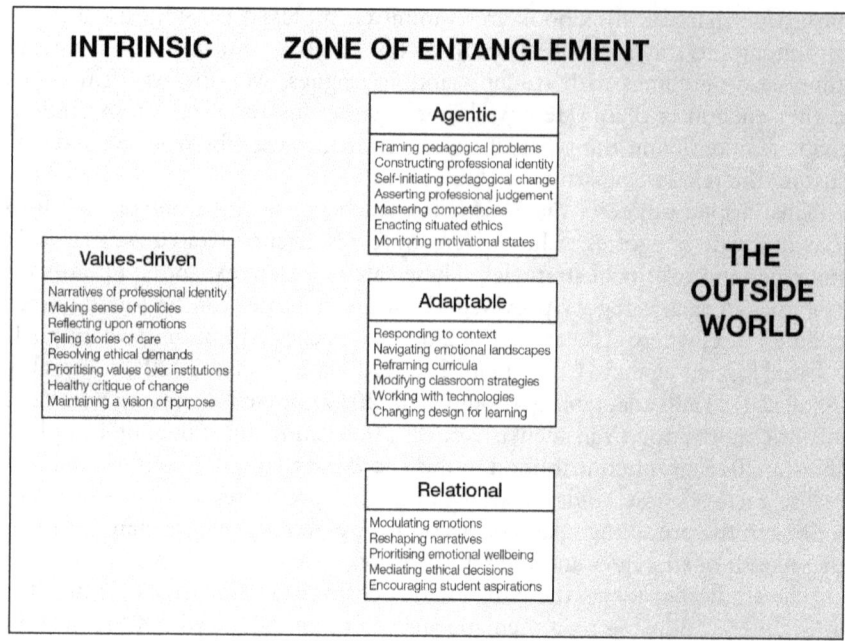

Figure 12.1 A representation of four categories for teachers' success strategies: value-driven, agentic, adaptable and relational

& Deci, 2000). However, rather than mapping teaching strategies into these existing psychological constructs, we feel it is more appropriate to use the categories of values, agency, adaptability and relationality that align more closely with practices that teachers will recognise and that were inductively arrived at through our findings. Further, there are many possible ways to organise these categories, and many practices sit at the intersection between them. An example of this is Edwards' (2005) notion of relational agency that is both relational and agentic. The emergent framework that structures this chapter represents just one way of making sense of teachers' strategies for success, one that we feel resonates with the stories told by the teachers in this book. Figure 12.1 supports a holistic understanding of our data through the four categories.

Value-Driven Success Strategies

Teachers use a number of strategies to ensure clarity around their values. It is these values that provide a source of orientation, perhaps even a moral compass, amidst the complexity of the teaching profession. The central theme of many of the chapters in this book is that teachers need to do work to ensure that they have a clear sense of their values: their educational philosophies, their personal ethics and their sense of purpose, among other things. This section describes the strategies that enable teachers to have their work grounded in such values, the wellspring of intrinsic motivation.

A primary way that teachers establish their values is through the construction and deconstruction of narratives, as Chapter 4 elaborated. The personal/professional identities of teachers are shaped by the stories that they tell, where these stories are powerful for framing the purpose behind teachers' actions, a precursor to agency. A theme running through Chapter 4 is that reflection upon narratives to provide opportunities to resolve contradictory beliefs and values is important for long-term emotional well-being.

A place where such reflection upon narratives occurs is the sense-making that teachers undertake in refracting policies on a micro level. As Chapter 6 describes, teachers need strategies to work through contradictions between policy and classroom realities without surrendering professional judgement. For example, this is seen in issues like national assessments that are bound to meet data-driven imperatives. Teachers find joy in their work through strategies of "[p]ursuing knowledge, not presuming knowledge; [r]especting self, students and others; [and a]ccepting difference as strength, not weakness", all of which enable them to connect to their values in the face of policies that may feel hostile.

Strategies to connect to values are intricately ties to teachers' emotional geographies and to their motivation, a theme of Chapter 3. For example, Arthur is a teacher who recognises that emotional engagement is a part of his motivation, saying in Chapter 4 that "I want to feel the same kind of emotional engagement with my teaching that I feel with my artistic practice and with [my] artistic discipline". Teachers need to have the critical emotional reflexivity (Zembylas, 2014) to notice what is going on with their emotions as a part of linking their values to their motivation and actions.

Chapter 10 engages directly with the sense of what it means to be a teacher and the continuities in teaching. When teachers have core educational values, they can permit those values to steer their daily choices, even when institutional pressures are strong. For example, Chapter 6 describes the frequent occurrence of *ethical dilemmas* faced by teachers in the context of challenging policies that can be addressed in connection to values. This resonates with Chapter 9, which recognises teachers' strategies for employing *situated ethics*, recognising teachers' abilities to read situations and act with integrity amid competing demands. This is yet another place where teachers' justice-oriented commitments can be brought to light in local, relational settings.

Further, in Chapter 2, teachers are described as designers of learning experiences that come fulfilling and a source of well-being they are grounded in a sense of purpose. Chapter 11 makes a similar point regarding the importance of teachers' values in guiding their adoption of technologies. Idealism is perhaps out of fashion in the present century, yet Chapter 10 suggests that idealism about the role of teacher can provide some continuity in a landscape with precious little to hold onto. The challenges of navigating the COVID-19 pandemic—a time of rapid change for teachers—showed the value of such idealism, as shown in Chapter 5. Success strategies include adapting practice while keeping sight of why the work matters. Here teachers were facing heightened pressures yet were able to remain professional and innovative and to draw genuine pleasure from their work through connection to their values.

Agentic Success Strategies

Teachers use agentic strategies to bring their values into the world. Agency is closely linked to motivation, with agency arising when the means to meet a goal stems from the teacher's desire to achieve it, and the intensity of their desire influences the strength of their efforts to achieve it (Deci et al., 1996). This category describes the ways that teachers use agentic strategies in their design for learning, narrative sense-making, collaborative resilience and technological discernment in crisis, policy refraction to preserve professional judgement, self-regulation and epistemic fluency to manage complexity, situated ethical discernment and ideal-driven calibration of practice towards students' flourishing. Read ecologically, these strategies translate motivation into deliberate, context-sensitive action distributed across relationships, resources and structures (Priestley et al., 2015) and are energised by autonomous motivation that sustains persistence, creativity and well-being (Ryan & Deci, 2000).

In Chapter 2, teachers are conceptualised as designers of rich learning who are informed by educational principles to act autonomously and iteratively in response to contextual demands, institutional constraints and student diversity. As such, they frame pedagogical problems by seeking sound solutions and feedback to enhance their design efficacy. By adopting the identity of educational designers, teachers are empowered to construct their own frame to meet the challenges of designing for learning.

A professional identity that reflects a sense of agency is recognised as a critical factor for thriving in the workplace. In Chapter 4, teachers are represented as narrative constructors where they make sense of their professional identities and practices to mediate interpretations of successes and failures. Storytelling is accepted as a mechanism internally to reflect and externally to present strategies for navigating institutional structures, work-related expectations and pedagogical values. By constructing their professional identity through narrative agency, the teachers make sense of their experiences to align their actions with their evolving educational goals and personal values.

The teachers' professional and personal stories reflect their experiences, such as when they became change agents during the COVID-19 global crisis. The role of teachers as pandemic navigators was detailed in Chapter 5, through the strategies implemented to adapt with agility to online learning platforms. Teachers explained how they handled the uncertainty of asynchronous and synchronous instruction, while managing professional and personal boundaries, by drawing on collective knowledge and collaborating with colleagues to recalibrate their teaching philosophies creatively. In uncertain and digitally shifting contexts, teachers self-initiated pedagogical change, reflecting both proactivity and technological discernment. At the forefront of their actions during this unprecedented stress was their students' well-being; while their own well-being was being challenged. Through their adaptive resilience to address the many challenges, the teachers exhibited agency within the professional workplace. Intriguingly, the interruption caused by COVID-19 became a catalyst to disrupt the cycle of discomfort that is threatening the very professionalism of teachers. For instance, some teachers found themselves with an increased sense of autonomy and collaboration, and revitalised connections with parents and communities (Perryman et al., 2024). Yet, there is a reported "rapid return to pre-pandemic normal" (Perryman et al., 2024, p. 810), despite the OECD (2020) encouragement to reimagine teacher professionalism after the pandemic by rethinking key elements of knowledge, collaboration and autonomy.

With moves towards greater accountability, the professional status and autonomy of teachers have become increasingly eroded (Saha & Dworkin, 2009). Chapter 6 discusses how partly autonomous teachers have responded by reinterpreting education policies to align with their professional values, beliefs and practices. Through this policy refraction, they can potentially wield a stronger influence when responding to ideologically framed policies where the importance of context would otherwise have been forgotten. Policy refraction is positioned as both a professional necessity and a strategy for preserving teacher agency, by enabling them ethically and partly autonomously to mediate conflicting policy demands. Yet this autonomous enactment of policy refraction requires ethical energy that takes its toll emotionally, intellectually and physically. The complexities discussed by the teachers in the chapter included the ethical dilemmas encountered and the agentic enactment of policy refraction that led to them trusting their own professional judgements. When teachers are empowered to assert their professional judgements, they reflect on their work to adapt situationally within complex, dynamic environments.

For teachers, being epistemically open to different ways of thinking enables an internal sense of agency to navigate professional challenges and enhance their teaching effectiveness. Teachers' epistemic fluency competencies are discussed in Chapter 8 in terms of their professional awareness, management and problem-solving as self-regulated learners. Mastery of these competencies is also important for students, so modelling of these strategic skills supports students in becoming self-regulated learners. Ultimately, teachers' capacity to self-regulate not only enhances their own professional success but also fosters dynamic, responsive learning environments that prepare students to become resilient, autonomous learners.

Chapter 9 positions teachers as situated ethicists who must draw on their moral identities and professional judgement when enacting ethical decisions. The chapter reveals that teacher agency in ethical decision-making is not only a matter of compliance or resistance but also a complex, relational and iterative process. Teachers' moral agency emerged in their ability to discern and act on what they believed to be *the right thing* in diverse, sometimes contradictory contexts. At times, their agency was curtailed by hierarchical structures, yet they sustained motivation not through rigid adherence to compliance, but through purposeful, informed and value-driven actions within the dynamic realities of teaching.

Teachers' actions and decisions are not arbitrary but guided by a personal teaching philosophy and a commitment to situated ethics, which help them make nuanced judgements tailored to their learners and settings. Chapter 10 explores the concept of the teaching idealist, by investigating how teachers articulate what teaching means to them and the ideals that drive their professional practices. Their agency is sustained by the emotional and motivational rewards they gain from seeing their students flourish and from the belief that their work contributes to students' holistic growth. These ideals shape decisions about relationships, curriculum and teaching methodologies, yet they are not static or universally agreed upon. They are personal, context-specific and dynamic, and serve as sources of motivation and resilience, helping teachers maintain their passion and navigate challenges in their work. Contributing to the resilience of these teaching idealists is a strong social conscience, a belief in the transformative power of education and a commitment to building relationships. Through the monitoring of motivational states, they find professional satisfaction and sustain their passion for teaching as agents of cultural and societal influence.

Adaptable Success Strategies

Teacher adaptability refers to strategies that enable teachers to respond to change. Of all of the categories, this is the one that is most influenced by the external world: when something difficult is coming at you as a teacher, how do you respond? This is perhaps most salient in Chapter 5, which relates teachers' stories of navigating the pandemic. New policies were being developed at short notice (especially regarding technology-mediated distance learning), and teachers were able to respond through a mix of innovation and care (Perryman et al., 2024).

The pandemic is just one of many examples explored in this book. Teachers regularly have to contend with new technologies where, at the time of writing, generative artificial intelligence (AI) is a pertinent theme (Zhai, 2024). Yet teachers have a habit of coming up with clever ways of adapting to new learning environments, just as they did during the pandemic. One teacher in Chapter 11, Paul, describes his way of navigating technological shifts by staying close to what matters: "I've always been more interested in helping the students construct meaning rather than giving them meaning, and that hasn't really changed".

Chapter 2 recognises teachers as professional designers, as crafters of learning experiences that respond to the reality of the context: "*this* particular class of students, *this* learning environment, *this* curriculum, *these* resources, *this* much time and so on" (Chapter 2). To do this, they need to be adaptable, recognising and responding to changes in that context. That applies during their design for learning and also to what is happening during a class, at learn time.

Adaptability requires teachers to respond to shifting emotional landscapes too, a theme that traverses multiple chapters. Chapter 3 quotes Keira, a teacher, saying that "I think teaching is about accepting who you are and accepting who others are and helping them be the best that they can be". Teachers need to be attuned to themselves and to their students, on cognitive as well as emotional levels, in order to be able to respond to them. Some of these emotional changes are in response to policies, which teachers refract through their practices, discussed in Chapter 6. They also adapt to changes in their own emotional landscape, which Chapter 4 addresses in the context of teachers' self-narratives. A teacher, Rosie, observes that "You're only one person, so you're always trying to work out what's the way that you can be most effective with the least amount of damage to yourself in terms of your own emotional wellbeing".

Chapter 10 describes teachers as self-regulated learners, and it identifies the need to be a *lifelong* learner to adapt to changing contexts and goals. A common experience is for teachers to realise that changes take time and continued adaptation, something that is reflected upon by Serene when she recalls: "I remember during my interview to become a teacher, I [said], 'I want to change everything; I want to change the system; I want to change that'. Then that didn't happen". Keeping an adaptive rather than a defensive mindset by attributing causes to changeable conditions that are under the teachers' volitional control (Weiner, 2005) enables adaptability for future development and self-regulatory mastery (Peel, 2020).

Relational Success Strategies

Teacher motivation and resilience emerge not merely from personal commitment or isolated professionalism, but also from ethically grounded, emotionally attuned and relationally sustained commitments to students, colleagues and communities (Beltman, 2021; McInerney et al., 2015). Across the chapters in this book, teacher motivation and resilience are framed as relationally situated practices that are deeply tied to their ethical responsibilities, emotional labour and commitment to student growth.

Chapter 3 demonstrates the teachers' emotional resilience as they modulate their emotions, not to suppress their feelings, but to protect and nurture positive student relationships. Emotional labour is utilised by teachers to develop positive, beneficial relationships. The elements of the teaching profession that require emotional labour (Walsh & Baker, 2022) are recognised to make a clear distinction between emotional work and emotional labour, with the latter being the teachers' resilience for managing the relational highs and lows of their day-to-day emotional interactions.

A significant source of emotional labour is highlighted in Chapter 7, which identifies the role of teachers as relationship brokers: in the classroom with students, with parents/carers and with other teachers. Often, teachers are required to "broker damaged relationships successfully such as those that may occur between student and colleague, teacher and management, student and parent, student and student, etc.", a significant source of emotional labour.

Consideration of how teachers reshape narratives collaboratively suggests that resilience also involves dialogic meaning-making. In Chapter 4, the teachers' personal stories evolve in dialogue with colleagues, school leaders, students, parents and the wider school community through shared understanding and collective sense-making. This chapter foregrounds the importance of relationships in the narratives that teachers construct and deconstruct as they navigate their professional identities. When professional challenges are confronted, meaningful relationships often serve as protective factors in complex or emotionally taxing situations.

Constructive relationships influence how teachers shape, sustain and sometimes reframe their professional identities. Furthermore, relationships can become a source of comfort and motivation for teachers amidst upheaval such as what was experienced during the COVID-19 pandemic. In Chapter 5, teachers' professional resilience and motivation were often anchored in their ability to maintain or manage relationships under pressure. During these challenges, relational bonds among teachers often strengthened. On the other hand, teachers experienced relational strain and feelings of isolation as an outcome of inconsistency in decision-making, a lack of support and perceived inequities within the system. The chapter illustrates how the pandemic revealed both the fragility and the power of educational relationships. Where those relationships were supportive, responsive and flexible, teachers were more able to sustain their motivation and resilience. The teachers prioritised their students' emotional well-being, even while under pressure themselves, highlighting the teachers' enduring capacity for professional resilience and innovation during times of rapid change.

From a different perspective, the COVID-19 interruption opened a space for teachers to refocus on care and connection rather than managing everyday compliance. Chapter 6 presents the ethical decision-making of teachers as they shape and are shaped by the contradictions between imposed policy directives and their commitments to prioritising their students' and their emotional well-being. Here their resilience involves navigating competing values while maintaining relational integrity with students and other stakeholders. Teachers' ethical resilience depends on their ability to sustain respectful, trusting relationships despite policy environments that often disregard the relational core of education. In these acts of policy refraction, teachers reaffirm their professional identity through their loyalty to students, collegial support and a commitment to fairness and care. Professional relationships, therefore, are foundational for teachers' motivation and resilience.

Against this backdrop, Chapter 9 highlights that relational trust enables teachers to remain principled even in complex or ambiguous circumstances. Importantly, professionalism is shown to be a relational practice where teachers navigate ethical dilemmas with mediated decision-making and responses that affirm teaching is a profoundly human and ethical profession. Moreover, ethical professionalism is shaped by trust: trust in oneself, in students and in the professional judgement of peers. Teachers often find themselves in emotionally charged situations where they must advocate for student well-being, sometimes in tension with policy, leadership expectations or parental demands. Relationships become both the context and the compass for these decisions.

Similarly, teaching idealists are driven by relationally grounded aspirations that extend beyond students' academic outcomes. Chapter 10 portrays teaching idealists who thrive on fostering students' holistic growth and supporting their journey to find their way in life. Central to their professional identity is their belief in the transformative power of education, which is enacted through meaningful and authentic relationships with students. These connections serve as a motivational reward for their work, sustaining their resilience amid challenges. Professional satisfaction emerges from mutual growth; as students flourish, so do their teachers as they encourage student aspirations. Teaching becomes a synchronistic phenomenon where their relationships with students are not incidental; they are essential.

Discussion

This is a chapter about the strategies that teachers adopt that work for them, enabling them to succeed on their own terms. It is worth taking a moment to recollect that there are, in Australia and many other countries, professional standards for teachers. They are required to know the content and related ways to teach it, and to assess students' learning accurately to ensure that what they are doing is effective. Yet these normative prescriptions of "good teaching practices" omit the very situational nature of what it is that motivates and sustains teachers. As has been highlighted in this book, teachers find motivation in caring for students as individuals, designing teaching for connecting to them in meaningful ways, being idealistic about the goals of the profession and so much more. The emotional labour that teachers encounter can be a rollercoaster ride of reward, triumph, disappointment and hurt, because of the investment made by individual teachers. Teaching is a caring vocation and for many teachers they are drawn by a calling to teach.

Highlighted by the teachers represented in this book is the rewarding nature of teaching as they observe their students' academic, emotional and social growth. Those serendipitous events of "Ah, I get it!", when the student grasps a new concept that bestows a shared satisfaction and sense of relief. Does the lure of teaching come from that joyous sound of a class of students and their teacher laughing together as they share a moment of spontaneous hilarity? Is it in the enigmatic fun that abounds from intrinsic learning? And then there are the mixed feelings encountered at the end of the school year, as teacher and students farewell one another. Yet, for students they are enlivened by what is ahead, and for teachers, knowing they have done their best reassuringly feeds their motivation to commit to the work they do.

The success strategies discussed in the book, and summarised here, provide an understanding of how early career and experienced teachers sustain their motivation and resilience despite an at-times hostile education system. There is a complex sense-making at play throughout the teachers' stories shared, reconciling the intrinsic sense of "how things should be" with the extrinsic encounter with "how things are". This plays out in terms of individuals, relationships, policies, educational goals, technologies, curriculum and pretty much everything else involved in being a teacher.

Clarà (2017) recognises the value of stories that teachers tell about their experiences in providing insights into their inner worlds. Subsequent work demonstrates that teachers who are able to reflect upon situations of adversity and to find coherence between values and reality are, to some degree, protected from emotional exhaustion and burnout (Clarà et al., 2023). Our hope is that the teacher strategies shared in this book might be of value to other teachers searching for such acceptance within their own emotional experience.

Conclusion

The chapter has built up an image of a profession that succeeds through a strong sense of purpose, with values that are reified through narrative and reflection. These values are brought into the world through the exercising of agency when opportunity presents, whether that is through responses to policies, designs for learning or relational initiative. This nexus of values and agency is inherently social, playing out in the relationships with others, especially students, parents/carers and other teachers. For this reason, teachers have many success strategies relating to caring for, nurturing and sustaining these relationships. This idealised teacher, whom we might refer to as "the self-determined teachers", has their house built upon shifting sands: as has been discussed, change is the only constant in the teaching profession. Thus, the final category of success strategies has been described as *adaptability*, the ability to change when the situation demands it.

These strategies for success, as shown in Figure 12.1, are not intended as a prescription, nor do we intend any normative portrayal of what it means to be a motivated or resilient teacher—quite the opposite. The sharing of these success strategies, drawn from interviews with teachers discussing their emotional experiences, is intended to provide examples of what some teachers find useful and that might, for that reason, be useful to others.

References

Amitai, A., & Van Houtte, M. (2022). Being pushed out of the career: Former teachers' reasons for leaving the profession. *Teaching and Teacher Education, 110*, Article 103540. https://doi.org/10.1016/j.tate.2021.103540

Beltman, S. (2021). Understanding and examining teacher resilience from multiple perspectives. In C. F. Mansfield (Ed.), *Cultivating teacher resilience: International approaches, applications and impact* (pp. 11–26). Springer Nature.

Biesta, G. (2015). What is education for? On good education, teacher judgement, and educational professionalism. *European Journal of Education, 50*(1), 75–87. https://doi.org/10.1111/ejed.12109

Brun, L., Dompnier, B., & Pansu, P. (2022). A latent profile analysis of teachers' causal attribution for academic success or failure. *European Journal of Psychology of Education, 37*(1), 185–206. https://doi.org/10.1007/s10212-021-00551-3

Clarà, M. (2017). Teacher resilience and meaning transformation: How teachers reappraise situations of adversity. *Teaching and Teacher Education, 63*, 82–91. https://doi.org/10.1016/j.tate.2016.12.010

Clarà, M., Vallés, A., Franch, A., Coiduras, J., Silva, P., & Cavalcante, S. (2023). How teachers' appraisals predict their emotional experience: Identifying protective and risk structures in natural appraisals. *Teaching and Teacher Education, 130*, 104166. https://doi.org/10.1016/j.tate.2023.104166

Cong-Lem, N. (2021). Teacher agency: A systematic review of international literature. *Issues in Educational Research, 31*(3), 718–738.

Deci, E. L., Ryan, R. M., & Williams, G. C. (1996). Needs satisfaction and the self-regulation of learning. *Learning and Individual Differences, 8*(3), 165–183. https://doi.org/10.1016/S1041-6080(96)90013-8

Edwards, A. (2005). Relational agency: Learning to be a resourceful practitioner. *International Journal of Educational Research, 43*(3), 168–182. https://doi.org/10.1016/j.ijer.2006.06.010

Lemon, N., & Turner, K. (2024). Unravelling the wellbeing needs of Australian teachers: A qualitative inquiry. *The Australian Educational Researcher, 51*(5), 2161–2181. https://doi.org/10.1007/s13384-023-00687-9

Loughland, T. (2019). *Teacher adaptive practices: Extending teacher adaptability into classroom practice*. Springer.

McInerney, D. M., Ganotice, F. A., King, R. B., Morin, A. J., & Marsh, H. W. (2015). Teachers' commitment and psychological well-being: Implications of self-beliefs for teaching in Hong Kong. *Educational Psychology, 35*(8), 926–945. https://doi.org/10.1080/01443410.2014.895801

Molla, T., & Nolan, A. (2020). Teacher agency and professional practice. *Teachers and Teaching, 26*(1), 67–87. https://doi.org/10.1080/13540602.2020.1740196

OEDC (2020). Organization for Economic Cooperation and Development: *Professional collaboration as a key support for teachers working in challenging environments*. OECD Publications Service.

Palmer, P. (1998). *The courage to teach: Exploring the inner land-scape of a teacher's life*. Jossey-Bass.

Peel, K. L. (2020). Everyday teaching practices for self-regulated learning. *Issues in Educational Research, 30*(1), 260–282. http://www.iier.org.au/iier30/peel.pdf

Peel, K. L., Kelly, N., & Danaher, P. (2024). Australian teachers' causal attributions along a motivational continuum in supporting their resilience. *Issues in Educational Research, 34*(1), 163–182.

Perryman, J., Leaton Gray, S., Hargreaves, E., & Saville, K. (2024). 'Feeling Overwhelmed': Pedagogy and professionalism in a pandemic. *Pedagogy, Culture & Society, 32*(3), 795–814. https://doi.org/10.1080/14681366.2022.2133157

Priestley, M. R., Biesta, G., & Robinson, S. (2015). *Teacher agency: An ecological approach*. Bloomsbury Publishing.

Ryan, R. M., & Deci, E. L. (2000). Self-determination theory and the facilitation of intrinsic motivation, social development, and well-being. *American Psychologist, 55*(1), 68. https://doi.org/10.1037/0003-066X.55.1.68

Saha, L. J., & Dworkin, A. G. (2009). Introduction: New perspectives on teachers and teaching. In L. J. Saha & A. G. Dworkin (Eds.), *International handbook of research on teachers and teaching* (pp. 3–11). Springer. https://doi.org/10.1007/978-0-387-73317-3_1

Seligman, M. E. P. (1990). *Learned optimism: How to change your mind and your life.* Vintage Books.

Shah, M. (2012). The importance and benefits of teacher collegiality in schools–A literature review. *Procedia-Social and Behavioral Sciences, 46,* 1242–1246. https://doi.org/10.1016/j.sbspro.2012.05.282

Vansteenkiste, M., Simons, J., Lens, W., Sheldon, K. M., & Deci, E. L. (2004). Motivating learning, performance, and persistence: The synergistic effects of intrinsic goal contents and autonomy-supportive contexts. *Journal of Personality and Social Psychology, 87*(2), 246260. https://doi.org/10.1037/0022-3514.87.2.246

Walsh, M. J., & Baker, S. A. (2022, July 11). What is emotional labour—and how do we get it wrong? *The Conversation.* https://theconversation.com/what-is-emotional-labour-and-how-do-we-get-it-wrong-185773

Weiner, B. (2005). Motivation from an attribution perspective and the social psychology of perceived competence. In A. J. Elliot & C. S. Dweck (Eds.), *Handbook of competence and motivation* (pp. 73–84). Guilford.

Zembylas, M. (2014). The place of emotion in teacher reflection: Elias, Foucault and 'critical emotional reflexivity'. *Power and Education, 6*(2), 210–222. https://doi.org/10.2304/power.2014.6.2.210

Zhai, X. (2024). Transforming teachers' roles and agencies in the era of generative AI: Perceptions, acceptance, knowledge, and practices. *Journal of Science Education and Technology.* https://doi.org/10.1007/s10956-024-10174-0

Recommended Further Reading

Fosen, D. M. (2016). *Developing good teacher–student relationships: A multiple-case study of six teachers' relational strategies and perceptions of closeness to students* [Doctoral dissertation, University College London, UK]. https://discovery.ucl.ac.uk/id/eprint/1474062/

Hawn, A. (2019). *Data-wary, value-driven: Teacher attitudes, efficacy, and online access for data-based decision making* [Doctoral dissertation, Columbia University, US]. https://academiccommons.columbia.edu/doi/10.7916/d8-8yme-sb59

Juutilainen, M., Metsäpelto, R. L., & Poikkeus, A. M. (2018). Becoming agentic teachers: Experiences of the home group approach as a resource for supporting teacher students' agency. *Teaching and Teacher Education, 76,* 116–125. https://doi.org/10.1016/j.tate.2018.08.013

Toward, G., & Henley, C. (2021). *Celebrating teachers: Making a difference.* Crown House Publishing Ltd.

Vaughn, M., Parsons, S. A., Burrowbridge, S. C., Weesner, J., & Taylor, L. (2016). In their own words: Teachers' reflections on adaptability. *Theory Into Practice, 55,* 259–266. https://doi.org/10.1080/00405841.2016.1173993

Appendix
Interview Protocol
Emotional Experiences of Australian Teachers

Brief description of the project

- Introduce the researchers
- Disclose the researchers' interest
  - Much can be learned when researchers value and appreciate the knowledgeable voices of teachers, who reflect on their experiences as practitioners in contemporary educational settings.
  - We recognise that teaching is both a crucial and sometimes a challenging profession.
- Purpose of the study is to investigate how teachers respond to rewarding and challenging situations.
- Clarify that this is an international research project that is designed to collect data through surveying and interviewing teachers to elicit their personal experiences in relation to their roles as teachers.
- Explain the data collection format
  - Provide the link to establish a connection for the researchers and teacher participant through the ZOOM video conferencing session. Ensure Consent Forms have been signed and returned.
  - Introduce researchers' interests in the research and the purpose of the study to establish a supportive and relational atmosphere.
  - Explain that the online survey requires teacher participants to read the questions and statements and record their responses.
  - Provide the link for the teacher to participate in the survey and arrange for the ZOOM link to be re-established in 30 minutes.
  - Conduct an informal conversation over approximately 40 minutes in the style of a semi-structured interview following the protocol topics for questioning.
- Offer opportunity for the teacher participant to ask any procedural questions.
- Request permission to video record the interview.

Participant	Teaching Position
Time and date of interview	Location/Link: ZOOM

Topics and suggestions for questions

1 Career as a teacher

- What initially led you to the teaching profession? Tell me the story about how you came to be a teacher.
- What areas have you taught in? Which did you particularly enjoy and why?
- What makes your job interesting?
- Where do you see yourself in five years from now?
- What do you see as the varied roles you play as a teacher?

2 Situations experienced as a teacher

- Think about a good day at school. What makes a teaching day a satisfying day for you?
- What emotions/feelings are associated with being a teacher for you?
- What comes to mind as positive emotions for you that are linked with your teaching experiences?
- Can you recount a challenging situation that you have experienced?
- How did you feel about this challenging situation at the time, and how has that changed or stayed the same?

3 Relationships with colleagues, students, parents, administration

- Consider a situation where you developed a relationship with someone in your roles as a teacher that led to a good outcome.
- In what ways have you experienced any of the benefits of working in a trusting and respectful environment?
- How do you deal with conflict and tensions in the workplace?
- In what ways do other teachers share their values about education with you?
- From your experience, what does it look like when other teachers are struggling to manage in situations at work?
- Can you share an experience where you felt the relationship between you and a colleague/s adversely affected you as a teacher?
- Can you share an experience where you felt the relationship between you and a student/s adversely affected you as a teacher?

4 Specific tasks

- Think about a specific task that you do in your teaching that you feel strongly about and explain why you feel in this way?
- How do you know when you are doing something in your work that is worthwhile?
- From your experience, can you recount when you have been conflicted in the tasks that you have add to perform?

5 Issues

- What aspects of your work keep you awake at night?
- When are you the most concerned and worried about in fulfilling your teaching roles?
- What is one big picture issue that influences your work as a teacher?

Appendix: Interview Protocol

Participant	Teaching Position
Time and date of interview	Location/Link: ZOOM
Topics and suggestions for questions	

6 *Continuity and change*

- Sometimes our perceptions of things that happen in our teaching are affected by our emotions. Can you share any incidents that you can recall where this has happened to you?
- Consider a situation when you have changed your view on something. How did this influence your subsequent decision-making?

Final Question

- What does it mean to you to be a teacher?

Debrief

- We thank you for your time participating in this research.
- Express appreciation. We thank you for your time participating in this research.
- Now that your involvement has been completed, we would like to explain that overall, we are interested in resilience—the ways in which teachers respond to adversity in their professional lives. During the interview we have referred to your emotional experiences during your time as a teacher as this research is based upon the notion that teachers' narratives matter here—that the subjective stories that are told around events determine how well teachers are able to deal with those events. It is also based upon the idea that if we understand resilience better than it can be, to some degree, taught.
- The research is also considering whether resilience relates to burnout, stress and attrition.
- We will send a summary of the research findings to you within 12 months so that you can observe the findings from this work.
- We thank you once again for all of your involvement with this research.

Index

accountability 85, 88, 94, 116, 153, 170, 176, 181
adaptability 2, 125, 177–8, 182–3, 186
adaptable strategies 177–8, 182–3, 186
affordance/s 72, 80, 163
agency 1–2, 5, 14, 25, 37, 40–1, 46–7, 50, 52, 57, 62–3, 67, 79, 84, 112, 117, 120, 125–6, 135–6, 138, 140, 164, 169, 171, 177–9
agentic strategies 177–8, 180–2, 186
attrition 131, 176
authenticity 35, 52, 97, 152, 154, 160, 185
autonomy 2, 11, 18, 22, 24–5, 27–8, 30–1, 37, 85–6, 88, 93, 113–14, 123–4, 131, 135–42, 180–1

basic psychological need/s 18, 21–2, 25, 30, 177
boundary/ies 63, 72, 99, 105, 108, 154, 180
boundary crossing 99, 108
boundary object/s 99, 108
boundary work/er/s 98–9, 108
bullying 38, 40–1, 90
burnout 7, 36, 40, 42, 67, 72, 101, 119, 137, 176, 186

change agent/s 64, 67, 180
collaboration 19, 22, 25, 31, 47, 62, 76, 78, 91, 97, 118, 126, 180–1
collegiality 61, 78, 107, 163, 177, 184
commodification 42, 47
communication 19, 22, 35, 47, 50, 97, 75–6, 105, 116, 140, 147, 149
competence 18, 22, 24–5, 27, 30, 91, 108, 112, 121–2, 124, 126, 152, 177
corporatisation 42, 47
counternarrative/s 56, 58

courage 8, 47, 144, 148, 150, 176
COVID-19 pandemic 2, 6–8, 35, 40, 51, 67–80, 86–8, 150, 179–82, 184

decision-making 25, 47, 69, 97, 119, 131, 133–7, 139–43, 172–3, 181, 184–5
declarative proposition/s 2, 5–6, 10, 12, 14, 51, 67
deprofessionalisation 1, 94
design capabilities 17–19, 22, 30–1
design cycle/s 19–20, 22, 24
design expertise 17–22, 25, 27, 31
design processes 26, 29
designers for learning 2, 17, 24
designing for learning 17–18, 24–8, 162, 172, 180
dilemma/s 85, 87–9, 93–4, 120, 130–4, 140–3, 179, 181, 185
discourse/s 1, 3, 53, 61, 138, 142, 163, 166–7
discursive dissonance/s 136, 143, 165
dual teacher roles for design 17, 30

EdTech 172
emotion/s 4–5, 10, 12, 34–5, 39, 47, 50, 61. 90, 114–17, 120, 122–3, 125, 138, 141–2, 170, 179, 183
emotion/al work 34–5, 183
emotional competence 112, 126
emotional connectedness 47
emotional connection/s 39–40, 42
emotional exhaustion 40–2, 47, 186
emotional labour 34–6, 38–9, 41–8, 50, 132, 183–5
emotional labourer/s 2, 34, 38
emotional regulation 12, 116, 125
empathy 20, 47, 118, 122–3, 125–6, 176

empowerment 17, 53, 60, 111–12, 117, 120, 125, 152, 180–1
engagement 26–7, 36, 43, 52, 58, 68–9, 72, 74, 79–80, 107–8, 114, 117, 132, 134, 173, 179
epistemic fluency 111, 113, 180–1
essence of teaching 154, 156–7
ethics 87, 98, 107, 131–3, 136, 139, 142, 160, 178
ethos 132, 138
expertise 58, 61, 71, 108, 122, 137, 141

frame-activity model 19–22, 24, 30
framing 37, 53–5, 58, 60–3, 76, 100, 104, 108, 133–6, 139–42, 171–3, 177, 179

goal/s 18–9, 25–6, 28, 61, 84, 99, 111–13, 123, 125–6, 147, 149, 154, 160, 169, 172–3, 180, 183, 185–6
goal setting 47, 148

humanistic perspective 118–19, 125–6

identity/ies 1, 3, 6, 10–12, 14, 24–5, 38, 51–3, 62–4, 80, 83, 114, 133–5, 149, 166, 179–81, 184–5
ideology/ies 50, 53, 84–6, 181
inequity/ies 69, 77, 133, 169, 184
informal learning 21, 54, 60, 91
innovation/s 6, 11, 20, 27, 43–4, 79–80, 84, 94, 163, 165, 171, 180, 182, 184

joy/s of teaching 47, 69, 93, 150, 152, 155, 179, 185

La relación entre las narrativas y el desarrollo de la resiliencia en los profesores (NARRES) 1, 3–5, 7–9, 14, 18
leadership 8, 30–1, 34–5, 39, 42–3, 52, 54–6, 58–9, 62–4, 69, 74–5, 77–80, 87–8, 115, 120, 122, 124–6, 137–9, 142, 154, 184–5
learntime 17, 24, 29–30
lifelong learning 111, 117, 124–6, 183

meaning-making 10, 52, 158, 184
mediation 4, 83, 85–6, 89, 92, 97–8, 180–1
mentoring 97, 102, 120, 139
metacognition 29–30, 112, 125

metaphor/s 6, 51, 68, 85, 158
motivation 1–3, 10, 14, 18, 22, 24–8, 30–1, 37, 44, 50–3, 61, 63, 68, 70–1, 73, 76, 79–80, 100, 107, 111–12, 114–15, 117–19, 121–2, 124–6, 132, 135–6, 139, 141–3, 148, 150–2, 155, 157–9, 165, 171, 176–7, 179–180, 182–6

naming 11, 37, 53–5, 60–2, 100, 104, 134–6, 139, 141–2, 177
narrative construction 2, 50–2, 54, 57, 61–4, 179–80, 184
narrative deconstruction 2, 50–2, 54–5, 57, 59, 61–4, 179, 184
narrative reconstruction 52, 55–7, 59, 61–3
NARRES see La relación entre las narrativas y el desarrollo de la resiliencia en los profesores (NARRES)

online learning 43, 71, 88, 106, 180
online teaching 35, 40, 67–8, 70–3, 78, 88, 106
optimism 47, 151–2, 176

pandemic navigator/s 2, 67–8, 71–4, 76–80, 179–80, 182
personal growth 45, 48
philosophy/ies 22, 25, 98, 102, 147, 150, 159–60, 163, 166, 170, 172, 177–8, 180, 182
policy/ies 1, 3, 31, 36, 41, 44, 59, 79, 83–9, 92–4, 97, 108, 122, 125–6, 142, 149, 165, 167, 176, 179, 181–6
policy refraction 83–5, 88, 93–4, 179–181, 183–4
positioning 1, 11, 53, 58, 92, 108, 134–5, 138, 142–3, 160, 181
praxis 47, 98, 147
problem-solving 19–20, 26, 47, 119, 124, 181
professional competency/ies 111, 114, 124
professional development 31, 44, 46, 63, 69, 71, 77, 80, 107–8, 142, 170
professional knowledge 85, 94
professionalism 3, 11, 25, 30, 37–40, 42, 44–6, 53, 80, 85–6, 88–91, 93–5, 97, 100, 108, 114, 131, 135, 149, 177, 181, 183–5

psychosocial 5, 7, 11, 22, 37–9, 41, 43, 45, 53, 99–101, 104, 108, 177

reflective practice 17, 63, 113
reflexivity 31, 52, 113, 179
reframing 55, 61, 162–73
relatedness 18, 22, 24–6, 28, 30, 177
relational strategies 177–8, 183–4
relationality 177–8
relationship broker/s 97–100, 103, 108, 183–4
resilience 1–7, 14, 31, 39, 46–7, 50–2, 61, 63, 68, 70–1, 73, 76, 79–80, 84–5, 102, 108, 111, 122, 132, 136, 139, 141–4, 150–2, 155, 157–9, 168, 176, 180–66
role modelling 34, 98, 120, 122–3, 125–6

self-awareness 42, 47, 84, 111–15, 119, 121, 124–6, 160
self-care 47, 57, 63, 119, 123, 159
self-concept 64, 133, 160
self-determination theory 18, 22, 24, 30
self-efficacy 57, 68–9, 76, 112, 120, 126
self-reflection 57, 111–2, 118, 122, 126, 153
self-regulated learner/s 5, 111–5, 117, 119–21, 123–6, 181, 183
self-regulated learning 111–15, 117–8, 120–1, 124–6
self-regulation 112, 180
sense-making 10, 92, 179–80, 184, 186
shaming 11, 37, 53–5, 60–2, 100, 134–5, 137, 139, 141, 177
situated ethicist/s 131–2, 134–5, 139–44, 181
situated ethics 132–4, 136–9, 141–3, 179, 182
stress 6, 10, 24, 36–7, 43–5, 47, 52–3, 55, 57, 63, 67, 69–75, 80, 87, 90, 100, 114–16, 119, 135, 151, 162, 165, 181
student–teacher relationship/s 35, 59, 64, 92, 98, 100–1, 103, 106, 139, 147, 155, 159–60, 183–4
success strategy/ies 1–3, 13–4, 18, 22, 24–5, 28, 30–1, 39, 50–2, 55–7, 59–64, 67, 70–3, 76–7, 79–80, 114, 124, 126, 132–3, 136, 139–42, 148, 151–5, 158, 163–4, 167, 169, 171, 173, 176–8, 180–3, 186

support for teachers 17–8, 24–5, 30–1, 41–2, 47, 57–8, 60, 62–3, 69, 71, 75, 78, 87, 105, 107, 111, 119, 123–4, 126, 132, 141, 152, 163, 176–7, 184

teacher education 3, 31, 94, 107–8, 132, 142, 177
teacher narrative/s 4, 51–2
teacher professionalism 38, 85, 181
teacher registration 92, 94
teacher/s' work 3, 11–12, 14, 24, 37, 51–3, 68–70, 73, 75–7, 80, 94, 114, 132–4, 136, 140, 150, 153, 156–7, 173
teaching by design 11, 37, 53, 100, 165, 173, 177
teaching idealist/s 51, 141, 147–8, 15, 158–60, 182, 185
teaching standards 25, 85, 87, 92, 94, 107–8, 142, 185
technology/ies 19, 67–8, 70–2, 76, 80, 85, 121, 162–73, 179, 182, 186
technology reframer/s 162–5, 173
testing of students 84–5, 88–9, 176
time management 116, 121, 123
transformation 4, 11, 24, 52, 61, 68, 95, 108, 152, 160, 163–6, 182, 185
triadic reciprocation 112–3, 124
trust 88–9, 98–9, 101, 104, 132, 151, 154, 181, 184–5

value/s 22, 24–6, 35, 41, 43, 45–6, 48, 54, 58, 63–4, 71, 79, 83–5, 89, 91, 98–9, 113, 117–20, 124, 136, 147, 152, 158–60, 165, 167, 169, 172–3, 177–81, 184, 186
value-driven strategies 177–8, 182
valuing teachers 12, 176
violence 38, 83, 133
vocation 51, 149–50, 185
voice/s 30, 34–5, 51–2, 67, 69, 72, 88, 99, 120–1, 140, 143, 150, 154, 158

well-being 3, 5, 7, 22, 40–1, 48, 59–60, 63, 68–9, 77, 79, 87, 105–6, 111, 131, 159–60, 172, 175, 179–81, 183–5
work–life balance 29, 97
workload/s 3, 8, 57, 68–9, 73, 77, 114, 122

For Product Safety Concerns and Information please contact our EU representative GPSR@taylorandfrancis.com
Taylor & Francis Verlag GmbH, Kaufingerstraße 24, 80331 München, Germany

www.ingramcontent.com/pod-product-compliance
Lightning Source LLC
Chambersburg PA
CBHW071409300426
44114CB00016B/2241